Ed Bolden and Black Baseball
in Philadelphia

Ed Bolden and Black Baseball in Philadelphia

COURTNEY MICHELLE SMITH

McFarland & Company, Inc., Publishers

Jefferson, North Carolina

ISBN (print) 978-0-7864-7849-1
ISBN (ebook) 978-1-4766-2743-4

LIBRARY OF CONGRESS CATALOGUING DATA ARE AVAILABLE

BRITISH LIBRARY CATALOGUING DATA ARE AVAILABLE

Front cover: Ed Bolden with his 1940s Philadelphia Stars team
(John W. Mosley Photograph Collection, Charles L. Blockson
Afro-American Collection, Temple University Libraries,
Philadelphia, Pennsylvania)

Printed in the United States of America

*McFarland & Company, Inc., Publishers
Box 611, Jefferson, North Carolina 28640
www.mcfarlandpub.com*

Table of Contents

Introduction

Ed Bolden, nicknamed "the Chief," dominated black professional baseball in the Philadelphia area from 1910 to his death in 1950. During that era, Bolden led two different baseball franchises. His first franchise, a Hilldale team known as the Hilldale Giants and the Hilldale Daisies, ranked as one of the top black professional baseball teams in the immediate post–World War I era. Hilldale captured a World Series title in 1925, but increasingly poor economic conditions stalled Hilldale's progress and led to the franchise's demise in the early 1930s. Bolden endured a messy divorce from his first franchise, but he rebounded with a new franchise that bore his name, Ed Bolden's Philadelphia Stars. He remained at the helm of that franchise until his death. Throughout his career with Hilldale and the Stars, Bolden earned a reputation for demanding high standards from his players. Bolden's legacy, however, goes beyond his demands for fair and clean standards from his players. Bolden established a legacy of leadership that transcended baseball and that revealed the limitations that black business leaders faced in a segregated world.

Organized black baseball was first played in Philadelphia in the 1860s, and it continued for approximately the next ninety years. During its formative years and beyond, the black game in Philadelphia represented an important and vibrant product of the area's longstanding African American community, which dates to 1684, a mere three years after William Penn secured his charter for Pennsylvania. In that year, a British mercantile ship carrying one hundred and fifty African slaves landed in Philadelphia. The colony's Quaker settlers purchased the slaves and used slave labor to clear the land and construct new buildings. Over the next two decades, approximately one in fifteen Philadelphian families owned slaves. African slaves, therefore, played a role in settling the new colony and embodied part of Philadelphia's society and culture almost from the time of the city's founding. Despite the fluctuations in the city's slave population, black Philadelphians left an indelible mark upon the city's society and culture and stood poised to taste a measure of freedom in the era following the American Revolution.[1]

Pennsylvania passed a gradual emancipation act in 1780, and that act laid the foundation for Philadelphia to house one of the United States' largest communities of free blacks in the Antebellum Era. Philadelphia's free black community produced leaders—including Bishop Richard Allen, Absalom Jones, James Forten, and William Still—who presaged future leaders in the black baseball world. Black Philadelphians faced a great deal of racism and hostility from white Philadelphians; therefore, they relied upon their own institutions for support and autonomy. Allen and Jones established the Free African Society (FAS) in 1787, the same year when George Washington and other Founding Fathers gathered in Philadelphia to write the Constitution. The FAS represented the first community institution for free black Philadelphians, and its policies confined membership to the affluent elite of free black Philadelphia society. Its policies also established high moral standards for behavior for all members. For example, the FAS barred its members from certain activities, such as gaming, that could bring shame upon black Philadelphians and all black Americans. The FAS provided relief to its members and opportunities for them to congregate with other members and foster the growth of future leaders. In addition to providing leadership in local Masonic lodges, FAS leaders also successfully pressed for the formation of independent black churches. In Philadelphia in 1794, Allen founded a church that he would later name Mother Bethel African Methodist Episcopal (A.M.E.) Church. The Mother Bethel A.M.E. Church grew into the most important black-led institution in North America. It offered black Philadelphians a place to worship and a place to organize community-wide activities against key issues, such as slavery.[2]

Elite black Philadelphians' antislavery activism persisted throughout the rest of the Antebellum Era. In 1813, James Forten protested a proposed state bill that barred blacks from immigrating to Pennsylvania. In the 1820s and 1830s, he also questioned the motivation of organizations like the American Colonization Society (ACS) who wanted to send free black Americans to Liberia or other locations in the Caribbean. The complaints from Forten and other Philadelphians provided William Lloyd Garrison with ammunition for his *Thoughts on African Colonization*, a pamphlet that convinced many abolitionists to withdraw support from the ACS. Forten and other black Philadelphians also worked with Garrison to publish his abolitionist newspaper *The Liberator* and to promote the efforts of the American Anti-Slavery Society. Leadership did not remain confined to black men; elite black women from Philadelphia society took positions within the Female Anti-Slavery Society. Black Philadelphians, furthermore, provided aid to the region's Underground Railroad "stations." William Still and others interviewed runaway slaves, took inventories, offered money to those housing and feeding runaway slaves, and helped runaway slaves reach their final destinations.[3]

Following the American Civil War, the black Philadelphia community produced leaders who followed in the footsteps of their forebears. The post–Civil War black Philadelphia community also provided support for the formation of new cultural institutions, such as baseball teams. Baseball flourished in post–Civil War America; white and black fraternal organizations established baseball clubs, and professional teams appeared in major cities. Philadelphia's first two black baseball teams adopted the names the Excelsiors and the Pythians. In October 1867, the Excelsiors defeated the Brooklyn Uniques 42 to 37 in the first official game featuring two black teams, a game the Brooklyn Daily Union touted as the "colored championship."

Despite the Excelsiors' impressive feat, the Pythians left a greater mark on Philadelphia's and black baseball's history. The Knights of Pythias, a fraternal organization, established the Pythians baseball team. The club held its first meeting in March 1867 and established a code of conduct reminiscent of the high moral standards the FAS established for its members. The code banned all gambling and prohibited alcoholic beverages from the Pythians' meeting room. Additionally, the code included fines for foul language and unbecoming conduct and made members responsible for damage done to the meeting room's furniture. Similar to the FAS, elite black Philadelphians supported and joined the Pythians. The Pythians included William Still among their membership, though he did fall behind in paying the one-dollar yearly membership fee. Jacob C. White Jr., the Pythians' secretary, served as Philadelphia's first black school principal and as the first black board member of the Mercy-Douglas Hospital.[4]

The Pythians' roots extended deep within elite black Philadelphian society. Octavius V. Catto, who served as the Pythians' captain, worked as a teacher at the Institute for Colored Youth (ICY) in Philadelphia. Catto's father William, who served as a minister, led a successful movement to pressure the ICY's Quaker administration to develop an academic-focused curriculum for its black student body. When he attended the ICY as a student, Catto became friends with Jacob C. White Jr., the future secretary of the Pythians. Other members of the Pythians' leadership—president James W. Purnell and vice-president Raymond W. Burr—came from local families involved in the Underground Railroad and civil rights. On New Years' Day in 1867, the St. Thomas African Episcopal Church, a church Absalom Jones established in 1792, held a ceremony for the Pythians and presented Catto with a ceremonial wooden bat. Worshippers at St. Thomas included many of Philadelphia's elite black families, and members of the Pythians came from those elite families. The ability of the Pythians to afford the yearly membership dues and to have the leisure time to play baseball reflected their elite status. Few Pythians worked at skilled or semi-skilled jobs; players belonged to other fraternal and civic groups. The Pythians' games represented social events for black Philadelphians. Some Pythians games included lavish entertainment such as picnics, dances, lunches, dinners, and other forms of entertainment. The menu for one game in July 1867 included ice cream, ham and tongues, pickles, cheese, cigars, and wine.[5]

Catto's leadership and renown extended beyond the Pythians. Due to his academic acumen and his relationships with white politicians, Catto stood as one of the most respected black men within Pennsylvania. As Robert E. Lee's army moved northward in 1863, Catto volunteered to serve in the Union Army, and many ICY students followed him into the Union Army. Catto led a company of black soldiers to Harrisburg, but his company returned to Philadelphia since Major General Darius N. Couch refused to induct them into military service. When he returned to Philadelphia, Catto publicly protested Couch's decision and helped to spark a successful movement to get black Pennsylvanians into the Union Army. Catto did not return to the Army, but he did earn an appointment as a major and inspector for the Pennsylvania National Guard's Fifth Brigade. In addition to supporting the Union cause, Catto pressed for civil rights. He attended the National Convention of Colored Men in Syracuse in October 1864; one month later, members of the newly formed Pennsylvania State Equal Rights League elected Catto as their corresponding secretary. After the Civil War, he led a three-man committee of the league to successfully lobby the state legislature for a bill desegregating Philadelphia's streetcars. Ultimately, Catto's support for the Union cause and civil rights activism demonstrated his strong leadership qualities and continued the legacy of strong leadership from Philadelphia's black elite. Catto's actions also foreshadowed the leadership he demonstrated as the Pythians' captain.[6]

During their brief existence, the Pythians challenged baseball's unwritten color line. In 1867, the Pythians amassed an impressive record of nine victories and one defeat. The Pythians' rivals included the Excelsiors and the Washington Mutuals. The Mutuals' roster included Charles R. Douglass, Frederick Douglass's son, and the elder Douglass attended one of the Pythians-Mutuals games as a spectator. The Pythians, however, only faced other black teams. After the successful season, Catto took steps to have the Pythians compete against white teams by applying to join a new organization called the Pennsylvania Convention of Baseball Clubs. Delegates from white teams involved in the organization met in Harrisburg, and Catto sent vice-president Raymond Burr to represent the Pythians. Two delegates from the Philadelphia Athletics supported the Pythians' petition, but they asked Burr to withdraw the petition since a majority of the delegates opposed the Pythians' membership. Burr refused; he also refused a subsequent request for the Pythians to withdraw their petition. Ultimately, the credentials committee repeatedly ignored the Pythians' request, and Burr finally withdrew the application. The Pythians faced further rejection when Catto applied for membership in the National Association of Base Ball Players. In rejecting the Pythians, the Association set an ominous tone for the future of black baseball. Delegates at the meeting passed a resolution barring membership to all baseball teams that included one or more black players. Baseball's unofficial color line suddenly became more official.[7]

Despite those setbacks, the Pythians did participate in interracial competition. After another successful season in 1868, the Pythians stood poised to enjoy continued success in the 1869 season. In June of that season, an anonymous letter to one of the city's newspapers raised the possibility of a game between the Pythians and one of the city's white teams. At the end of July, another anonymous letter called upon the Athletics to play the Pythians. The Pythians never faced the Athletics, but they did face the prestigious Olympic Club in September at the Olympics' home grounds on Twenty-Fifth and Jefferson Streets. The Olympics won the game 44 to 23, and the game drew attention from newspapers across the country. Other interracial games followed, including a game between the Pythians and the City Items at the Athletics' home field on Seventeenth Street and Columbia Avenue. The Pythians won the game 27 to 17, and the team's players earned praise from one of the local newspapers for their level of competition. Most importantly, the Pythians showed that black teams could compete against white teams and left a lasting legacy for black baseball.[8]

Sadly, the Pythians disappeared from the black baseball world following Catto's death in 1871. While he led the Pythians, Catto continued his civil rights activism beyond black baseball. He worked to ensure that black men in Philadelphia could vote, a right recently granted to them through the Fifteenth Amendment. On Election Day in 1871, violence erupted between white and black voters. Despite the danger, Catto resolved to vote, and he proceeded to walk through the dangerous streets. Catto purchased a pistol after enduring two separate confrontations with unruly whites and one direct threat on his life, but he did not have any ammunition. He continued his walk; a white man named Frank Kelly approached Catto and shot him three times. Catto died instantly, and the Pythians as well as the rest of the black community in Philadelphia lost one of their most important leaders. During his short life, Catto represented an important link between Philadelphia's antebellum past and twentieth-century future. He carried on the legacy of leadership from the city's black elite, and he promoted a baseball team, an important outlet for black achievement and entrepreneurship in the twentieth century. Both Catto and the Pythians set high standards for future black baseball teams from the Philadelphia area and for the men who would lead those teams.[9]

Following the Pythians' demise, the color line in professional baseball hardened. There were, however, integrated teams in professional baseball. By 1878, John "Bud" Fowler had become the first African American in so-called organized baseball, having joined the International Association's Lynn, Massachusetts, Live Oaks that season. A year later, William Edward White, a Brown University student, became the first black man to play in the majors when he filled in for one game for Providence's Joe Start. In the 1880s, George Stovey was a standout left-handed pitcher in the minor leagues, and Moses Fleetwood Walker joined both major and minor league teams. The presence of black players bothered some white players, most notably Cap Anson of the National League's Chicago White Stockings. In 1887, Anson refused to take the field in an exhibition game against Stovey's minor league team from Newark. Stovey's team, which played in the International League, accommodated Anson's demand and substituted a white player for Stovey. By the next day, newspapers were reporting that the owners, in a secret meeting, had decided "to approve of no more contracts with colored men." Owners of teams in the National League and the American Association, the other major league at that time, already abided by a tacit agreement along the same lines, and no black player had appeared on their rosters since Walker in 1884. That agreement filtered to the International League and other minor leagues and remained in place until October 1945.[10]

Even as segregated play became entrenched, the evolution of baseball in Philadelphia continued. The Philadelphia Phillies of the National League first appeared in 1883, and the Philadelphia Athletics of the American League first appeared in 1901. In that same year, the city's next great black team, the Philadelphia Giants, first appeared. Unlike the Pythians, the Giants did not rely upon Philadelphia's black elite for support or leadership. Instead, the Giants leadership consisted of Walter Schlichter, the white sports editor for the Philadelphia Item, and Sol White, a respected black baseball player and author. The success of Schlichter's and White's Giants reinvigorated black baseball in the Philadelphia area. The team's interracial partnership also set a trend for black baseball in the twentieth century.[11]

For a brief period in the early twentieth century, the Philadelphia Giants ranked among the top black baseball teams in the country. In 1903, Schlichter and White advertised the Giants as the "World's Colored Champions," even though no league or championship series existed to support their claim. Another team, E.B. Lamar's Cuban X Giants, challenged the Philadelphia Giants' claim, and the two clubs engaged in a rivalry over the next two seasons. Schlichter used his newspaper columns, and White used his baseball guide to promote the Giants and downplay the success of the team's rivals. They also pursued top players, including noted pitcher and future black baseball leader Andrew "Rube" Foster. The peak of the team's success came in 1906. During that season, the Giants' roster included Foster, shortstop Grant "Home Run" Johnson, outfielder Pete Hill, and second baseman Charlie Grant. In the middle of the season, the Giants joined the short-lived International League of Independent Base Ball Clubs. The Philadelphia Phillies permitted the Giants to rent eighteen-thousand-seat Baker Bowl for a playoff game, and the Giants' players received a cup for winning the league's championship. Foster and his teammates, however, earned only $100 for Sunday games and even less for games played during weekdays. The Giants' poor finances prompted Foster and eight of his teammates to leave at the end of the 1906 season and search for a better financial situation in the Midwest. Afterwards, the Giants collapsed, and the Philadelphia area lacked a strong representative in the growing black baseball world.[12]

Within a few years of the Giants' demise, a group of young black men in Darby established a new baseball team called Hilldale. In 1910, Hilldale's first season, Darby resident Ed Bolden joined the team and put the young squad on a path toward greatness. Bolden worked in black professional baseball for nearly the next forty years, first with Hilldale and then with the Philadelphia Stars. His leadership harked back to the leadership that

Allen, Catto, and other black Philadelphians demonstrated in the nineteenth century. Bolden established high standards for behavior for Hilldale's players, and he spearheaded the all-black Hilldale Baseball Corporation to provide support for the franchise. During his time with the Stars, Bolden reached out to other local leaders and made sure that his team maintained connections to Philadelphia's black community. Honorary pallbearers at Bolden's funeral in 1950 included attorney Raymond Pace Alexander, Philadelphia Postmaster Raymond Thomas, Judge Herbert Millen of the municipal court, Stars manager Oscar Charleston, and Lloyd Thompson from the Hilldale Baseball Corporation. Those pallbearers reflected the dual career Bolden maintained in black professional baseball and in Philadelphia's center city post office. They also attested to the influence and respect Bolden earned within Philadelphia's black community.[13]

Bolden's long career mirrored the trajectory of black professional baseball from the 1910s to the early 1950s. He slowly built Hilldale into a top professional team; both he and the team took full advantage of black professional baseball's growth in the 1920s. Bolden briefly headed his own league, and Hilldale won black baseball's second-ever World Series. As black professional baseball faced financial crises in the late 1920s, Bolden entered the lowest point of his career. He experienced a personal breakdown and later left the Hilldale Baseball Corporation in disgrace after a dispute with his business partners. Bolden spent several seasons in black baseball's wilderness as the sport confronted the reality of the Great Depression. After a false start with the Darby Phantoms, Bolden made a comeback with the Stars at the same time as Gus Greenlee's Negro National League started to reimpose a league structure upon black professional baseball. With the Stars, Bolden endured all of the highs and lows related to membership in the Negro National League. Bolden guided the Stars to the 1934 championship, his second championship in black professional baseball. Bolden also faced all of the troubles confronting owners in the Negro National League—including disputed records, disrespect for player contracts, and financial losses. During the final years of his life, Bolden endured the inexorable decline of the Stars as black players in the Major Leagues diverted attention and support away from black professional baseball.

In addition to mirroring black professional baseball's history in the twentieth century, Bolden's career built upon a legacy of leadership from Philadelphia's black elite. Bolden assumed leadership positions and supported goals, such as the integration of the Major Leagues, that resembled goals Philadelphia's black leaders supported in the nineteenth century.

Even though Bolden lived in Darby, he developed and fostered relationships with Philadelphia's black community. Those relationships translated into support for both the Darby-based Hilldale team and the Stars. Bolden turned to the *Philadelphia Tribune*, the region's largest black newspaper, to promote both of his franchises and to reach his franchises' fans. His career, therefore, highlights the critical link between black professional baseball and black communities who patronized black baseball teams. Bolden spent his career maintaining that link and making both of his franchises part of the Philadelphia region's rich history.

Bolden's story also serves as a way to examine the history of the Philadelphia Stars and the role that white booking agents occupied within the world of black professional baseball. The Stars existed during the decades when black teams confronted the Great Depression, World War II, and integration in the Major Leagues. Those obstacles provide insight into the pressures Bolden faced as he built the Stars' roster and chased a third championship. Throughout his time with the Stars, Bolden worked

Ed Bolden, pictured here (in jacket, tie and hat) with his Philadelphia Stars in the 1940s, worked in black professional baseball in different capacities for most of his adult life. His work leading leagues and two professional franchises brought him both praise and scorn (John W. Mosley Photograph Collection, Charles L. Blockson Afro-American Collection, Temple University Libraries, Philadelphia, Pennsylvania).

with Ed Gottlieb, a white Jewish booking agent based in Philadelphia. Gottlieb's connections to black professional baseball extended beyond the Stars, and his presence occasionally attracted the ire of other owners in the Negro National League. Criticism of Gottlieb intensified as all-black baseball teams faced extinction in the wake of Jackie Robinson's signing with the Brooklyn Dodgers in 1945.

Overall, Bolden's story reflects the multifaceted world of black professional baseball in the twentieth century. His story charts the rise of black baseball from sandlots to professional leagues. His story also charts black baseball's struggles through economic depressions and two world wars. Bolden's story, furthermore, provides insight into the less glamorous aspects of Negro League baseball. Through Bolden, stories emerge about conflicts over umpires, necessary relationships with white booking agents, and a growing dependency upon Major League ballparks to stage events. His occasional ruthlessness in dealing with players provides insight into the pressures owners faced and into the lack of togetherness that often characterized relationships between owners. Bolden's story, finally, reveals the connections between black baseball teams and their local communities. Bolden worked hard to cement relationships with the local newspapers, civic leaders, and his fans. Once his Stars and other black teams lost support from black newspapers and fans, they struggled to remain relevant. Bolden's death presaged the Stars' demise by approximately two and a half years. In both life and death, Bolden paralleled the trajectory of black professional baseball in the United States.

CHAPTER ONE

A Team in Darby,
1911–1919

As the twentieth century entered its second decade, the segregation that characterized much of American society characterized professional baseball. The so-called Jim Crow laws fostered segregation in housing, employment, public transportation, public accommodations, and places of entertainment. Similarly, a "gentlemen's agreement" kept African Americans out of Major League Baseball. Occasionally, black teams would compete against teams composed of white major leaguers. Those games provided opportunities for black ballplayers to prove their mettle and demonstrate their competitiveness against their white counterparts. Some teams, such as Connie Mack's Philadelphia Athletics, carried racially mixed rosters by signing Native American or Cuban players. Major League Baseball, however, remained off-limits for African American players.[1]

Since they lacked access to the stability associated with Major League Baseball, most black professional baseball teams faced precarious existences. Unlike their white counterparts, black professional teams did not enjoy the benefits of regularly scheduled games, respected player contracts, and an organized postseason to determine a champion. Black professional teams faced competition from other black teams in the same or nearby areas for ballparks and for fans' attention as well as money. Those teams relied upon leaders who could schedule regular games, advertise the team in local black newspapers, secure access to well-maintained ballparks, and provide a solid foundation for continued growth. Several such leaders emerged during this era in both the Midwest and the East. Those leaders included Andrew "Rube" Foster in Chicago, C.I. Taylor in Indianapolis, and Ed Bolden in Philadelphia.[2]

Bolden's leadership with Hilldale continued the legacy of strong black leadership in the Philadelphia area. His early years with Hilldale established a pattern for his leadership within black baseball, a leadership that persisted for nearly forty years. Similar to earlier black leaders from Philadelphia, Bolden enforced high standards upon his players. Like the FAS, Bolden sought to foster self-help by developing a corporation for Hilldale using black capital. He also reached out to the region's largest black newspaper, the *Philadelphia Tribune*, to promote Hilldale and form relationships with Philadelphia's black community. Bolden's grand ambitions led him into clashes with other black baseball moguls, most notably Foster. Through Bolden, a story emerges about black leadership in the early twentieth century and about the realities men like Bolden faced as they sought to match their ambitions to a segregated society.

Enter "The Chief"

Darby Borough, located approximately five miles outside of Philadelphia, likely housed settlers before William Penn acquired his charter for the colony of Pennsylvania. In the early twentieth century, Darby welcomed residents who sought to leave the congestion of Philadelphia. Since officials in Darby sought to prohibit blacks from settling in the borough, black residents in Darby gathered in an area known as the Hill. The concentration of black residents in one region of Darby, combined with the continued popularity of baseball, created the conditions for the appearance of a black baseball team. The team that appeared, Hilldale, took its name from the area of Darby that was home to its black residents. It initially represented little more than a sandlot team for black teenagers and did not show any hints of its future greatness.[3]

Established in 1910, Hilldale emerged at a time when the Philadelphia area lacked a standout black professional baseball team. The once-mighty Philadelphia Giants still fielded a team, but their championship-contending years had passed. Other teams based in the greater Philadelphia area included the South Philadelphia Giants, the Anchor Giants, the Philadelphia Defiance, the Southwark B.C., the Bon Tons, the Central Social Athletic Club, and the Evergreen Hall team from southern New Jersey.[4] Similar to Hilldale, many of those teams used the *Tribune* to advertise their games and to solicit opponents. For example, the Bon Tons' manager George Henry announced in the *Tribune* that he had assembled "one of the strongest teams in the city" and scheduled games against both Hilldale and the East Philadelphia Giants.[5] He also asked "to hear from Morton Stars, Somerville Giants, La Mott Giants, East End Giants, Peerless Giants or any first class team desiring a strong attraction and offering a reasonable guarantee."[6] Hilldale, therefore, faced a great deal of competition in reaching and attracting black baseball fans in the greater Philadelphia area.

Little information exists about Hilldale's inaugural season. Ironically, a box score from Hilldale's earliest recorded game appeared in the *Philadelphia Inquirer*, a newspaper that typically provided scant coverage to Hilldale and other black baseball teams. The box score, which featured a game between Hilldale and the Lansdowne F.C., offered few details about the game or any of the players on either team.[7] In its first season, Hilldale carried a roster full of teenagers who lived and worked in the communities near Darby. The club's leadership reflected its youthful roster. Nineteen-year-old Austin Devere Thompson served as the team's first manager; his younger brother Lloyd played second base. At one point during the season, the club asked Darby resident Ed Bolden to keep score of one of their games. By the end of the 1910 season, Austin Devere Thompson left the club, and Bolden replaced him as the franchise's new leader.[8]

Bolden, who earned the nickname "the Chief," lived his entire life in Delaware County, Pennsylvania. Born on January 17, 1881, in Concordville, a town approximately twenty miles outside of Philadelphia, Bolden moved to Darby as a child and attended Darby's public schools. He had a wife, Nellie, and a daughter, Hilda. Starting in 1904, Bolden worked at Philadelphia's Central Post Office, and he consistently earned high marks for his performance.[9] A performance review from 1921 indicated that Bolden handled approximately twenty-five cards per minute, or over fifteen hundred cards per hour, and did not make any mistakes.[10] Bolden continued to work full-time at the Central Post Office when he assumed control of Hilldale. With his steady and respectable job and older age, Bolden provided Hilldale with more mature leadership than it had enjoyed under Austin Devere Thompson. He set out to distinguish Hilldale from its competitors in the Philadelphia area and to place the young club on a firm foundation.

To promote his team, Bolden turned to the *Philadelphia Tribune*, the region's leading black weekly newspaper. The *Tribune* typically devoted one page to both local and national sports that involved African American athletes. For its baseball coverage, the newspaper typically relied upon managers like Bolden to submit stories and box scores from their team's games. Occasionally, the newspaper printed notices reminding managers about deadlines for submitting materials for publication in the *Tribune*. In one such notice, an editor clearly conveyed a sense of frustration and annoyance at managers who ignored deadlines for submitting materials: "We have repeatedly requested you to send in your score by Tuesday noon each week. If you don't see your games published it is because you have not complied with this rule. A game played on Saturday could easily be sent in by Tuesday and not Wednesday or Thursday as some seem to think. If you don't get it here on Tuesday keep it at your office."[11]

Since the baseball teams had the ability to write their own game stories, Bolden and other managers sometimes used the *Tribune*'s sports page to solicit opponents. In one story summarizing several of Hilldale's recent games, Bolden called upon "all uniformed teams to get in touch with Hilldale."[12] That same story referred to Hilldale as a "fast aggregation of young lads" and as "the pride of Darby and the surrounding community."[13] Another similar solicitation included a request to hear from "all good, fast colored uniformed teams" and the famous phrase "[t]he bigger they are, the harder they fall."[14] Both solicitations ended with Bolden's name, his identification as Hilldale's manager, and his home address of 300 Marks Avenue in Darby.

In addition to soliciting future opponents, Bolden also used the *Tribune*'s sports page to promote his team and the favorable conditions of Hilldale's home grounds. As part of a story on a game Hilldale lost to Evergreen Hall, Bolden described the poor conditions of the opponents' home field. Wooden blocks served as bases, and trees dotted left field. He commented that to "get back on our skinned diamond is like walking from the kitchen into a beautiful parlor."[15] As new baseball seasons approached, stories in the *Tribune* touted new players Hilldale had signed over the winter, competition for positions on the roster, new uniforms, and improvements made to the team's home grounds at Tenth and Summit Streets in Darby. Several preseason stories declared that Hilldale planned to have its biggest season to date and to play against the top class of teams from the Philadelphia area.[16]

At one point, the on-field competition between Hilldale and other local teams seeped into the *Tribune*'s sports coverage. In the afternoon portion of a double-header scheduled for May 30, 1912, Hilldale had arranged to play a team identified as the "S" Club. When the "S" Club failed to appear for the game, Bolden referred to them as the "biggest lemon in amateur baseball" and sarcastically said that "as Darby is such a great distance from Philadelphia we will look for them about Christmas."[17] Later that same month, the Bon Tons' club manager, Leon Nelson, used the *Tribune*'s sports page to issue a challenge to Bolden. In his description of a recent game between the Bon Tons and Hilldale held in Darby, Nelson claimed that biased umpires cost his team a certain victory. Nelson then dared Bolden to accept a rematch on the Bon Tons' home grounds, promising him the "fair and square match" Hilldale allegedly denied the Bon Tons in Darby.[18] Bolden responded to Nelson's claims in the next edition of the *Tribune*. Showing no sympathy for Nelson's complaints, Bolden declared that the "sooner the Bon Tons get away from the 'pimp' idea that their own umpires can win their games for them on foreign soil, the sooner they will become a winning team."[19] Bolden proceeded to highlight the concessions Hilldale made to the Bon Tons during the game and credited the Hilldale players for winning the game in the pivotal seventh inning. He ended his response to Nelson with one final invective— "Just play clean, fast ball for nine full innings and you will get better results next time."[20]

Near the end of the same baseball season, Bolden once again used the *Tribune's* sports page to defend himself and his team against charges of cheating through biased umpires. The person who brought the new charges raised questions about several umpire decisions during the game and used the term "robber team" to describe Hilldale.[21] Bolden defiantly declared that "[r]ibaldry and kicking cannot win games on the Hilldale grounds" and highlighted inaccuracies in the person's recollections of the game.[22] He also boldly predicted, "Hilldale will stand in the forefront of the other good colored teams of Eastern Pennsylvania" at the end of the 1912 season.[23] By using the *Tribune's* sports page to respond to cheating allegations, Bolden engaged in both offensive and defensive actions. He aggressively refuted charges leveled against Hilldale and defended his team's reputation. At the same time, his defense served as a way to advertise Hilldale and to make the team a more attractive opponent for area clubs.

The freedom Bolden enjoyed on the *Tribune's* sports page resembled the relationship between black baseball managers and black newspapers in other cities. In the Midwest, black professional baseball thrived largely due to the leadership of Andrew "Rube" Foster. After leaving the Philadelphia Giants, Foster built the Chicago American Giants into arguably the best black professional team in the Midwest, if not the entire country. Foster worked closely with Chicago's leading black newspaper, the *Chicago Defender*, to promote the Chicago American Giants. He also used the newspaper as a proxy in his battles with C.I. Taylor of the Indianapolis ABCs. Taylor, similarly, used the *Indianapolis Freeman* to promote his club and to respond to Foster's allegations about the outcome of games as well as a championship series held in 1916. A close relationship between black baseball managers and black newspapers, therefore, represented the norm in black baseball, although this would be less true as time wore on.

That relationship provided black baseball teams with the kind of support, specifically with scheduling games and reaching fan bases, that they lacked due to the absence of formal leagues.[24]

In addition to resembling the relationship Bolden had with the *Tribune*, Foster's career in Chicago foreshadowed Bolden's ambitious plans for Hilldale—competing at the professional level. Until the start of the 1917 season, Hilldale competed at the amateur level and faced nonprofessional competition. Hilldale's players earned money by getting a portion of the gate receipts, not by signing professional contracts. Turning professional carried risks for Hilldale, particularly since the team would need to operate without the support of a league structure. Bolden, however, appeared ready to assume those risks. Despite those risks and the looming threat of American military involvement in World War I, Bolden made a wise and well-timed decision. His decision put Hilldale in an ideal position to follow even grander ambitions in the next decade.

Self-Help and Civic Mindedness Grow in Darby

As baseball season began in April 1917, President Woodrow Wilson asked for and received from Congress a formal declaration of war against Germany. With America formally involved in World War I as a combatant, both black baseball teams faced the possibility of losing players to the armed services. In September, the *Chicago Defender* reported that Foster's Chicago American Giants lost its entire pitching staff to the United States Army. During the following season, Foster lost four additional players to the Army, including first baseman Leroy Grant and two more pitchers. Hilldale also felt the sting of the American military in the 1918 season. When the government issued a call for Class A1 men, the team lost star catcher Louis Santop, outfielder P.F. "Specks" Webster, and Tom Williams. These players joined the nearly 400,000 African Americans who served at the time of World War I.[25] When announcing the losses, Bolden immediately assured fans that he would find the best available players to replace the departing stars. The losses, however, underscored one of the obstacles all black professional baseball teams faced in the World War I era.[26]

While the war threatened to undermine the development of black professional baseball, the Great Migration promised to bolster the sport in Northern cities like Philadelphia. The Great Migration referred to the increase in African American migration from the South to northern cities. African American migrants came to cities like Philadelphia in order to seek better opportunities, to take advantage of war-related labor shortages, and to escape endemic Southern racial discrimination. The migration led to a fifty-eight percent increase in the city's African American population between 1910 and 1920. The largest number of African Americans arrived in Philadelphia between 1915 and 1920; by 1920, the African American population of Philadelphia stood at 134,229. The rapid population increase did cause some tensions between black and white Philadelphians, and a riot briefly erupted in the summer of 1918. The population increase, however, helped to provide Bolden with a strong foundation to transform Hilldale into a professional team. As it had before World War I, Darby remained an African American satellite community in Philadelphia's suburban area. Public transportation lines linked Darby to Philadelphia, so Hilldale could readily take advantage of the population increase and build a larger fan base. Both the public transportation lines and the *Tribune* provided Hilldale with access to Philadelphia's black baseball fans and vice versa.[27]

To execute his ambitious plans for Hilldale, Bolden again relied upon the *Tribune* to broadcast his moves and to build anticipation among Hilldale's fan base. The first signs of Bolden's grand ambitions appeared at the end of the 1916 season. In a retrospective of the 1916 season, Bolden actually provided a brief retrospective of Hilldale's six-season history. He spoke of Hilldale's impressive growth from a "team of small boys in 1910 under the management of ... a genial Philadelphia Post Office clerk."[28] The retrospective also hinted that Hilldale had reached its full potential as an amateur team. Bolden referenced Hilldale's new home ballpark, Hilldale Park, located at Ninth and Cedar Streets in Darby, and the team's large fan base as two factors propelling the team to "greater heights."[29]

During the 1917 season, more indications about Hilldale's ambitions and new status appeared in the *Tribune*. In January, Bolden announced the arrests of four men who had caused a disturbance at Hilldale Park during the previous year's Labor Day game. He also announced the formation of a vigilance committee to prevent future disturbances and acts of vandalism at Hilldale Park. One month later, Bolden used the *Tribune*'s sports page to remind readers about the formation of the Hilldale Base Ball and Exhibition Company. Bolden, who served as the Company's president, had taken the step of incorporating Hilldale the previous November. With Bolden at the helm, the Hilldale Base Ball and Exhibition Company represented an African American corporation.[30] Bolden struck a note of racial pride in a biblical-sounding letter published in the *Tribune*. After paraphrasing a passage from the Book of Genesis, Bolden waxed poetically on the theme of growth and heartily thanked the "ladies and gentlemen of our race" for their support over the past seven years.[31]

In addition to incorporating Hilldale, Bolden signaled his team's new professional status by signing two key professional players—outfielder Otto Briggs and pitcher Frank "Doc" Sykes. Briggs had previously played for several teams, including C.I. Taylor's Indianapolis ABCs and the Anchor Giants. Aside from representing Hilldale's first professional player, Briggs's signing had greater significance for Bolden. Briggs later worked as a circulation manager for the *Tribune* and married the daughter of the newspaper's founder. Briggs's signing, therefore, provided Bolden with a link he could use to maintain his relationship with the *Tribune*. Bolden's signing of Sykes drew the attention of the *Chicago Defender*, which credited Bolden with making a good addition to his team. Prior to signing with Hilldale, Sykes pitched for some of the top eastern teams, including the Lincoln Giants and the Brooklyn Royal Giants.[32]

Hilldale opened the 1917 season with a great fanfare. The team welcomed a large crowd to Hilldale Park for the game against the R.G. Dunn team from the Main Line League. Prior to the game, the Morton Coronet Band paraded from Darby's business section to Hilldale Park. The band stayed at the park to play "The Star-Spangled Banner" and to provide musical entertainment throughout the game. The Reverend Hodson Waters, pastor of the Mount Zion A.M.E. Church in Darby, threw out the first pitch. Hilldale, alas, lost the game by the score of 8–1.[33]

While Hilldale continued to play local teams like the R.G. Dunn team, they also met white Major Leaguers during their barnstorming tours and faced some black professional teams. In October 1917, Hilldale lost two games to a team composed of Major League players; approximately one year later, they won an intense one-run game over the Major League stars. Hilldale also defeated the International All-Stars team led by Charlie "Chief" Bender, a future inductee into the Baseball Hall of Fame. The black professional teams Hilldale faced included the Atlantic City–based Bacharach Giants, the Cuban Stars, and Foster's Chicago American Giants. Both in Chicago and in Darby, the games between the Chicago American Giants and Hilldale drew large crowds. Foster and Bolden used the black newspapers in their respective cities to generate interest before the games and to provide game recaps. At this point, the relationship between Foster and Bolden seemed amicable. Neither man used the sports page of his city's black newspaper to level accusations or make demands. The games between Hilldale and the Chicago American Giants did plant a seed for future developments in black professional baseball. The games also demonstrated that black professional baseball had developed in the East and that eastern teams could compete against their Midwestern counterparts.[34]

Overall, during its first three seasons as a professional team, Hilldale enjoyed success both on and off of the baseball diamond. Bolden managed to schedule regular games at Hilldale Park, and those gate receipts helped fill the Hilldale Base Ball and Exhibition Company's coffers. In 1918, the Company realized a net profit of $1,576.22, and the team won twenty more games than it had during the 1917 season. The franchise's good fortunes continued into the 1919 season, and Bolden worked with local authorities to improve public transportation access to Hilldale Park. Advertisements for Hilldale's games in the *Tribune* typically included a notice about the appropriate streetcar line fans should take from Philadelphia to Darby. Before the 1918 season, the Philadelphia Rapid Transit Company ran one of its streetcars directly from Walnut Street to Hilldale Park. Starting in 1918, the Company devoted two additional streetcars to transporting fans from Philadelphia to Darby. While the additional streetcars did not directly service Hilldale Park, they gave fans in Philadelphia additional options for attending games in Darby.[35]

To keep filling the Hilldale Base Ball and Exhibition Company's coffers and to keep fans coming to Hilldale Park, Bolden worked to ensure that his team remained competitive. Following in the footsteps of his signings of Briggs and Sykes, Bolden added more talented professional players to Hilldale's roster. Those players included Arthur Dilworth, shortstop Dick Lundy, catcher Louis Santop, pitcher Tom Williams, outfielders Pearl Webster and George Johnson, pitcher Phil Cockrell, and infielder William Julius "Judy" Johnson. For Lundy and Cockrell, signing with Hilldale marked the start of a lengthy relationship they enjoyed with Bolden. Santop and Judy Johnson also blossomed into stars, and Johnson entered the Baseball Hall of Fame in 1975.[36]

Bolden's and Hilldale's actions attracted attention from people outside of the Philadelphia area. The *Chicago Defender* offered regular stories about Hilldale's games and carried announcements, perhaps submitted to the paper by Bolden himself, when the team signed new players. Bolden's team also drew interest from a powerful white sports promoter who wanted to expand his reach in black professional baseball—Nathaniel Colvin "Nat" Strong. Strong exercised a monopoly-like control over black professional baseball in New York City. After launching his career by selling sporting goods, Strong wisely invested in real estate and purchased both Brighton Oval and Dexter Park in Brooklyn. Strong rented the parks to black professional teams, and he then gained control over more ball-parks in New York City and surrounding areas. Any black team that wanted to play in New York City had to reckon with Strong and with his demands for payment in the form of gate receipts.[37]

Using Walter Schlichter as his emissary, Strong approached Bolden in order to bring Hilldale within his booking empire. Specifically, Strong proposed an amalgamation with Hilldale, an amalgamation that would give him control over both Hilldale and Hilldale Park. In a lengthy letter published in the *Tribune*, Bolden resolutely spurned Strong's offer and outlined the reasons for his refusal. Bolden's letter, addressed to Schlichter, included a sense of racial pride and emphasized the idea that the Hilldale Base Ball and Exhibition Company represented an African American enterprise.

> Mr. H. Walter Schlichter
> 803 Summer Street, Phila., Pennsylvania
>
> Dear Sir:—
>
> I succeeded in getting the Directors together and laid before them your, rather Mr. Strong's proposition to amalgamate our Corporation with him. The result was as I contemplated and coincided with my feelings. The success, good name, and reputation of our Hilldale Company has been acquired by nine years of untiring effort to give to our race an institution that we have finally perfected.
>
> The race people of Philadelphia and vicinity are proud to proclaim Hilldale the biggest thing in the baseball world owned, fostered and controlled by race men and in return we are modestly proud to be in position to give them the most beautiful park in Delaware County, a team that is second to none and playing the best attractions obtainable.
>
> That others propose to enter similar business in [an] adjacent neighborhood is not our affair.
>
> To affiliate ourselves with other than race men would be a mark against our name that could never be eradicated.
>
> We are personally responsible for the fame and success of Hilldale, to place it in jeopardy would be absurd.
>
> With due consideration for your intentions and efforts as an amalgamator I remain
>
> Yours Truly,
> Edward Bolden, Mgr.
> Hilldale B.B. & Exhibition Co., Inc.[38]

As Bolden letter indicated, Hilldale had established itself as a key African American enterprise in the Philadelphia area. Through his corporation, Bolden fostered a spirit of self-help reminiscent of groups that free black Philadelphians established in the eighteenth and nineteenth centuries. Bolden also demonstrated a civic-mindedness that probably helped to engender pride in the Hilldale Base Ball and Exhibition Company. Hilldale faced several baseball teams based in nearby Army camps. During one opening day, Hilldale honored two players, Briggs and Spottswood Poles, who had joined the Army.[39] In letters to Bolden, both players expressed an affinity for both Bolden and his team. In his letter, Briggs thanked Bolden for trying to arrange a game with his Camp Meade team and expressed dismay at news of Hilldale's recent losses. Briggs also assured Bolden that "wherever I am you will always find me climbing for the top and wishing Hilldale the best of luck."[40] Poles's letter contained an overt plea for a contract once he completed his military service. Bolden complied, and the centerfielder returned to the team at the start of the 1919 season.[41]

Another sign of Bolden's civic-mindedness came in September 1918 when Bolden arranged for a game at Hilldale Park to serve as a benefit game for Hilldale's players. Bolden used the game story in the *Tribune* to list the additional ways he supported both the local and wider communities. According to the story, the players "grasped Bolden's hand [and] voiced their appreciation and warm feeling."[42] Bolden then proclaimed that Hilldale "has financed more colored boys thru [*sic*] college, given more money to charity and war benefits and lifted to a higher plane Negro ball players and other athletes than any institution of its kind in the United States."[43] He closed his story by thanking fans for their support and patronage.[44]

By the end of the decade, Bolden had successfully molded Hilldale into a successful business enterprise and one of the top black professional teams in the East. The corporation's shareholders expressed their gratitude in November 1919 by passing a vote of appreciation and reaffirmed his position as Hilldale's manager as well as the corporation's president. Bolden had exercised shrewd judgment in guiding Hilldale. He spearheaded a corporation to provide the franchise with a financial foundation and turned the team professional at a time when it could take advantage of demographic changes in Philadelphia. Bolden, furthermore, minimized Hilldale's financial expenditures by rarely taking the team for games outside of the Philadelphia area. His actions, however, placed Hilldale on a path to venture outside of Philadelphia and to stand at the forefront of a key development in black professional baseball in the 1920s—the creation of formal leagues.[45]

CHAPTER TWO

The Rise, 1920–1925

Prior to 1920, attempts to create and sustain black professional leagues ended in failure. In 1906, the ambitious International League of Colored Baseball Clubs in America and Cuba (ILBCAC) formed under the guidance of William Freihofer and John O'Rourke. The original six teams in the Philadelphia-based league covered two countries and included two teams with predominantly white players—the Philadelphia Professionals and the Riverton Palmyra Athletic Club. The Cuban X Giants, Philadelphia Quaker Giants, Cuban Stars, and Havana Stars of Cuba constituted the remainder of the ILBCAC. In July, the Philadelphia Giants and the Wilmington Giants replaced two of the original teams, the Cuban Stars and the Philadelphia Quaker Giants. Although the league spawned the "World's Colored Championship" between the Philadelphia Giants and the Cuban X Giants, the league appeared to either disband or merge with a new league at the end of the 1906 season. Many of the same teams, including the Philadelphia Giants and the Cuban X Giants, joined the Brooklyn-based National Association of Colored Baseball Clubs of the United States and Cuba (NACBC). While the NACBC lasted longer than its predecessor, it experienced internal turmoil and dissolved after the 1910 season.[1]

During its brief existence, the NACBC faced many of the same challenges and realities that black professional baseball leagues encountered in the 1920s, 1930s, and 1940s. Members of the NACBC tried to prevent players from jumping their contracts and to impose salary caps. Players, however, still jumped their contracts and rebelled against salary limits by joining teams outside of the league. In future decades, different black leagues struggled with those same issues and, like the NACBC, saw internal conflicts arise among team owners. A good deal of the NACBC's infighting centered around white promoter Nat Strong. Strong dominated the NACBC's operation since he scheduled games and controlled the league's finances. Strong used his position to deny booking dates to teams outside of his organization and to receive high percentages of the gate receipts from games played in his ballparks. Strong's operation foreshadowed the involvement of white booking agents in black professional baseball and the leverage they exerted over teams and owners who lacked other options for scheduling games.[2]

Ten years after the NACBC's demise, Andrew "Rube" Foster made the next successful attempt to create a black professional baseball league. Prior to launching a league in 1920, Foster accumulated some key leadership experiences. As a player, Foster led a rebellion against the NACBC's attempt to impose salary limits and helped establish the Chicago-based Leland Giants as a premiere Midwestern team. Foster did more than play for the Leland Giants; he served as the team's manager and booking agent. He used his position of authority to net substantial guarantees or percentage of gate receipts and to take the team on barnstorming tours. In 1911, a dispute with the Leland Giants' owner led Foster to leave the team and to form the Chicago American Giants. With the American Giants, Foster continued to work as a player, manager, and booking agent. He formed a partnership with a white tavern owner, John M. Schorling, who also owned a ballpark at Thirty-Ninth and Shields, formerly home to the Chicago White Sox, that the American Giants used for their home games. Foster also took the American Giants on barnstorming tours on the West Coast, pitted his team against Major Leaguers, and reestablished an East vs. West Colored World Championship. Foster claimed several of those titles for the American Giants; he also claimed his team won championships in the West Coast and in other areas where they barnstormed.[3]

In February 1920, Foster's announcement that he had chartered the Negro National Baseball League (NNL) reflected both his bold leadership style and his national ambitions. The announcement came during a meeting of Midwestern baseball managers that Foster had called for the express purpose of forming a league. Foster, however, had incorporated the NNL in several Eastern states, including Pennsylvania and New York. His intention, in other words, was to bring Midwestern and Eastern teams under one organization. Such an action opened the door to potential partnerships and conflicts with Eastern black baseball leaders, including Nat Strong and Ed Bolden.[4]

Both the working relationship and the animosity between Foster and Bolden helped to define black professional baseball in the first half of the 1920s. Foster and Bolden possessed strong ambitions, and those ambitions occasionally clashed. The two men had disagreements over player contracts, and the threat of raids from NNL teams factored into Bolden's decision to join the NNL in 1921. Bolden, however, withdrew Hilldale from the NNL after the 1922 season, and then formed the Eastern Colored League (ECL) in late 1922. The formation of a rival league increased the tension between Foster and Bolden, but the two men did manage to put aside their differences and schedule an annual World Series between the champions of their respective leagues. Hilldale faced the NNL's Kansas City Monarchs in the first two World Series, winning the title in 1925.[5]

The era from 1920 to 1925 marked a period of great success for Hilldale and Bolden. With its ECL and World Series titles, Hilldale secured its place as one of the top teams in black professional baseball in the United States. Those titles marked the culmination of all of the work Bolden had done since he joined the team during its inaugural season. As the founder of the ECL, Bolden himself rose to the top of the eastern black baseball world. Though his career would continue for another two and a half decades, Bolden would never again enjoy the level of power he had when he ran the ECL. The success and power Bolden enjoyed did come at a price, namely a working partnership with white promoter Nat Strong. While Bolden could build an all-African American corporation to support Hilldale, he could not do the same for the ECL. Even at the height of his career, Bolden had to face limits upon his self-help ambitions, limits that arose from realities facing African Americans in the United States in the 1920s.

Setting the Stage for Organized Leagues

Following the end of the 1919 season, Foster penned a series of five articles called "The Pitfalls of Baseball" in the *Chicago Defender*. The articles provided insight into Foster's reasons for establishing the NNL and his ambitions for the new league. In the first article, Foster focused on the financial situation surrounding black professional baseball. He noted that most teams struggled to turn profits due to high operating expenses and a lack of lucrative games on their schedules. Travel expenses, player salaries, a lack of profitable weekday games, and an overreliance upon weekend games added to teams' financial burdens. Foster continued to analyze the issue of player salaries in his second article. After providing a brief overview of the salaries players earned in the first decade of the twentieth century, Foster defended the salaries he paid to his players and refuted claims that players earned paltry salaries. He argued that the amount of money the American Giants spent on salaries per month had never dipped below $1500. He pledged to spend no more than $2000 per month on salaries during the upcoming season, an amount he claimed no eastern club could surpass. Foster then compared the amount of money players earned to the amount people earned in other jobs, coming to the conclusion that the players earned just as much if not more than people in other occupations. He also pointed out that people in other occupations worked longer hours; by his calculations, ballplayers worked about only twenty hours per month.[6]

In his second article, Foster addressed another key issue that stood at the heart of his vision for black professional baseball—the need for a strong leader. As Foster explained, baseball as it existed "at the present among our people needs a very strong leader, and this leader to be successful must have able lieutenants, all of whom have the confidence of the public."[7] Foster held his own leadership qualities in high regard, particularly when he compared his background as a player and talent evaluator to the backgrounds of other promoters.. He referred to himself as "a student of the game" and as someone "whose intellect and brains of the game have drawn more comment from leading baseball critics than all the Colored players combined."[8]

Foster carried similar arguments into his final three articles. He criticized owners for wrecking successful teams and emphasized the need for greater organization in black professional baseball. He asserted that a league organization would protect owners from raids upon their rosters, support regular schedules, and place black baseball teams on firmer financial foundations. Foster used the American and National Leagues in Major League Baseball as examples for the kind of organization he envisioned for black baseball. One league, or circuit, would include teams from Midwestern cities like Chicago and Kansas City; the other circuit would include teams from Philadelphia, New York, and other eastern cities. Foster's final article revealed his frustration at other owners who resisted his plans and his race-based intentions for forming a league. As he argued, Foster wanted to avoid forming dependent relationships with white promoters. An organized league would promote African American agency and ownership within black professional baseball.[9]

Foster's decision to establish a league reflected larger movements present within American society in the 1920s. While the decade saw the Ku Klux Klan march in Washington, D.C., it also witnessed a flourishing African American cultural movement called the Harlem Renaissance, and with it the spirit of self-determination embodied in the New Negro. Since

Foster's plan encompassed teams located in prominent Midwestern and Eastern cities, organized leagues could take advantage of another development involving African Americans—continued population growth.[10]

The population growth that started in the World War I era in cities like Chicago and Philadelphia continued into the 1920s. For example, in Philadelphia, the African American population rose by over ten thousand people per year between 1922 and 1924. By the end of the decade, the city's African American population stood at close to two hundred and twenty thousand people, an increase of more than eleven percent over the population at the start of the decade. Philadelphia, therefore, continued to have the population needed to patronize black professional baseball and possibly even a league. Since Hilldale remained the top professional team in the region, any league that wanted to do business in the Philadelphia area would need to work with Bolden. With the Hilldale corporation under his control, Bolden stood as a formidable presence within Eastern black professional baseball. He enforced strict conduct rules upon his players, he used the *Tribune*'s sports pages to his advantage, and he operated a successful baseball franchise. Bolden, therefore, represented both a potential ally and a potential antagonist for Foster if he executed his plans for a national league organization. During the life of Foster's league, Bolden would fill both roles.[11]

Most importantly, both Foster and Bolden demonstrated how the era's spirit of self-help among African Americans influenced black professional baseball. The 1920s marked the height of Marcus Garvey's Pan-Africanist movement and his Universal Negro Improvement Association (UNIA). As part of his movement, Garvey established the Black Star Line, a shipping fleet that sought to compete with similar white-owned companies. To fund the Black Star Line, Garvey appealed to blacks across the country and asked for their investments in his venture. Through the UNIA and the Black Star Line, Garvey and his supporters sought to promote racial progress through economic growth. In a similar vein, Foster's and Bolden's leagues sought to assert black leadership over a black enterprise. Their competing ambitions created a rift within black professional baseball and helped to define relationships between competing owners of black baseball clubs and leagues in the twentieth century.[12]

Staying Independent

Foster formally established his league, the National Negro Baseball League (NNL), at a meeting in Kansas City in February 1920. Foster attended the meeting as the representative of both the Chicago American Giants and the Cuban Stars, a travelling team. The other men in attendance included C.I. Taylor of the Indianapolis ABCs, J.L. Wilkinson of the Kansas City Monarchs, J.T. "Tenny" Blunt of the Detroit Stars, Joe Green of the Chicago Giants, and Lorenzo Cobb of the St. Louis Giants. John Matthews of the Dayton Marcos could not attend the meeting due to an illness; he sent Foster a letter of support and money to cover his team's obligations to the new league. The meeting also included reporters and editors from black newspapers, like the *Chicago Defender*. Not surprisingly, the attendees elected Foster temporary president of the NNL and *Chicago Defender* sports editor Cary B. Lewis as the NNL's secretary. Lewis joined with Dave Wyatt of the *Indianapolis Ledger*, Elwood C. Knox of the *Indianapolis Freeman*, and attorney Elisha Scott in writing the NNL's constitution. The owners accepted the constitution and paid a fee of five hundred dollars to formalize their membership in the NNL.[13]

Though the eight-team NNL did not include any teams based in eastern cities, Foster held onto his dream of building an eastern circuit. When he secured a charter for the NNL, he incorporated the new league in three eastern states—New York, Maryland, and Pennsylvania.[14] At one of the NNL's organizational meetings, Foster announced that he had received a letter from Nat Strong in which Strong pledged to "do anything [to] promote the best interests of baseball all over the country."[15] In April, Foster traveled east and helped to welcome a new franchise, the Madison Stars. He also succeeded in getting one eastern club, the Atlantic City–based Bacharach Giants, to join the NNL as an associate member. While Foster could not entice any other eastern teams to join the NNL, he did succeed in getting the league's teams more exposure by securing games at Dyckman Oval in New York City.[16]

Foster had ulterior motives for his actions in the East—he wanted to undermine Hilldale's operations and hurt Bolden for signing three of his players. In November 1919, Bolden signed outfielder Jess Barbour, third baseman Bill Francis, and ace pitcher Dick Whitworth. Even though the baseball season had ended before Bolden signed the players, Foster felt that Bolden had raided his roster. Foster's support of the Madison Stars represented a direct attempt to strike at Hilldale since the Stars used the Madison Athletic Park, a new structure at 34th and Reed, for their home ballpark.[17] Foster struck another blow against Bolden and Hilldale when he enticed the Bacharach Giants to join the NNL as an associate member. As an associate member of the NNL, the Bacharach Giants pledged to respect the contracts players had signed with other league teams. The

Bacharach Giants could, however, raid the rosters of non–NNL teams, like Hilldale. Soon after joining the NNL, the Bacharach Giants signed three Hilldale players—catcher Yank Deas, shortstop Dick Lundy, and Barbour. Bolden filed an injunction; a court rejected his argument, and the players did not return to Hilldale.[18]

The tension between Bolden and Foster, via the Madison Stars, appeared on the *Tribune*'s sports pages. Stories about the Stars' upcoming inaugural season appeared alongside stores about Hilldale's preparations for the 1920 season. In one of those stories, the team announced the signing of three former Hilldale stars, including Otto Briggs.[19] Another story touted the team as "controlled by financial and baseball magnates of untold ability" and as "one of the greatest business and sporting enterprises known before in Philadelphia."[20] The story tied the new franchise to an attempt to make Philadelphia a center of black baseball. It also pleaded with the *Tribune*'s readers to patronize the new franchise since "it [was] owned and controlled by people of our race."[21] A subsequent story reinforced the race-based reasons for supporting the Madison Stars. According to the story, an African American–owned team playing at Madison Athletic Park represented "something that has been needed a long while in Philadelphia (a ball park owned by the race)."[22] The story included call for racial solidarity—"United we stand, divided we fall"—in appealing for readers to support the new franchise.[23]

In the aftermath of those articles, the *Tribune* published an article praising Hilldale's ten-year-long progress from a sandlot team to one of the top black professional baseball teams in the United States. The article also extolled Bolden's leadership and delivered a business-minded argument for scheduling games with Hilldale. According to the article, Hilldale drew record-breaking crowds in its road games and attracted large crowds at its home ballpark in Darby. For those reasons, Hilldale represented one "of the best drawing and most largely patronized independent teams in the East" in 1919.[24] Hilldale, furthermore, defeated the top black teams in games at Hilldale Park and earned the respect of the Major League players it faced during the previous season. Bolden garnered praise as a wise and respected baseball manager who deserved credit for Hilldale's remarkable achievements. Bolden also received praise for the strict conduct he enforced upon his players and the fans who patronized Hilldale Park.[25]

Bolden directly used the *Tribune* to defend his signing of three former American Giants and to critique Foster's encroachments upon eastern baseball. In his open letter to Foster, Bolden accused Foster of trying to retroactively create and enact laws. Bolden asserted that he had signed the three players in November 1919, after their contracts with Foster had expired and before Foster established the NNL. He also chastised Foster for increasing the amount of money one of the players, the pitcher Whitworth, owed him. Bolden demeaned Foster's attempts to undermine Hilldale's operations within eastern black professional baseball. He reminded Foster of a time in 1917 when he traveled east and lost money because he did not schedule any games against Hilldale. Bolden argued that the same would happen to any NNL team that traveled east and ignored Hilldale. Bolden also raised another financial issue, one that carried larger implications beyond his current dispute with Foster. He argued that Hilldale "can make more money in a single day in New York than [it] can in a week in Detroit" and that the "cost of traveling expenses make it paramount that no lucrative possibility be overlooked."[26]

Despite Foster's aggressive tactics, Hilldale enjoyed a successful 1920 season. Darby mayor Burgess Grayson helped Hilldale open its home season by throwing the ceremonial first pitch, and the Keystone Band provided entertainment to the opening day crowd. In addition to leasing Hilldale Park in Darby, Bolden leased ballparks in Camden, New Jersey, and Wilmington, Delaware, for Hilldale to use on a regular basis. Due to the ongoing feud between Bolden and Foster, Hilldale mostly faced local white amateur or semi-pro teams throughout the 1920 season. For the first time in its history, Hilldale won over one hundred games. The team claimed several titles, including the Delaware County championship and an independent championship. It claimed the latter championship after emerging as the winner of a three-team tournament held at Baker Bowl, the Philadelphia Phillies' home ballpark. Baker Bowl also hosted two contests pitting Hilldale against teams composed of Major League players. Hilldale lost to a team Casey Stengel assembled, but it shut out a team featuring Babe Ruth.[27]

Hilldale fared well as an independent team, yet Bolden lacked any defense against NNL teams raiding his roster and signing away his best players. Bolden, consequently, brought Hilldale into the NNL as an associate member for the 1921 season. Bolden's decision marked a turning point in Hilldale's history and in his own career. By joining the NNL, Hilldale came into the same orbit as the other top teams in the country. For Bolden, joining the NNL provided him with protection against player raids and access to a successful organization. Teams in the NNL made money during the 1920 season, and a slight geographical realignment in the 1921 season portended potentially higher profits. Hilldale's membership in the NNL also represented a gateway for Bolden to assume and assert greater leadership within black professional baseball.[28]

Into the Fold

Harmony reigned at the NNL meeting held in Indianapolis in December 1920. The men in attendance, including Bolden, unanimously elected Foster as the league's president and secretary for the upcoming season. Each of the owners also paid a $1000 "good faith" deposit and agreed to a new league constitution. The constitution mandated fines for owners and managers who engaged in ungentlemanly conduct and required players to maintain conduct standards both on and off the field. Other rules passed at the meeting gave NNL teams the right to refuse to play against non-league teams, pledged to respect contracts players had with other league teams, and imposed new measures to prevent players from jumping their contracts. The recent animosity between Bolden and Foster never surfaced at the meeting. As the *Chicago Defender* stressed, Foster and the other owners treated Bolden like a long-standing member of the NNL. Bolden also resolved any lingering conflict with John Connor, the Bacharach Giants owner who had signed three Hilldale players soon after joining the NNL in 1920. The two men acted as cordial friends, even sharing a hotel room for the meeting's duration.[29]

With its associate membership in the NNL, Hilldale embarked upon another successful season. The team won over one hundred games for the second consecutive season, compiling winning records against both NNL teams and the local white teams that still filled its schedule. With one hundred and seven wins, Hilldale surpassed its win total from the 1920 season by five games. Similar to the 1920 season, Bolden secured a park in Camden for Hilldale to use on Wednesdays. The team still played home games at Hilldale Park on Thursdays, Saturdays and holidays; Pennsylvania's blue laws prevented Hilldale from playing in Darby on Sundays. Louis Santop, Judy Johnson, Dick Whitworth, Otto Briggs, and Phil Cockrell all played key roles in Hilldale's success. Hilldale's winning ways culminated in a six-game series in October against the Chicago American Giants. Hilldale prevailed by winning three of the games in the series; Chicago won two games, and one game ended in a tie.[30]

Hilldale's success came in the midst of some troubling signs for the overall health and long-term stability of the NNL. Unlike the previous season, several NNL teams lost money due in part to declining attendance. The financial troubles accompanied franchise instability. The Columbus Buckeyes, formerly the Dayton Marcos, folded; the St. Louis franchise shifted from the St. Louis Giants to the St. Louis Stars. NNL teams, moreover, played an uneven number of games. In September, Foster claimed the NNL title for his American Giants despite the fact that the Monarchs had a higher win total and that the six-game series remained with Hilldale. The NNL's troubles prompted Foster to pen another series of articles in the *Chicago Defender*. Those articles covered issues, including leadership and the use of African American umpires, shaping both the present and future state of black professional baseball. In those articles, Foster took aim at owners and managers who he felt made bad decisions and needed to learn how to properly run successful baseball teams. He also faulted players for their poor conduct and African American umpires for not grasping baseball's rules. Foster, in other words, assigned blame to everyone but himself and his Chicago American Giants. In his first article, he asserted that he had made a great sacrifice in joining the NNL since the American Giants could make more money as an independent team. He also asserted that any criticism he received came from ignorant people who failed to understand and appreciate his leadership.[31]

For Bolden, the end of the 1921 season marked a time for him to reconsider Hilldale's membership in the NNL. Membership in the NNL granted access to games with other league teams, but members could not schedule games with NNL "outlaws." Those "outlaws" included eastern teams, such as the Brooklyn Royal Giants, that Hilldale had faced in past seasons and that fell under the control of Nat Strong. Bolden, along with other NNL owners, also resented Foster's relationship with white businessman John Schorling and chafed at Foster's decision to schedule frequent home games for his American Giants. Schorling owned the American Giants' home ballpark, and the frequent home games kept money flowing into the team's coffers. The frequent home games also saved the American Giants the expense of long eastern road trips. That burden fell to other NNL teams, such as the Kansas City Monarchs. Due to those circumstances, Bolden explored the possibility of withdrawing from the NNL and joining forces with Strong. Before he could make the move, Foster struck back with threats of player raids and the denial of games with NNL teams. Bolden and Foster met in February 1922, and Bolden decided to keep Hilldale in the league for another season.[32]

The off-season tension presaged a tough 1922 season. By the end of the season, the Bacharach Giants, Cleveland Tate Stars, and the Pittsburgh Keystones folded. The latter two clubs had joined the NNL at the start of the season; the Keystones had incurred a $28,000 debt before disbanding. Other NNL teams also incurred debts and suffered from declines in attendance. The $1,000 mandatory annual deposit for all NNL teams, demands for ten percent of gate receipts, and the need to share gate receipts with white ballpark owners added to the NNL's woes and made it difficult for Foster to entice new owners. Foster also suffered some personal difficulties in both 1921 and 1922. While traveling to New Orleans in November 1921, authorities in Atlanta briefly arrested Foster over charges that he owed money to several players. Foster lost his daughter to pneumonia and, in November 1922, suffered from an illness that confined him to bed.[33]

The NNL's instability, combined with Hilldale's own struggles, compelled Bolden to withdraw from the league after the 1922 season concluded. Hilldale still compiled an impressive overall record of ninety-four wins, fifty-seven losses and two ties. Hilldale, however, ended the season with a losing record against NNL teams and against other black professional teams, such as the new Harrisburg Giants, not affiliated with the league. Issues related to money and long-distance travel added to Bolden's ire. Hilldale made an expensive trip to the Midwest to face the Detroit Giants and American Giants, but only few of the Midwestern NNL teams traveled to Darby. Hilldale's association with the NNL again precluded it from potentially profitable games against eastern terms deemed "outlaws." Additionally, with Foster at the helm of the NNL, Bolden could not exert much influence over league affairs. For those reasons, Bolden formally severed Hilldale's ties with the NNL in December 1922. Bolden asked for the $1000 he submitted to the NNL when Hilldale originally joined the league, but Foster refused. Foster cited Bolden's intentions to raid NNL team rosters and the rule barring the return of the deposit in his decision refuse Bolden's request. An eastern versus western battle had emerged within black professional baseball.[34]

The break between Bolden and Foster seemed unavoidable. Prior to joining the NNL, Bolden had enjoyed a great deal of freedom in running Hilldale and in scheduling games. Hilldale's membership in the NNL blocked raids on its roster, but it limited the amount of power Bolden could extend over his own franchise and over black professional baseball in eastern states. Bolden had to follow Foster's dictates, lacked access to teams located in eastern states, and faced the prospect of financial losses. By withdrawing Hilldale from the NNL, Bolden set the stage for his next bold leadership step within black professional baseball—forming his own league.

East Versus West

Bolden officially established the Mutual Association of Eastern Colored Baseball Clubs, or the Eastern Colored League (ECL), on December

16, 1922, at the Southwest YMCA in Philadelphia. Six teams constituted the charter members of the ECL—Hilldale, the Original Atlantic City Bacharachs, the Baltimore Black Sox, the Cuban Stars, the Brooklyn Royal Giants, and the Lincoln Giants. In addition to Bolden, the baseball men in attendance at the ECL's inaugural meeting included Nat Strong, Alex Pompez, James Keenan, Charles Spedden, and Thomas Jackson. Each of those men represented one of the ECL's teams. For example, Strong represented the Brooklyn Royal Giants, Alex Pompez represented the Cuban Stars, and Thomas Jackson represented the Bacharach Giants. In a departure from the NNL's practices, the ECL drew leaders from each of the six league teams. Officials from each team served as commissioners; those commissioners would annually select a chairman and a secretary. The commissioners also would craft laws governing the ECL's owners, players, and other officials. At the inaugural meeting, the commissioners elected Bolden as the ECL's first chairman and James Keenan as the first secretary.[35]

Not surprisingly, Bolden's departure from the NNL and his formation of the ECL provoked strong reactions. In an article in the *Baltimore Afro-American*, Foster accused Bolden of establishing the league merely as a cover for Strong's influence within eastern black professional baseball. Foster took aim at one of the reasons for Bolden's departure from the NNL: the small number of league teams which traveled to eastern states. He noted that NNL rules, which Bolden agreed to when he joined the league, did not require teams to travel east or west to play games against other league teams. Foster also questioned Bolden's leadership and his decision to work with Strong, a man whom Foster claimed extracted high percentages of gate receipts from black baseball teams. He further accused Bolden of raiding NNL teams and threatened to strike back against eastern teams.[36]

A similarly worded article, probably written by Foster, appeared in the *Chicago Defender* and poked at Bolden's leadership. The article wondered why Bolden did not extend invitations to teams based in Richmond, Harrisburg, Washington, D.C., and Norfolk. To respond to its own question, the article reported on a "serious" rumor from people with knowledge of "the inside of the Eastern situation"—"because Nat Strong, a white man, did not book those clubs they were Ku Kluxed."[37] The article also presented Foster's version of the events that nearly propelled Bolden out of the NNL prior to the 1922 season and raised questions about Bolden's membership on the Philadelphia Baseball Association (PBA). Established in 1922, the PBA attempted to regulate the approximately sixty baseball franchises that joined the association. Though the PBA included both white and black clubs, the association segregated those clubs into different divisions. The article noted another form of discrimination within the PBA: white teams collected ten percent of the gate receipts, while black teams collected considerably less. Since Bolden sat on the PBA's board of directors, the article questioned his appointment as the ECL's chairman and the type of leadership he would demonstrate in the new league. The article lamented "that unless he shows a racial change in judgment in the new league, Colored baseball in the East has gone back a decade, gone back to the days when Nat Strong offered ball clubs $100 flat and two 15-cent meals for a Sunday game."[38]

As he had done in the past, Bolden used an open letter to respond to Foster's charges. He derisively compared Foster to the deposed German Kaiser. He also sarcastically referred to Foster as the self-appointed "Czar of Negro baseball" who had resorted to the "poison pen" and engaged in "unscrupulous measures."[39] To respond to Foster's criticism of his decision to work with Strong, Bolden highlighted Foster's partnership with Schorling and even used the term "chattel."[40] Bolden also noted that J.L. Wilkinson, the Monarchs' white owner, served as the NNL's secretary and that Foster took high percentages of the gate receipts from NNL games. According to Bolden, Foster's actions in regards to the gate receipts violated NNL regulations. Bolden concluded that since the NNL "could offer us no benefits, no protection, we followed the only course that a sagacious one would pursue and resign."[41]

The animosity between Bolden and Foster persisted as the 1923 season approached. In February, Foster traveled to several eastern states, including Pennsylvania, to make preparations for the NNL's upcoming season. He hinted to the *Chicago Defender* that he hoped to schedule games at the Polo Grounds and Shibe Park, moves designed to undercut Strong and Bolden in their respective regions. Foster also came to Philadelphia prepared to meet with Bolden, but the meeting never transpired. He blamed Bolden's strange schedule—Bolden allegedly worked all night and slept during the daytime—for the missed meeting. When the ECL published its schedule, the *Chicago Defender* compared it very unfavorably to the NNL's schedule. The newspaper pointed out that the Baltimore Black Sox had only thirty-one scheduled games against other ECL teams. By contrast, the newspaper boasted that each NNL team had one hundred and five games on its league schedule.[42]

After that tumultuous off-season, the ECL enjoyed a mostly successful 1923 season. Bolden and the other team owners worked amicably and reported attendance increases, which they attributed to fan interest in the league's pennant race. The ECL's financial arrangements helped to breed the harmonious atmosphere among the league's owners. Visiting teams received a guarantee ranging from $150 to $300 as well as an option for forty percent of the gate receipts. Such an arrangement resembled financial arrangements prevalent within independent baseball. The NNL maintained a different arrangement, one that had rankled Bolden. In the NNL, the league itself assumed ten percent of the gate receipts; the visiting team received forty percent of the receipts, while the home team received the remaining fifty percent. The ECL also benefitted from raids that owners, including Bolden, had conducted on NNL rosters. Like their NNL counterparts, the ECL teams did not play balanced schedules, and none of the teams completed their schedules. Despite those shortcomings, Bolden's venture succeeded, and the league's success translated into renewed success for Hilldale.[43]

The 1923 season marked the start of another reign of dominance for Hilldale within eastern black professional baseball. Hilldale's ability to attract large crowds at both Hilldale Park and its away games bolstered the ECL's financial health. Additionally, Hilldale completed all but one of its scheduled games, more than any other team in the ECL. After falling below one hundred victories in the 1922 season, Hilldale rebounded with an astonishing one hundred and thirty-seven victories in 1923. Thirty-two of those wins came against ECL teams; Hilldale lost only forty-seven games, and seventeen of those losses came against its ECL foes. With those victories, Hilldale easily captured the ECL pennant. The team added the PBA championship and five victories over two teams of barnstorming Major League players to its impressive accomplishments. Those games happened despite a ban Major League Commissioner Kenesaw Mountain Landis had imposed against white Major League teams barnstorming against Negro League teams.[44]

Bolden's key offseason acquisitions, some of whom he signed away from NNL teams, played key roles in Hilldale's successes. Jessie "Nip" Winters strengthened a pitching staff that still included Phil Cockrell; the two of them had a combined total of over sixty wins. George Carr, Jake Stephens, Frank Warfield, and Clint Thomas added depth to a roster that already had Louis Santop, Otto Briggs and Judy Johnson. Catcher Raleigh "Biz" Mackey finished the season with the ECL's highest batting average. Shortstop and team captain John Henry "Pop" Lloyd also finished the season with one of the league's highest batting averages, but his presence marked one of Bolden's few disappointments in 1923. The thirty-nine-year-old Lloyd commanded a high salary, yet an injury in the middle of the season removed him from the lineup. Friction developed between Lloyd and the other players, particularly when Lloyd blocked a salary increase for one of his teammates. In September, Bolden suspended Lloyd for ten days; he later made the suspension permanent. Bolden cited unspecified business matters in his decision to suspend one of his star players. W. Rollo Wilson in the *Pittsburgh Courier* reported on rumors of jealousy among Hilldale players, particularly one unnamed player who wanted Lloyd's job, as a factor in his dismissal from the team.[45]

The controversy surrounding Lloyd did not obscure Hilldale's achievements and the ECL's success. At the end of the season, the *Philadelphia Tribune* carried yet another retrospective article on Hilldale's rise under Bolden's tutelage. The retrospective praised Hilldale as an "organization built upon the sure foundation of fair sportsmanship, whose accomplishments have made glad the heart of every school boy of our race."[46] It also credited Hilldale for encouraging others to "soar to the heights they have reached in their chosen profession."[47] At a league meeting held in December in Philadelphia, the ECL owners reelected Bolden as the chairman and Keenan as the secretary-treasurer. Bolden and his fellow owners expanded the ECL to eight teams by welcoming the Washington Potomacs and the Harrisburg Giants. The peaceful meeting closed with the owners agreeing to meet at a future date to craft a league schedule and to reaffirm regulations in regards to player contracts.[48]

While Bolden tasted success in 1923 and oversaw the ECL's expansion, Foster endured a tough and frustrating season. NNL franchises based in Toledo and Milwaukee folded; Foster and other NNL owners also faced the constant prospect of ECL owners raiding their rosters. Additionally, Foster saw his league's gate receipts decline, and he lacked any clear options on replacing the two lost franchises. Foster, furthermore, began to dismantle his American Giants once they slipped out of first place. His team finished the season in third place; the Monarchs won the NNL pennant. In past years, black professional baseball hosted a championship series pitting an eastern champion against a western champion. With both the NNL and the ECL, a championship series seemed like a logical way to conclude the baseball season. Foster's lingering resentment over Bolden's actions prevented the NNL and ECL champions, the Monarchs and Hilldale, from facing each other in a championship series. Such a step needed more time, and the possible intervention from an independent arbiter, to develop.[49]

We Are the Champions

Similar to the 1923 season, Hilldale rose to the top of the eight-team ECL and won over one hundred games in 1924. The team officially opened its ECL season with a celebratory opening game against the Harrisburg Giants at Hilldale Park. A concert from the Cornucopia Band preceded a pennant-raising ceremony honoring Hilldale's ECL championship; the Pennsylvania Boxing Commissioner threw out the first ball. Even with the dismissal of Lloyd, Hilldale's roster boasted talented players—Santop, Johnson, Carr, Briggs, Stephens, Cockrell, Winters, Warfield, and Mackey. With those players, Hilldale won forty-seven of the sixty-nine ECL games it played and captured its second consecutive league pennant.[50]

In September 1924, officials from both the ECL and the NNL discussed plans for a World Series pitting Hilldale against the Monarchs, the two-time NNL champions. Before the two leagues could schedule a championship series, Bolden and Foster had to resolve their differences in regards to contract jumpers and the $1000 Bolden believed Foster owed him since he had left the NNL. Commissioner Landis offered to arbitrate the dispute, but Bolden and Foster managed to resolve their differences without his influence. Bolden waived his demands for the return of his $1000 deposit, and the two men worked out an agreement in regards to player contracts and contract jumpers. A national commission composed of both ECL and NNL officials, including Bolden and Foster, made the arrangements for the World Series. The plan the commission produced tried to ensure that both leagues would benefit directly and indirectly from the series. The two teams would play the first two games in Philadelphia, travel to Baltimore for game three, travel to Chicago for games four and five, and then travel to Kansas City for the last three games. Thirty-five percent of the gross receipts from the eight games would go to Hilldale and the Monarchs, with the winning team obtaining sixty percent of those receipts. The remaining percentage of the gross receipts would go to the second and third place teams in each league, to the team owners, and to the national commission.[51]

Though Hilldale played well, the Monarchs triumphed and captured the World Series title. Since game three ended in a tie, the two teams played ten games in the series; the Monarchs won five games, and Hilldale won the remaining four. Hilldale scored more runs and collected more hits than the Monarchs; the team also grabbed a lead in the series, winning three of the first five games. The Monarchs, however, made a comeback by winning two of the games played in the Kansas City and scoring a decisive 5–0 victory in the tenth game. Hilldale's batters struggled against the Monarchs' pitcher Jose Mendez, who started in the decisive game and notched a shutout. A poorly timed error from Santop and a poor pitching performance from Cockrell also factored into Hilldale's loss in the series.[52]

Bolden and the rest of the franchise accepted the defeat in the World Series. Neither he nor any of Hilldale's players complained about bad calls or hinted that the Monarchs won the series by engaging in dirty tactics. After the series ended, a group of Hilldale's fans greeted the team at the Broad Street Station, ushered them into cars, and led them on a parade down Broad Street. A brass band provided music for the parade, which disbanded at George Robinson's New Roadside Hotel. Several nights later, Bolden joined his players for a banquet at the New Roadside. Robinson, who had supported Hilldale during the season, organized the banquet that brought together Hilldale's prominent supporters and the team in a celebration of the team's accomplishments. Though the players felt despondent over the loss, many of them delivered thankful speeches during the banquet. Bolden and the team's supporters, including Attorney Mercer Lewis and the legendary Sol White, also delivered speeches praising the team and added to the festive atmosphere.[53]

Overall, the first World Series produced mixed results. Foster gushed that "[e]xcusing the first two games in Philadelphia, I saw eight of the best played games of baseball I had ever witnessed."[54] His praise for the Monarchs seemed reserved, yet he lauded Hilldale for having "the most wonderful outfield I have ever seen" and extolled Winters's pitching performances. Foster's mostly positive review, however, contained some hints at deeper problems with both the series and with black professional baseball. He and the Negro National League's other commissioners each received $200 from the series' gross receipts. While Foster did not complain about the small amount, he did note that "the three weeks of time, the loss to my club during my absence was worth thousands to me."[55] Foster also acknowledged that teams could have made more money barnstorming during the series' three-week-long duration than they did through the series' gate receipts. Overall, the World Series' receipts totaled $52,114; after factoring in expenses like railroad fares, the two leagues split $23,463,44. Kansas City's sixteen players split $4,927.32, and Hilldale's seventeen players split $3,284.88. The club owners, Wilkinson and Bolden, also received a share of the gate receipts. Bad weather and the scheduling of some games during weekday afternoons led to some significant swings in attendance figures during the series. Overall, over 45,000 fans patronized the ten-game series. A Sunday game in Kansas City drew the largest crowd of 8,865 fans, while a mere 584 fans witnessed a Monday afternoon game in Baltimore.[56]

Even though the 1924 World Series yielded some mixed results, it helped to promote a spirit of harmony between the two leagues. The animosity that had characterized Bolden's and Foster's relationship a few years earlier had dissipated. The two leagues even held a joint meeting in Chicago in December 1924. At the meeting, the ECL owners again elected Bolden as the chairman and Keenan as secretary-treasurer. Additionally, Bolden formally delivered a note of thanks to Foster for his "fair and unprejudiced articles in reference to the Eastern League" and for his "encouraging attitude" toward eastern baseball.[57] Once the joint session for the ECL and NNL owners started, Bolden moved that Foster act as the session's chairman. The other owners unanimously supported Bolden's motion. The owners then came to an agreement in regards to each league's territorial rights; they used Pennsylvania's western border as the dividing line between the two leagues. They also reached agreements that established uniformity in player contracts across the two leagues and that aspired to prevent owners from raiding each other's rosters.[58]

On the baseball diamond, the 1925 season mirrored the 1924 season, with Hilldale capturing the ECL title and the Monarchs winning the NNL title. With its roster full of talented players, Hilldale once again won over one hundred games. Though it faced some tough competition from the Harrisburg Giants, Hilldale accumulated one hundred and twenty-one victories on its way to its third consecutive ECL pennant. Eight of Hilldale's regular players ended the season with a batting average of over .300, and Carr led the league with an average of over .400. Cockrell, Winters, and Rube Currie bolstered Hilldale's pitching staff; Warfield, Thomas, and Briggs each stole over thirty bases.[59]

In a rematch of the 1924 World Series, Hilldale easily prevailed over the Monarchs by winning five of the six games played in the series. Hilldale's players dominated the Monarchs in all facets of the game. After the series ended, Bolden and his players basked in the glory of their victory. They received favorable coverage and praise in the *Tribune* and gathered for another banquet at the Hotel Brotherhood. At the banquet, the players received gold baseballs. One of the speakers, Dr. Charles A. Lewis, lauded Hilldale as helping lead the country to a more progressive age, and foretold a future with an integrated Major Leagues. Another speaker, Magistrate Amos Scott, praised the efforts of Bolden and the Hilldale corporation. He also stated that the city of Philadelphia appreciated Hilldale's success and remarkable performance during the 1925 season. Bolden also spoke at the banquet, and he used the opportunity to briefly sketch Hilldale's growth from a sandlot team to a World Series champion. Speeches from other members of the Hilldale corporation and community supports as well as other forms of entertainment added to the banquet's festive atmosphere.[60]

Bolden, Hilldale's supporters, and Hilldale's players justifiably basked in the World Series victory, but larger problems threatened to overwhelm black professional baseball. Bad weather and fewer games during the World Series translated into significantly lower attendance figures, resulting in lower gate receipts. Total attendance for the World Series dropped to 20,067, while the gross receipts fell to $21,044.60. Those figures included an exhibition game played in Jersey City on the day after Hilldale clinched the World Series. After deductions for taxes, park rentals, travel expenses, and other items, the players on Hilldale's winning team shared a meager $1,233.11. The Monarchs players shared an even more meager $822.08.[61]

The problems threatening both the ECL and the NNL went beyond the disappointing World Series results. For the first time since he established the league, Bolden faced criticism from other ECL owners about his leadership and handling of league affairs. Both Bolden and Foster faced criticism, particularly from black newspapers, over their decision to use white umpires. Their use of white umpires, along with their continued association with white promoters, rankled black sportswriters and fans at a time when African Americans faced declining economic fortunes. The 1925 season brought both Bolden and Hilldale to the top of the black baseball world, but it also provided a window into an unhappy future. In the upcoming years, growing criticism and Hilldale's struggles exacted a personal toll on Bolden and led to his temporary exile from black professional baseball. Bolden demonstrated strong leadership in taking Hilldale from a sandlot team full of teenagers to a championship team replete with multiple Hall of Fame players. Sustaining that success in the face of an oncoming economic disaster proved impossible.[62]

CHAPTER THREE

The Fall, 1925–1930

Over the first fifteen years of his career in black professional baseball, Bolden established himself as the next in a long line of African American leaders in the Philadelphia area. He led Hilldale on a steady progression from a sandlot team to a World Series champion. Additionally, Bolden asserted leadership within the larger world of black professional baseball. He spearheaded the formation of an African American corporation to support Hilldale. He also established a league, the Eastern Colored League (ECL), that brought together top eastern black professional baseball teams and that mirrored a similar organization Andrew Rube Foster established in the Midwest. Though all owners shared governance powers within the ECL, Bolden served as the league's first chairman and represented the ECL's public voice in the *Philadelphia Tribune* and other black newspapers. In the ECL's first three seasons, Hilldale reigned as the league's dominant team, winning three pennants on its way to its World Series victory over the Kansas City Monarchs in 1925.

Starting in 1925 and accelerating over the next four years, Bolden faced dissent and criticism that steadily undermined his leadership and standing within black professional baseball. Most of the criticism that Bolden faced stemmed from his tendency to use white umpires, instead of black umpires, in both regular season and postseason games. Even though Bolden led an African American corporation, some people within black professional baseball and in the black press regarded his use of white umpires as a betrayal. As Bolden endured the dissent and criticism, Hilldale's standing within the ECL dropped, and the team faced financial difficulties. The combined problems took a personal toll on Bolden, and he suffered a nervous breakdown in September 1927. Bolden's breakdown temporarily took him away from black professional baseball. Once Bolden returned, he pursued aggressive actions designed to protect Hilldale at any cost. His actions precipitated the demise of two leagues, the ECL and the short-lived American Negro League (ANL). He also faced mounting criticism for his continued use of white umpires and his association with white businessmen.[1]

Bolden's seemingly heartless and cutthroat actions stemmed from an increasingly dire situation facing Hilldale and other black teams. An economic downturn hit African Americans in Philadelphia and other major cities several years before the stock market crash grabbed newspaper headlines. The downturn hurt already vulnerable African Americans and weakened, or even eliminated, their ability to patronize teams like Hilldale. Though Bolden earned high marks at his full-time Post Office job, his annual salary stood at only $1,900. Similarly, many people within Philadelphia's growing African American population found employment in modest-paying or low-paying jobs. The economic downturn both limited the number of jobs available to African Americans and limited the buying power of their annual salaries. Such a situation meant that Bolden had to fight for every dollar from African American baseball fans in the Philadelphia region. It also meant that Bolden explored another option for maintaining Hilldale's operations—a partnership with a white businessman.[2]

For Bolden, the year 1930 marked the ugliest year in his black professional baseball career. His experiences during that year reflected the limits of the effectiveness of the self-help philosophy that had guided him since he had established the Hilldale Corporation. Garvey's Pan-Africanist movement floundered in the late 1920s as Garvey faced deportation from the United States and his business ventures faltered. Similarly, Bolden's determination to lead a black enterprise and to foster a black corporation floundered as economic conditions among his base of supporters diminished. His determination to uphold high standards, combined with a personal health crisis, unearthed a streak of ruthlessness in his actions. His willingness to turn to white capital as a means of support triggered a fierce response from other members of the corporation and black sportswriters. That fierce response demonstrated the sense of pride that Hilldale instilled and the persistence of the hope that black capital could support black enterprises. That fierce response also drove Bolden from black professional baseball and, for a time, seemed to close the door on his career.[3]

Race and Umpires

Umpire-related issues bedeviled Bolden and other baseball owners for many years. Unlike the arrangement in Major League Baseball, ECL and NNL teams selected their own umpires for their home games. As a result, confrontations between players and umpires and allegations of umpire bias marred many games. Prior to the start of the 1924 season, Bolden and other ECL owners felt compelled to adopt new regulations for on-field conduct. The new regulations designated the field captain or playing manager as the only people eligible to resolve on-field controversies or deliver protests against umpires' calls. The new regulations also prohibited players from engaging in umpire baiting. Players faced ejection and fines for baiting umpires; they faced a fine of $100 for assaulting umpires. Bolden and the other owners also imposed some regulations upon umpires because they believed that "the appearance of [the] umpires and their efficient service have a tendency to upbuild organized baseball."[4] For the umpires, the new regulations called upon them to arbitrate unbiased games, use discretion when removing players from games, and to act promptly when ejecting players. Umpires faced expulsion for failing to adhere to the vague guidelines.[5]

The 1924 World Series between the Kansas City Monarchs and Hilldale sparked some renewed discussion about the use of black umpires. Prior to the World Series, a national commission composed of Bolden, Foster, and other representatives from the ECL and NNL made arrangements for the series. As part of those arrangements, the representatives chose white umpires to work at all of the games. The use of white umpires drew some mild criticism from writers in the *Pittsburgh Courier*. One writer lamented that the use of white umpires contradicted the overall spirit of the series and represented an insult to the black umpires whom both leagues had used during the season. The writer, however, reasoned that the leagues used the umpires in order to avoid any claims of bias toward Hilldale or Kansas City.[6] A few weeks later, the *Courier*'s W. Rollo Wilson mentioned black umpires in his regular column. Wilson used his column to "respectfully invite the [ECL's] attention to the proposition advanced by us some time since—NEGRO umpires, paid by the league, rotated among the cities of the league."[7] As Wilson reasoned, if "colored men can play baseball they can umpire baseball games and should be given the chance to do so."[8]

The twin issues of race and umpiring blossomed again during the 1925 season. For the first time, the ECL decided to use a rotating crew of umpires, and it hired a white man, Bill Dallas from the *Evening Ledger*, as the crew's leader.[9] In response, *Tribune* sports editor J.M. Howe drew a cartoon depicting the ECL as an Uncle Tom character. Speaking for the ECL, Bolden wrote a letter strongly objecting to the cartoon and defending

Dallas's hire. Bolden decried the cartoon as "untimely and unfair," particularly since the ECL's decision to hire Dallas reflected its desire to provide teams with "a system of competent umpiring."[10] Bolden praised Dallas as conscientious, capable of making decisions regardless of a player's race, and more experienced than other umpires in the ECL. The ECL, therefore, made a logical and sound decision to make Dallas the leader of its umpiring crew.[11]

Even with the rotating crew of umpires, controversy and conflicts continued to mar many ECL games, and similar incidents engulfed the NNL. In the middle of the season, two NNL umpires wrote a letter to the *Pittsburgh Courier's* Rollo Wilson. The umpires asked for patience and understanding for their fellow umpires, who occasionally made mistakes. They also chastised the newspaper for publishing managers' and owners' complaints, which they regarded as propaganda for the league, and asked for more balanced coverage.[12] One month after their letter appeared in the *Courier*, Rube Foster announced that he had released most of the NNL's umpires. One of the released umpires, Bert Gholston, had co-written the letter published in the *Courier*. When he announced his decision, Foster used the opportunity to criticize the "wretched" umpires, whose work "had been anything up to the standard."[13] He detailed the umpires' shortcomings—bad decisions that led to on-field disruptions, lack of knowledge about baseball's rules, and not using the correct hands to call balls and strikes.[14] Shortly after Foster unleashed his rant against the NNL's umpires, an ECL game between Hilldale and Harrisburg featured fights both on the field and in the stands. The game prompted Wilson to lament the normality of rowdy baseball in the ECL and about the poor state of umpires in the league. He noted that one of the umpires at the Hilldale-Harrisburg game called time to get a drink of water; the pause seemed to help Hilldale's pitcher. The umpire also refrained from punishing a player who threw dirt at him to protest a call. Wilson cautioned that such actions threatened the ECL's integrity and had the potential to drive fans away from ECL games.[15]

As the 1925 season reached its conclusion, concerns and anger involving umpires remained potent. After his release, Gholston blamed race as the key factor in the ongoing conflicts between teams and umpires. He accused several NNL teams of planning to physically attack black umpires and of refusing to respect black umpires' decisions. He also claimed that the lack of respect for black umpires touched the entire league and not simply a few teams.[16] Wilson again devoted space in another one of his regular columns to the umpire situation, boldly proclaiming, "EASTERN LEAGUE UMPIRES HAVE NO MORE AUTHOR-ITY THAN A KU KLUXER WOULD HAVE AT A BANQUET OF THE 'HELL FIGHTERS' IN HARLEM!"[17] He provided some details on more evidence of biased umpires in recent ECL games and disavowed the rotating umpire system, a system he once advocated. Though Wilson focused his ire at the "bimboes" who worked as umpires, he placed some of the blame upon the ECL and umpire supervisor Dallas.[18] He reasoned that the lack of support they provided to competent umpires compelled those umpires to favor the home teams and, therefore, exacerbate grievances against all umpires.[19]

Wilson's diatribe foreshadowed reactions from black sportswriters concerning the ways Bolden conducted his business. For Wilson, the treatment accorded black umpires likely rankled him because it played into ugly stereotypes concerning African Americans. If black umpires could not effectively assert their authority over black players, then Bolden and other officials had no choice but to use white umpires. The image of white umpires restoring order over black players within a black league could lead to suggestions that African Americans could not govern their own affairs. The use of white umpires, furthermore, could lead to broader suggestions that black men could not occupy positions of authority and that segregation statutes maintained a proper sense of order in American society.

Umpire-related controversies plagued Bolden and the ECL again in 1926, particularly since the owners discontinued the use of a rotating umpire system. Instead, the league reinstated the policy of allowing home teams to hire umpires. Consequently, visiting teams frequently complained about biased calls, and players engaged in altercations with umpires. In one altercation, Hilldale's Phil Cockrell punched an umpire after the umpire changed his mind on a call. According to the accompanying story in the *Tribune*, the fight brought local cops out onto the field, and one of the cops hit Cockrell in the back of his head as he left the diamond. Bolden tried to assert leadership on the issue by fining Cockrell $100 and suspending him for five days. Through his actions, Bolden probably intended to make an example out of Cockrell and to discourage other players from attacking umpires. Bolden's actions, however, seemed like a desperate attempt to assert his authority over and bring order to an increasingly unruly ECL. Criticism surrounding umpires represented only one of several serious problems plaguing Bolden and the rest of the ECL. The other problems targeted Bolden's leadership and deeper questions about the way black baseball should operate in American society.[20]

Everyone's a Critic

Prior to the 1925 season, the criticism Bolden faced typically came from people outside of the ECL, particularly Foster and his emissaries in the *Chicago Tribune*. Starting in the 1925 season, however, Bolden started to face pronounced criticism from people associated with the league he founded. In June, Oscar Charleston, player-manager of the Harrisburg Giants, wrote a letter in which he decried the ECL as a farce. While Charleston never specifically referred to Bolden in his letter, he did refer to unnamed men who are "hoodwink[ing] and fool[ing fans] out of hard earned cash."[21] He bemoaned the lack of clarity in determining which games counted toward the ECL's standings and which ones counted as exhibitions. Charleston also referred to incidents marring two recent games between Harrisburg and Hilldale. In one game held in Darby, Charleston claimed that the supposedly unbiased umpires consistently made calls favoring Hilldale. On the following day, the teams met in Lancaster, and the umpires called the game after three innings due to rain. The umpires' decision rankled Charleston because it came after a mere fifteen minutes of rain and because Harrisburg had a four-run lead. ECL rules, as Charleston pointed out, gave umpires the option of calling a game after thirty minutes of rain, not fifteen. Several other factors angered Charleston. First, the rain had stopped, and the grounds' crew had started to prepare the field for the resumed game. Additionally, Hilldale and Harrisburg stood in contention for first place in the ECL, and the umpires emerged from Hilldale's dugout when they called the game. Charleston, therefore, concluded that the umpires called the game in order to protect Hilldale's position in the league's standings. He also concluded that the decision came at the expense of his team and that similar actions would ultimately undermine the ECL.[22]

Bolden delivered a sharp rebuke of Charleston's claims in a letter published in the *Tribune*. Without admitting to Charleston's claims of biased umpires, Bolden reiterated his commitment to building a strong system of umpires in the ECL. He then referred to a letter from an unnamed umpire who refused to work any games at Harrisburg due to threats he had received from the players. Bolden also disputed Charleston's claims of biased umpires at the recent game in Darby, noting that the umpires made several calls favoring Harrisburg. To counter Charleston's claims of more biased umpires at the game in Lancaster, Bolden provided a different version of events. He asserted that the rain delay lasted for longer than thirty minutes and that the rain had left the field unusable.

The umpires had to call the game, and the ECL's rules supported their decision.[23]

In the same edition of the *Tribune*, editor J.M. Howe both defended Bolden and acknowledged the veracity of some of Charleston's grievances. Howe admitted that poor calls marred the game played at Darby, but he flatly denied that the ECL's umpires deliberately made bad calls to favor one team. He also concurred with Charleston on the lack of clarity in regards to games that counted toward the ECL's standings, as opposed to games that counted as exhibitions. Howe highlighted a problem Bolden referred to in his response to Charleston: the problem of umpire baiting. Finally, Howe sounded an alarm about the dangers of too much criticism directed at the ECL. He expressed faith in the ECL's leaders to fix the league's problems provided that they worked together to achieve common goals. Howe's final sentence nicely summarized his viewpoint: "Let the league live, but make it live RIGHT."[24]

Shortly after that controversy flared, Bolden found himself immersed in more criticism stemming from the failure of the Wilmington Potomacs franchise and questions about the legitimacy of Hilldale's record. George Robinson, the Potomacs' owners, announced the club's dissolution in July; his team's players went to other clubs. At the same time, the ECL published league standings that showed Hilldale in front of the second-place Harrisburg Giants. William Nunn in the *Pittsburgh Courier* suggested that Bolden, who oversaw the publication of the standings, manipulated the standings in order to put Hilldale in first place. Echoing Charleston's and Howe's criticism, Nunn called for publication of a list of all games officially counting as games toward the ECL's standings. He also wondered if the ECL's team managers knew ahead of time whether or not a game counted as official league games.[25]

Not surprisingly, Bolden went on the offensive against the *Pittsburgh Courier*. He accused the newspaper of spreading lies and propaganda against Hilldale and the rest of the ECL. He also accused the newspaper of colluding with Charleston and not reporting on instances when Charleston himself and his players fought umpires and players from opposing teams. In response to Nunn's suggestion that he had engaged in underhanded tactics to boost Hilldale, Bolden accused Robinson of engaging in underhanded tactics to boost the rosters of three of Hilldale's competitors. Those competitors included Charleston's Harrisburg Giants. The *Courier* flatly denied Bolden's charges and republished the ECL standings that prompted Nunn's column. Those standings clearly showed that Hilldale played and won three league games in the span of one week. According to those same standings, Harrisburg played seven league games and lost five of those games. As Nunn did in his column, the newspaper demanded Bolden release a list of official ECL games. The newspaper also demanded that Bolden assert better leadership in regards to the ECL's umpires and to the on-field assaults he mentioned.[26]

On the heels of that heated exchange, Bolden faced more criticism from Robinson, the former owner of the dissolved Wilmington Potomacs. Robinson's criticism came in the form of a lengthy letter in which he defended his actions, took offense at Bolden's claims against him, and openly questioned Bolden's leadership. He framed his criticism of Bolden by recalling the banquet he organized for Hilldale following the 1924 season and other ways he had shown support for Bolden and the ECL. Robinson then recounted events that led to Bolden's hiring of William Dallas to serve as the umpires' supervisor. According to Robinson, Bolden selected Dallas because the two enjoyed a friendship. Robinson further claimed that Bolden and Nat Strong, who exercised control over the ECL schedule, crafted a schedule that advantaged Hilldale and other ECL teams at the Potomacs' expense. The Potomacs never played games Bolden promised them and lacked access to one of the ballparks under Strong's control. To refute Bolden's claims he acted underhandedly in dispersing his players, Robinson provided details about the deals he made with other clubs. He recalled a conversation he had with Bolden about one of his pitchers. Robinson claimed he rejected the deal because he felt Bolden made an unsatisfactory offer. In his conclusion, Robinson made a dramatic statement: "I want to make it known that in my estimation the Eastern Colored League is the poorest operated business proposition I have ever known!"[27]

The criticism Bolden endured frayed his control over the ECL's affairs. In one of his regular columns in November 1925, Wilson issued a call for Bolden to resign his position and for the ECL to choose someone not affiliated with any of the teams as his replacement. Wilson reasoned that such an unaffiliated chairman would better address the ECL's problems related to umpires and scheduling. At the start of the 1926 season, James Keenan of the Lincoln Giants refuted rumors that the ECL owners had decided to replace Bolden as the league's commissioner. As the season progressed, however, the ECL faced mounting problems related to the umpires and uneven schedules. In July, the ECL once again contracted to seven teams when a new franchise, the Newark Stars, failed to survive its inaugural season. Shortly after the Stars folded, six of the remaining seven ECL owners met to discuss problems with uneven schedules, access to ballparks, and the possibility of continuing with only six teams. Tellingly, Nat Strong did not attend the meeting, and the other owners did not count his Brooklyn Royal Giants as one of the six teams staying in the ECL.[28]

All of the criticism, combined with the internal ECL problems, presaged Bolden's removal as the league's chairman in January 1927. In a letter released to the press in August 1926, Bolden reiterated his devotion to enforcing player discipline, maintaining balanced schedules, and the betterment of the game of baseball. He also tried to make the argument that he alone should not face the sole blame for all of the ECL's problems. As he noted, "the Eastern Colored League is ruled by a majority vote of the Commission and it is unkind to hold me personally responsible for the action of the league."[29] Bolden's letter ultimately proved futile. The ECL's 1927 season started with James Keenan leaving the league and then returning in time for the annual meeting with NNL owners. At that meeting, the ECL owners elected Isaac Nutter, an attorney from Atlantic City, as the new league president. As the president, Nutter enjoyed authority over Bolden, who served as the league's secretary-treasurer. By creating a new position and electing an outsider to that position, the ECL demonstrated a readiness to move ahead without the league's founder at the helm. For Bolden, his departure from the league's leadership marked the start of a troubling period for him, a period marked by professional and personal tribulations.[30]

Down But Not Out

As Bolden faced rising dissension and instability, Foster suffered a similar fate in the Midwest. The NNL suffered from franchise instability, uneven schedules, and financial shortcomings. Prior to the 1925 season, Foster dramatically offered his resignation, but the other owners rejected his offer and reaffirmed his leadership of the NNL. Foster, however, adopted a hard line with his owners and vowed to no longer advance them money to help their teams' finances. He also adopted a hard line with his own team by releasing many of his veterans and rebuilding the Chicago American Giants' roster. Later in that same season, a gas leak at Foster's boarding house in Indianapolis nearly killed him. Players found Foster unconscious and slumped against a gas heater; he had a burn on his left arm from the lit heater. An ambulance rushed Foster to a local hospital, and someone from the Chicago American Giants contacted Foster's wife to urge her to join her husband in the hospital. Foster regained consciousness later the same afternoon, and he soon returned to his home in Chicago.[31]

Foster's personal difficulties persisted into 1926. In the middle of the season, Foster appeared to take an absence from leading the NNL, and the owners discussed the possibility of electing a temporary replacement. Foster's absence later became permanent when he suffered a mental breakdown. According to one of the stories, Foster had exhibited mentally unbalanced behavior for several weeks and had a physical altercation with a police officer. The same story also claimed that Foster had terrorized the other occupants of his home. Other stories related to this situation had Foster looking for fly balls in Chicago's streets, hitting someone with his car, and locking himself in his office bathroom. Police arrested Foster in his home, and Foster then underwent psychiatric care in a Chicago hospital. Foster never recovered, and he died in 1930 while still under psychiatric care. In his absence, the Chicago American Giants returned to the World Series, and the other NNL owners elected Dr. G.B. Key of St. Louis as the new president. The NNL, however, faced continued financial difficulties, and the league sorely lacked the kind of leadership Foster had demonstrated earlier in the decade.[32]

While Foster's world crumbled, Bolden inched closer to his own breakdown. In a bad yet appropriate omen for the 1927 season, rain washed out Hilldale's home opener against Harrisburg. Hilldale ended the season with eighty-four victories, but it amassed a losing record against ECL teams in the first half of the season. In June, Bolden issued indefinite suspensions for George Carr, Nip Winters, and Namon Washington due to their lack of discipline and indifferent playing. All three players had failed to appear for recent games in New York. The suspensions only lasted for a few weeks, but the return of the three players failed to end Bolden's troubles. White semi-pro baseball had declined in the Philadelphia area , leaving Hilldale with fewer lucrative dates on its non–ECL schedule. Bolden and other owners tried to fill the void by scheduling more black independent teams, but those games failed to produce enough revenue. The growth of black independent teams, like the Homestead Grays, posed a threat to Bolden and other ECL owners since those teams could entice players to jump their contracts. The ECL passed laws mandating tough punishments for contract jumpers. ECL president Nutter, however, neglected to enforce those punishments, thereby opening the door to continued contract jumping. On top of those setbacks, ECL teams continued to play unbalanced schedules, a financial scandal rocked the Baltimore Black Sox, and the Lincoln Giants withdrew from the league.[33]

The seemingly continuous difficulties plaguing both Hilldale and the ECL temporarily forced Bolden out of black professional baseball. In September, Bolden suffered a nervous breakdown as he prepared to serve as one of the commissioners for the upcoming World Series. Bolden spent time in a hospital receiving treatment, and he appeared to make a quick recovery. About a month after his breakdown, Wilson reported seeing Bolden at a football game and having a discussion with him about his plans for the upcoming season. Wilson made a prudent prediction— Bolden would return to Hilldale with a fighting attitude. The other members of the Hilldale corporation, however, seemed less assured of Bolden's imminent return. They chose Charlie Freeman, a former Hilldale player and vice president of the corporation, as the new leader. Freeman then went to work making decisions, such as hiring former Hilldale star Bill Francis as the field manager for the upcoming season. A brief item in another one of Wilson's columns provided some insight into the Hilldale corporation's actions. According to Wilson, Bolden's physicians advised him to stay away from baseball and to avoid the stresses associated with running a team. Without a definitive plan for Bolden's return, the other members of Hilldale's corporation had to move on without their longtime leader.[34]

As Wilson predicted, Bolden returned to work in early 1928 with an aggressive attitude. In his first public statements since his breakdown, Bolden reflected on what he saw as the shortcomings of organized baseball, specifically of the ECL. He refrained from criticizing his own leadership, instead blaming the narrow-mindedness and selfishness of the other commissioners for the ECL's weaknesses. Bolden then made moves to reclaim control over Hilldale. At a meeting in March, Charlie Freeman, James Byrd, and Lloyd Thompson tendered their resignations. They had held the positions of president, treasurer, and secretary within the corporation. Their replacements included Bolden as the president, George Mayo as vice-president, Mark Studevan as treasurer, and Thomas Jenkin as secretary. Bolden took an additional step to emphasize his resumption of control over Hilldale. In one of his first acts upon resuming Hilldale's presidency, Bolden named Mayo, the corporation's vice-president and a former player, as the field manager. Mayo replaced the recently hired Bill Francis, the man whom the deposed Freeman had selected for Hilldale's field manager for the 1928 season.[35]

Bolden made similar moves against the already-fragile ECL. After regaining control of Hilldale, Bolden withdrew his team from the league he founded and announced that the team would operate as an independent franchise. Bolden's move dealt a near-death blow to the ECL since the league also lost Strong's Brooklyn Royal Giants and the Harrisburg Giants. His move also garnered a fiery response from ECL president Nutter, who effectively declared war on Bolden and Hilldale by accepting the application for a new Philadelphia-based franchise. Nutter also denounced both Bolden and Strong and issued a defiant proclamation: "Both Hilldale and the Brooklyn Royal Giants will seek admittance to the league again after they see we intend to fight and that neither can make baseball a paying proposition without the League."[36]

In explaining his decision to withdraw Hilldale from the ECL, Bolden cited lack of cooperation, uneven schedules, lack of ballpark ownership, and financial concerns as key factors in his decision. Bolden explained to the *Pittsburgh Courier*'s Wilson that the ECL "has not been a money-maker" and that "[w]e are through losing money in an impossible league."[37] He later elaborated on the financial problems forcing Hilldale out of the ECL by noting that the team had to borrow money in each of the previous three seasons and lost $21,500 in 1927.[38] In an open letter to the *Tribune*, Bolden sharpened his criticism of the other ECL owners who undermined his plan to use rotating umpires and who did not play all of their scheduled league games. He also cited Hilldale's past success as an independent franchise and the recent financial losses it sustained as a member of the ECL. Although the ECL president had rebuked Bolden, Bolden praised Nutter as a "thoroughly capable man" who remained "sincere in his efforts to build organized baseball."[39] Bolden did warn that "it would take a Hercules to [build an organized league], especially if handicapped by lack of parks, and co-operation."[40]

The ECL floundered for a few months before finally disbanding in June, thereby confirming Bolden's comments about organized baseball. Bolden helped to speed the ECL's demise by securing access to ballparks in Philadelphia and thwarting the league's attempts to establish a new franchise. Hilldale appeared to thrive without an organized league in the eastern states, finishing the season with one hundred nineteen victories. The lack of a league structure gave Bolden more flexibility in scheduling Hilldale's opponents. Hilldale still faced local teams and its former rivals in the ECL. Games against two traveling clubs, the House of David team and a team of Japanese all-stars, filled Hilldale's schedule. Bolden had no trouble adding top-notch players, including his one-time nemesis Oscar Charleston, to Hilldale's roster. At the end of the season, Hilldale won a series over the Homestead Grays, a series the *Tribune* billed as an unofficial championship series for the state of Pennsylvania. Hilldale reversed its financial losses, yet the team failed to attract large crowds at many of its games. The ongoing economic downturn for the Philadelphia area's African Americans made baseball a luxury and left the future of teams like Hilldale in doubt.[41]

While Hilldale and other eastern teams competed without a league structure, discussions emerged about reestablishing an eastern league. Speaking for the Eastern Sports Writers Association, both the *Tribune's* Randy Dixon and the *Pittsburgh Courier's* Rollo Wilson called for a new eastern league. According to them, eastern baseball needed an organized league because "the public will never again patronize 'independent' baseball as it did in the days before it knew the association brand of the game."[42] They included Hilldale and most of the former ECL teams as the members of the proposed league. Both men pointed to Bolden as the only person who could establish and lead the new league. To support their choice, they briefly related Bolden's success in leading Hilldale from a sandlot team into the "BIGGEST NEGRO CORPORATION IN SPORTS!"[43] They also listed the great players in Hilldale's history, Hilldale's on-field success, and Bolden's honorable intentions for organized black baseball. Bolden initially demurred on the idea of reestablishing a league, noting all of the financial and logistical problems that had undermined the ECL. One of his former players, Otto Briggs, expressed similar sentiments in an article published in December. By that time, however, Bolden had developed a firmer opinion about reestablishing an eastern league. He supported the formation of a new league, and he announced his support in the *Tribune*. Unbeknownst to Bolden, his involvement in the establishment of another eastern league marked the beginning of the end of his tenure with Hilldale, a tenure that would have a very ugly ending.[44]

We Mean THROUGH!

In many ways, the American Negro League (ANL) seemed like both a redux of the defunct ECL and an attempt to correct the defunct league's ills. Bolden and other owners gathered in Philadelphia in January 1929 to formally establish the ANL and select league officers. At the meeting, the owners unanimously elected Bolden as league president, James Keenan as vice-president, Rollo Wilson as secretary, and George Rossiter as treasurer. Five of the six ANL teams had played in the ECL—Hilldale, the Bacharach Giants, the Baltimore Black Sox, the Cuban Stars, and the Lincoln Giants. The sixth team, Cum Posey's Homestead Grays, officially operated as a traveling team, but they played their home games in Pitts-burgh. As a president, Bolden enjoyed greater authority over the five other ANL owners than he had enjoyed over the ECL owners. Under his direc-tion, the ANL issued new regulations designed to prevent player attacks upon umpires. The ANL owners agreed to use a system of rotating umpires. Players faced a $50 fine along with a thirty-day suspension with-out pay for attacking an umpire or engaging in fights on the field. Players, furthermore, faced a $5 fine for arguing with an umpire and delaying the game. Other laws prohibited ANL teams from facing opponents who car-ried suspended players on their rosters or playing in ballparks that per-mitted suspended players to compete. The owners also instituted a reserve clause and agreed to fine players who did not report to their teams by opening day. To prevent contract squabbles, the league fixed each roster at fifteen starting on June 15. Afterwards, laws prevented ANL teams from borrowing players from other league teams and from using players within five days after announcing their signing to the league president.[45]

Despite Bolden's efforts to build a solid organization, the ANL endured a tumultuous existence. The teams managed to play almost all of the league games on their schedules, but the owners seemed to lack the willpower to enforce the league's laws. As an example, Biz Mackey went on a barnstorming tour and did not report to Hilldale until early June. Instead of following the league's laws and suspending Mackey one day for every day he failed to report to Hilldale, Bolden allowed Mackey to play starting on June 25. The same happened to three players from the Bacharach Giants. Posey presented some additional problems for Bolden. In July, Posey signed several players who had contracts with teams in the NNL. According to a statement from the NNL's president, Posey defended his actions by noting the lack of an agreement between the two leagues in regards to contacts. Posey's actions reawakened the possibility of a war between ANL and NNL owners over players. His on-field antics, specif-ically his tendency to bait and argue with umpires, added to the problems Bolden faced as the ANL's president.[46]

Two outsiders, former ECL president Nutter and Syd Pollock, brought additional stress upon Bolden in his role as the ANL's president. As soon as Bolden and the other owners established the ANL, Nutter issued an ultimately empty threat to file an injunction should any former ECL play-ers join ANL teams. He also threatened to use proceeds from games played in New Jersey to pay outstanding debts owed to the ECL.[47] Pollock, a white Jewish booking agent who owned the independent Havana Red Sox, wrote a scathing article in which he questioned Bolden's leadership. The ANL forbade any of its teams from facing the Red Sox, and Pollock demanded an explanation for the regulation. He noted the league's lax enforcement of its laws involving the number of players permitted on rosters, the use of suspended players, and playing in ballparks that allowed suspended players. Additionally, Pollock lamented the lack of discipline on ANL teams as well as the lack of cooperation between independent eastern teams and ANL teams. Pollock claimed that he did not write his letter out of spite; rather, he merely wanted to highlight some facts about the ANL and to make fans aware of the league's shortcomings. Pollock, however, took direct aim at Bolden in the closing section of his letter by drawing unfavorable comparisons to the kind of leadership the NNL's current president demonstrated. He said: "[W]hat the eastern league really needs is another Judge Hueston … who will live up to their rulings and head the circuit with a real hand of discipline."[48]

While Bolden never responded to Pollock's charges, he received support from Posey and Wilson. Posey responded to Pollock's statements by claiming that the Red Sox had a fictitious record and had undermined the profitability of black baseball in the Pittsburgh area. He made other charges against Pollock, and Pollock reacted with an indignant and lengthy letter in the *Pittsburgh Courier*.[49] Wilson issued a more heartfelt defense of Bolden's actions. He called Pollock's attacks "unfounded, unjust, and unethical" and "jealous, ignorant, and evil."[50] Wilson also outlined the trying economic conditions confronting black baseball and all of the responsibilities Bolden shouldered. Bolden worked the night shift at Philadelphia's Central Post Office six days per week, and then he turned his attention toward both the ANL and Hilldale. Wilson called Bolden's double duty as Hilldale's and the ANL's president "a job which few men would attempt and fewer still would succeed at."[51] He closed his letter with one final reason to admire Bolden—he did not draw a salary as the league's president.[52]

Hilldale's on-field and off-field struggles, as well as a scary incident at Hilldale Park, compounded the stresses Bolden endured throughout the 1929 season. After a flurry of trades before the season began, Hilldale struggled against ANL competition and won only fifteen games in the first half of the ANL's season. Overall, Hilldale won only sixty-seven games, its lowest win total of the decade. In the midst of Hilldale's early-season struggles, Hilldale Park became the scene of a murder. During a May game against the Grays, a man entered the stands behind the visitors' dugout and shot and killed his common-law wife. The incident happened in the third inning with the Grays leading by the score of 5–0. After a delay, the game resumed, and Hilldale defeated the shaken Grays in extra innings. That game, played on a Saturday afternoon, came on the heels of a fight-filled game between the same two teams on Friday. In the previous game, violence erupted in top of the ninth inning when the Grays' players disputed an umpire's decision. Hilldale players also got involved, and fans then swarmed the field. Unable to restore order, the umpire called the game with the score tied.[53] Near the end of the season, two Hilldale players, Joseph Strong and Walter Jackson, fought over forty cents at a "questionable house" on Naudain Street in Philadelphia.[54] Strong sustained a fractured skull once Jackson hit him in the head with a brick. After a stay in the hospital, Strong returned to his home and assured the *Tribune* that he could still play on the same field with Jackson.[55]

Overall, the biggest problem Bolden confronted during the 1929 season involved umpires. Bolden's refusal to use black umpires elicited some criticism in the *Tribune*. One article noted that Bolden had used black umpires in the past and released those umpires due to bad game performances. According to the article, one of the released umpires had performed well for another ANL team, and black umpires regularly worked games in other league cities. "Dubbia Ardee," Dixon's pseudonym, also noted that Bolden retained a white umpire even though he made a bad call identical to the call one of the released umpires delivered. Bolden's decision prompted Dixon to declare that "[i]f there is any reason for hiring Nordic umps who are not one bit better than colored ones, we don't know of it."[56] Dixon also foretold a riot from Hilldale's fans if Bolden refused to alter his policies concerning umpires.[57]

In the same edition of the *Tribune*, an editorial elaborated on the issues Dixon mentioned and delivered some strong criticism to Hilldale's management. The editorial linked concerns about using black umpires to wider efforts to promote African Americans in leadership positions in a local fire company and other areas of civic life. It called upon the Hilldale corporation to set an example for other institutions by hiring black umpires. It also regarded Hilldale's use of white umpires as inexcusable and economically unfair to African Americans. The editorial further claimed that the use of white umpires gave whites the opportunity to regard African Americans as inferior and incapable of governing their own affairs. It warned Hilldale's management about the possibility of losing fans over this issue and asked some very pointed questions: "Are we still slaves? Is it possible that colored baseball players are so dumb that they will resent one of their own race umpiring their game? Or is it that the management of Hilldale is so steeped in racial inferiority that it has no faith in Negroes?"[58]

In the next edition, the editorial page reaffirmed its commitment to having black umpires at Hilldale's games. A letter questioning the wisdom of having black umpires prompted the second editorial. The letter doubted the ability of black players to respect black umpires by citing instances when they did not respect white umpires. The editorial countered with evidence of black umpires working games without any incidents. Additionally, the editorial repeated its claim that Hilldale's management refused to hire black umpires due to its collective sense of racial inferiority. Similar to the first editorial, the second editorial alluded to slavery to prove its point about Hilldale's racial sensibilities. The editorial sarcastically thanked God that "ball players are no longer slaves. They do not think that everything white is perfect and everything black is evil."[59]

Those concerns about the race of umpires working at Hilldale's games, combined with the team's on-field and off-field difficulties, led to a troubled off-season for both the team and the ANL. Dixon commented that both players and fans knew "[a]ll is not well in Hilldale camp."[60] Hilldale and other ANL teams, along with their counterparts in the NNL, suffered from attendance and financial shortages. Bolden issued a call for an ANL owners' meeting in early October, but the meeting failed to materialize. In one of his columns, Wilson hinted at rumors of ownership changes and even franchise dissolutions. At the end of October, the situation for all of black baseball grew bleaker when the stock market crashed. In February 1930, Bolden and the other ANL owners met at the Republican Club in Philadelphia to formally dissolve the league. Posey had previously informed his fellow owners that he intended for the Grays to resume playing as an independent franchise. Concerns about Hilldale's future also factored into the ANL's dissolution. Bolden announced that Hilldale had lost their longtime playing field in Darby. In reality, Bolden did not renew the lease at Hilldale Park. His decision represented the first step in a drastic plan designed to both destroy and rebuild the Hilldale franchise.[61]

After not renewing the lease, Bolden took additional steps to dissolve the Hilldale corporation. Bolden's moves prompted Wilson to lament, "What a pity it is that the members of the corporation could not adjust the personal differences which have shattered the morale of the outfit for the past three years!"[62] Other members of the Hilldale corporation fought back against Bolden's plans. Those members included two of the men Bolden had deposed when he returned following his nervous breakdown—Thompson and Freeman. At a meeting of the corporation's stockholders, Thompson and Freeman ousted Bolden and his allies, and Thompson took control as the new president. With Hilldale under his control, Thompson announced his intention to field a team. Thompson moved to renew the lease at Hilldale Park and make other preparations for the rapidly approaching 1930 season.[63]

Thompson's actions set up a confrontation with Bolden since the former Hilldale leader remained determined to build a new franchise. The new franchise, named "Ed Bolden's Hillsdale Club," would use Passon Field at 48th and Spruce Streets in West Philadelphia for its home ballpark. The field's white owner, promoter Harry Passon, would provide financial backing for the new club. Bolden proceeded to build a roster containing some of the same players who had played for Hilldale. Bolden, however, faced a setback to his plan when the Lincoln Giants announced that they would play two games per week in Philadelphia. With Thompson also making plans for the 1930 season, the Lincoln Giants' move meant that three black teams would operate in the Philadelphia area at an economically trying time. Facing that reality, Bolden dropped his plans to form a new club. Due to the continued existence of the Hilldale franchise, Bolden lacked any options for returning to the black baseball world in the 1930 season. Bolden's baseball career seemed over.[64]

In the eyes of the *Tribune's* Dixon, Bolden's baseball career had permanently ended. Dixon delivered a harsh assessment of Bolden, an assessment that touched upon issues of leadership and race:

> At last it looks as if Ed Bolden is fading from the picture. Once an omnipotent figure in Negro baseball. Once the czar of the East. Once the dictator. Once feared and respected. Bolden is through, readers, make no mistake.
>
> The history of the erstwhile postal clerk reads like a dime store bestseller.... It is all history now how Bolden wrecked his team when he went hog wild and administered the oft mentioned boot in the buttocks to several stalwarts, hiring them away from Darby loam with the info that their batting eyes were becoming dulled or their joints were beginning to annoy him with their frequent creaking as the case might have been.
>
> But as if this wouldn't suffice, Bolden proved himself a traditional cullud man by playing "Uncle Tom" and taking his advantages to the Nordic faction....
>
> When the American League folded up, Bolden came through with a subsequent statement that Hilldale had dissolved. The Dynasty had ended. He got Nordic backing. Made arrangements to take something that had been nurtured by colored people and was a colored institution and bend it in such a manner to as to fill the coffers of the Nordic. Not maliciously or intentionally perhaps, but such was the case or almost the case.
>
> Lloyd Thompson has stepped in and thwarted Bolden at every turn and now the man who was once a king is now a piker and Ed Bolden is through. We mean THROUGH![65]

As Dixon's assessment demonstrated, Hilldale carried a special meaning for the black community in Philadelphia. Hilldale represented something more than a baseball franchise. It represented a touchstone, an example of what black capital and black leaders could accomplish in the face of racism and segregation. It provided the region's African Americans with a relevant antidote to the ugly philosophies that guided segregation statutes. Bolden's actions, therefore, seemed like a betrayal to his base of supporters and a concession to racial stereotypes.

Dixon delivered a harsh assessment of Bolden's recent actions, but he erred when he declared Bolden's baseball career was over. Bolden remained on the sidelines in the 1930 season, but black baseball continued to survive in spite of the deepening economic depression. As long as black baseball survived, Bolden could resume his career and build another championship-caliber franchise. Hilldale's survival, along with the ugliness and heated words surrounding his departure, meant that Bolden needed to wait for the right opportunity to return to black baseball. Such an opportunity emerged in the early 1930s.

CHAPTER FOUR

Wilderness and Return, 1931–1933

The period from 1930 to 1933 represented a period of transition for Negro League baseball. Andrew "Rube" Foster's death and Ed Bolden's disgraceful exit deprived the sport of two of its most prominent leaders from the previous decade. With the loss of those two giants, power within organized black professional baseball shifted away from Chicago and Philadelphia toward the city of Pittsburgh. In 1932, Cumberland Posey, owner of the Homestead Grays, established the short-lived East-West League upon the ruins of Foster's defunct Negro National League. When that league floundered after one season, Gus Greenlee of the Pittsburgh Crawfords established a new NNL in 1933. Greenlee's league would last for the next sixteen seasons and would serve as the backdrop of the second act of Bolden's career.

Bolden returned to the ranks of black professional baseball in 1933 under the auspices of an independent team named Ed Bolden's Philadelphia Stars. The Stars differed from Hilldale in several respects. Unlike the Darby-based Hilldale club, the Stars made their home in West Philadelphia and carried Bolden's name in their official team name. While Hilldale had the support of an African American corporation, the Stars had the support of Bolden and Ed Gottlieb, a white Jewish booking agent and sporting goods merchant. Bolden's partnership with Gottlieb signaled a new reality for black professional baseball. The ideal of self-help and a black-owned enterprise running on black capital gave way to the need to use white capital in order to remain in business. Bolden remained an active owner and the franchise's public face; Gottlieb's connections helped the team secure bookings and ballparks.

Even though a new NNL existed in 1933, the Stars operated as an independent during their inaugural season. Bolden likely made that decision due to the angst he endured with three separate leagues in the

1920s. By keeping the Stars out of the NNL in 1933, Bolden gave his new franchise the opportunity to establish a fan base and avoid the new league's growing pains. As he did with Hilldale, Bolden relied heavily upon the *Philadelphia Tribune* to market his new club. Gottlieb's connections in the Philadelphia region enabled the team to play against local teams in front of large crowds. Through their efforts, the Stars enjoyed a successful 1933 season. The team never lost a series and earned praise as the "[b]est balanced Colored attraction in baseball."[1]

Most significantly, the Stars' successful season helped Bolden move beyond his messy divorce from Hilldale and to relaunch his career in black professional baseball. The Stars' debut season came at an opportune time. Hilldale's new leadership failed to stabilize the franchise's falling finances and made the decision to dissolve the franchise during the 1932 season. A team Bolden briefly led, the Darby Phantoms, never lived up to his high expectations. The Philadelphia black baseball market, therefore, had an opening, and Bolden seized the opportunity. His efforts succeeded in establishing a solid basis for the Stars and in making the Stars the region's new top black professional baseball team. Bolden's return, and the Stars' twenty-season history, began in Gottlieb's office in February 1933.

Ed Bolden in the Wilderness

Early in 1931, two hot rumors appeared on the Tribune's sports pages. Randy Dixon reported that "a new dynasty has already taken gigantic strides in its ultimate objective of placing baseball among Negroes on a plane never before attained in Philadelphia."[2] Those in charge of the new rumored dynasty had already secured a site for the team's home ballpark. For his second reported rumor, Dixon revealed that Bolden planned to return to black baseball after spending one year away from the sport. Perhaps still bitter over his previous experiences with Foster's NNL and the ECL, Bolden intended for his new team to compete independently.[3] One month later, a subsequent story from Dixon offered more information about Bolden's rumored comeback. Bolden planned to build his new team with the assistance of two key individuals—John Henry "Pop" Lloyd and Harry Passon. Lloyd played for Hilldale, and Passon co-owned the company that supplied Hilldale with equipment in the 1920s. This new team would use a Passon-owned ballpark, Passon Field, located at 48th and Spruce Streets in West Philadelphia.[4]

Dixon's article also contained information that threatened to thwart

Bolden's return to black professional baseball. John Drew, a wealthy African American from Darby, had assumed control of the Hilldale Daisies. Drew decided to take command of the team after several members of the financially insolvent Hilldale Baseball Corporation approached him for aid. As the article noted, Drew faced a tough task in leading Hilldale for its twenty-second season. The team still owed salaries to its players from the previous season, and its star player Judy Johnson had already agreed to play for the Homestead Grays. Hilldale, furthermore, possessed steep debts and lacked any assets.[5] Despite those daunting odds facing Drew and Hilldale, the team's continued existence ended the nascent partnership between Bolden and Lloyd. Lloyd declared that had he "known Hilldale was to have a team [he] surely would not have considered Mr. Bolden's offers" because he did not want to associate with a new team that challenged an established team.[6] Bolden suspended his plans to build a new baseball team, and he spent another season on the sidelines.

While Bolden remained in exile, two men from Pittsburgh asserted control over the direction of Negro League baseball—Gus Greenlee and Cumberland Posey. Greenlee owned the Pittsburgh Crawfords, while Posey owned the Homestead Grays. In 1931, Greenlee took his first stab at running a league by trying to keep the old Negro National League (NNL) afloat. His efforts failed, and the old NNL did not survive long enough to stage a world series at the end of the 1931 season. Posey, who maintained a regular column in the *Pittsburgh Courier*, claimed the world series title for his Grays. He also claimed that the Grays amassed an incredible record of one hundred and forty-three wins against only twenty-two losses. For the 1932 season, Posey built a new league, the East-West League, upon the ruins of the old NNL. In addition to the Grays, Posey included the Baltimore Black Sox and Hilldale among the eastern terms in his new league.[7] Posey praised Drew, Hilldale's new leader, and Lloyd Thompson, a former player who had joined Drew in operating Hilldale after Bolden's departure. Posey lauded Drew as a "business man with business principles" and Thompson as "one of the smartest, shrewdest and [most] businesslike men" to ever work in black baseball.[8] In that same column, Posey noticeably stopped short of heaping praise upon Hilldale's previous leader, Bolden. Posey called Bolden a "good baseball man," yet he accused him of "temporizing" in the face of internal dissension.[9]

Despite Posey's best efforts, the East-West League fizzled during its first and only season. The loss of franchises and persistent financial problems undermined the league's operations. Ed Gottlieb, Bolden's future partner, also factored into the league's swift demise. Gottlieb's dominating presence in the Philadelphia area made it difficult for the league to establish a strong base in the lucrative Philadelphia and New York markets. Gottlieb, along with his associate Nat Strong in New York City, controlled the ballparks that league teams used for their games. They took either five or ten percent of the profits from the games they booked, leaving little

Throughout the history of the franchise, the Philadelphia Stars players wore jerseys that combined the colors red, white, and blue. On opening day, Stars players, like the unidentified two pictured here, would sometimes debut a new uniform incorporating the patriotic color scheme (John W. Mosley Photograph Collection, Charles L. Blockson Afro-American Collection, Temple University Libraries, Philadelphia, Pennsylvania).

money left for the black teams. By July, Posey's Grays remained the league's only solvent franchise, leaving him with no choice but to disband the East-West League. The owners of the remaining league franchises abandoned the second half schedule and ceased paying salaries to their players. The Grays and other remaining franchises operated as independent teams; players received payment by sharing a percentage of the gate receipts with the owners.[10]

As Posey's East-West League lumbered through its brief existence, Bolden made the first steps toward his comeback in black professional baseball. Instead of trying to establish a new professional team in the Philadelphia market, Bolden chose to direct the amateur Darby Phantoms. The Phantoms belonged to the Inter-Urban League and won the league championship the previous three seasons. Bolden's leadership of the Phantoms began in February 1932 when, at the invitation of the club's members, he delivered a speech titled "Progressive Ideas in Modern Baseball" at the club's meeting. The club's members unanimously granted Bolden honorary membership and asked him to assume control of the Phantoms' sports department. Bolden agreed as long as the club afforded him absolute control of the Phantoms' basketball and baseball teams. The members agreed and approved other plans that included the organization of a boosters' club and the strengthening of the club treasury. With Bolden in control, the club rebranded itself as Ed Bolden's Darby Phantoms and prepared for the 1932 season.[11]

Under Bolden's direction, the Phantoms endured a rough season. Prior to the season's start, Bolden arranged for the Phantoms' players to learn about the skills they needed to perform at professional levels. The players would learn those skills through short talks with veteran professional players, some of whom played for Hilldale, and through analysis of charts drawn on blackboards. To toughen his young players, Bolden scheduled games between the Phantoms and local semi-pro clubs. Those plans signified that Bolden had high hopes for the Phantoms; he likely intended for the franchise to follow the same path that Hilldale followed on its way to a World Series championship. Bolden included some Hilldale veterans on the Phantoms' opening day roster, and he arranged for the team to play a Decoration Day game at Passon Field in West Philadelphia. The Phantoms, however, struggled against the semi-pro competition Bolden included on the schedule. By the end of May, Bolden displayed his impatience by dismissing several players from the team. He promised to replace those players with established stars, but his efforts failed to produce better results for the Phantoms.[12]

While Bolden toiled with the Darby Phantoms, his former team collapsed. As a member of the East-West League, Hilldale encountered the financial and scheduling problems that undermined the league. Beginning on June 15, the team stopped paying salaries to its players and began to pay them according to a percentage plan. After deducting expenses and allocating a share to the club, the team divided the remaining gate receipts or guarantee among the players. The new payment plan sparked rumors that several Hilldale players, including the manager Judy Johnson, planned to join other teams.[13] Additionally, the team raised ticket prices, and Drew tried to resist working with either Strong or Gottlieb in booking or promoting Hilldale's games. By the end of July all of those combined factors and poor attendance led Drew to dissolve the Hilldale franchise.[14]

In the *Philadelphia Tribune*, sportswriter Dick Sun provided a blistering critique of Drew's actions prior to Hilldale's dissolution. Sun accused Hilldale's management of provoking fans by raising ticket prices at a time when those fans faced a terrible economic depression. He also accused the management of failing to secure good players and of neglecting to use the newspaper to advertise Hilldale's games. At the end of his column, Sun reprinted the official statement from Hilldale's management. Through its statement, the team's management tried to assure the public that Drew's "only reason for suspending operations with his Darby Daisies is that the present season held no possibilities for operating a salaried club of the type [Drew] tendered to the fans last season."[15] The statement also included Drew's sober assessment of the present conditions facing teams like Hilldale: "The fans do not have money to spend on baseball."[16]

Despite the travails of Hilldale and the East-West League, the Philadelphia area remained an attractive location for black professional baseball teams. In a thoughtful assessment of the 1932 season, Ray Macey of the Darby Phantoms noted that a team in the Philadelphia area could easily fill its schedule with teams from New York, New Jersey, Baltimore, or Washington, D.C., Macey also noted that the Philadelphia area included many semipro and amateur teams, thereby enabling outside teams to schedule multiple games in the area during their road trips.[17] Even the existence of Pennsylvania's "blue laws," prohibiting games on Sundays, and a worsening economic depression failed to diminish the Philadelphia area's appeal. Multiple black teams, at one point four teams simultaneously, played games in the Philadelphia market in the 1932 season.[18] Macey predicted a "wild scramble for supremacy" in Philadelphia's black baseball market and felt confident that the area's fans would support a team "with the right kind of baseball management."[19] He, however, also predicted that black teams in Philadelphia and other areas would need to book their games through "certain agencies," white booking agents.[20] Macey seemed to lament their involvement and voiced a common concern in black baseball: "[O]ur sympathetic Nordic brother may be brought out to enter our business for strategic reasons, but who will pocket our gain?"[21]

A New Start, a New League

Even though both the 1931 and 1932 seasons witnessed the collapses of separate professional leagues, the dream of league-based black professional baseball remained alive. A meeting in Chicago in January 1933 set in motion the creation of the Negro National Baseball Association, popularly known as the Negro National League (NNL). The prominent moguls who gathered at that meeting included Greenlee, Posey, Robert Cole of the Chicago American Giants, Tom Wilson of the Nashville Elite Giants, and Jim Taylor of the Indianapolis ABCs. The moguls did not make any final decisions in regard to franchises or finances. They did select Greenlee as the NNL's temporary chairman; at a later meeting, the moguls elected him the league's president. In February, Greenlee traveled to Philadelphia to meet with eastern baseball moguls and to work on establishing an eastern circuit for the new NNL. Greenlee's efforts succeeded, and teams in both eastern and Midwestern states prepared to play in the NNL in the 1933 season.[22]

At a meeting in Philadelphia in March, Greenlee and other NNL owners added some dimensions to the new NNL. Despite high costs associated with travel, teams from the eastern circuit would travel to the western circuit, and vice versa. The teams, however, would receive help booking games in both circuits and would not play league games every day of the week. With those open dates, NNL teams could fill their schedules with games against non-league teams that attracted large crowds and generated large gate receipts. To avoid the fate of the East-West League, the NNL owners in the eastern circuit turned to Gottlieb to schedule their non-league games.[23]

As Greenlee prepared for the 1933 season, he faced a situation that illuminated the kind of owners who would dominate Negro League baseball in the 1930s and 1940s. In March, a jury found Greenlee not guilty in a case that involved the numbers lottery. A numbers lottery, or racket, existed in many African American communities. Similar to other lotteries, people participating in the numbers lottery bet on a combination of three numbers. Those running the numbers lottery then randomly drew and published the winning combinations. The case against Greenlee originated when Alberta Frey claimed she hit on a winning number and never received her $500 prize. Frey and her husband sought out the man who took the bet, a man identified as Harper. When Frey's husband could not find Harper, he then sought out Greenlee. A subsequent raid on a place known for conducting the numbers lottery resulted in Greenlee's arrest. During the trial, the prosecution did not produce solid evidence tying Greenlee to the bet Alberta Frey made or the gambling house. The judge, therefore, directed the jury to return its not guilty verdict.[24]

Greenlee's acquittal obscured the fact that he maintained some illegal business enterprises, including the numbers lottery, along with his legitimate businesses. His legal ventures included a taxi company and the Crawford Grill, a nightclub in Pittsburgh and the origin of his baseball team's name. Greenlee owned other establishments in Pittsburgh and served as a boxing manager. One of his most famous clients, John Henry Lewis, held the world's light heavyweight title for four years in the 1930s. All of those businesses gave Greenlee the means to own the Crawfords and the team's home ballpark, a rarity for black professional baseball in the 1930s. Greenlee, however, supplemented his legitimate business earnings with money he accrued from illegally selling alcohol during the Prohibition Era and by running the numbers lottery. His businesses, both legal and illegal, cemented his position as one of Pittsburgh's top black community leaders. As the Negro League evolved in the 1930s, it attracted other owners like Greenlee who operated the illegal numbers lottery in their local communities. Those connections to illegal business enterprises, like the involvement of white booking agents, represented the reality for the Negro Leagues as they operated during a difficult economic time in the United States.[25]

With his acquittal, Greenlee embarked upon the NNL's inaugural season. The season's highlight came with an idea Greenlee implemented, an all-star game known as the East-West Game. The East-West Game, which debuted in the same season as Major League Baseball's All-Star Game, included players whom fans selected through ballots printed in black newspapers. Notable players at the first East-West Game included Oscar Charleston, Satchel Paige, Norman "Turkey" Stearns, Judy Johnson, and James "Cool Papa" Bell. The East roster included four Philadelphia Stars—Raleigh "Biz" Mackey, Jud Wilson, Dick Lundy, and Rap Dixon. Greenlee secured Comiskey Park in Chicago as the site of the game. Due to the game's success, the East-West Game emerged as an anticipated, and financially beneficial, annual event.[26]

The East-West Game represented the lone bright spot for the NNL's inaugural season. In June, as the NNL owners prepared for the second half of the season, disputes over player contracts peaked and led to the Grays' dismissal from the league. The owner of the Detroit Stars claimed that Posey violated the league's code of ethics when he signed two players who allegedly had contracts with the Detroit franchise. John Clark, an associate of Greenlee, used a column in the *Pittsburgh Courier* to make further allegations against Posey. Posey responded in his own column in the *Courier* in which he defended his actions and accused other owners of conspiring to ruin the Grays. He accused Greenlee and other owners of working with Gottlieb to secure the best games in Gottlieb's territory and, therefore, denying the Grays opportunities to make money. To support his claims, Posey noted that a similar situation in 1932 had led to the demise of Hilldale and to the East-West League. Subsequent columns from Posey heaped more criticism upon Greenlee and the rest of the NNL. Posey claimed that the NNL did not include enough experienced people capable of running a professional baseball league and that the league contained very few top-level players.[27]

The NNL's rough first season and involvement with an illegal gambling enterprise formed the context for the Stars' inaugural season. Despite their independent status, the Stars maintained connections to the new NNL. In February 1933, Greenlee, Bolden, and other baseball men met in Gottlieb's office to officially launch the NNL's eastern portion. Gottlieb booked games for both the Stars and for the NNL teams when they traveled into the area. The Stars faced NNL competition and won four slots in the first annual East-West Game. By operating the Stars as an independent franchise, Bolden succeeded in keeping the Stars away from the problems that plagued the new league. Bolden, who maintained a partnership with Gottlieb, likely kept the franchise out of the NNL to secure the best booking dates in the Philadelphia region. With Gottlieb's help, Bolden's Stars built upon favorable preseason publicity and filled a void in the Philadelphia black baseball market.

Ed Bolden's Philadelphia Stars

The first inkling that Bolden intended to establish a new franchise came in February 1933. In his column in the *Pittsburgh Courier*, W. Rollo Wilson reported on a conversation he had with the "Chief." Bolden told Wilson that he felt "fit as a fiddle and ready to go."[28] Bolden also told Wilson that his new team could not use Hilldale Park in Darby "because the people have got out of the habit of going that far to witness a game."[29] For his new team, Bolden mentioned two unspecified ballparks in West Philadelphia that his team could use as its home ballpark. A few days later, the *Philadelphia Tribune* added some more details about Bolden's comeback. Bolden intended to work with Dick Lundy, a former Hilldale star, in building his new team.[30] The same edition of the newspaper featured an article that highlighted the stark reality facing Bolden and the Philadelphia Stars. In the Atlantic City area, seven banks that catered to African American clients had failed during the previous week. The newspaper estimated the losses at approximately $500,000. The financial depression that had harmed earlier leagues and had factored into Hilldale's demise remained very present in 1933. By launching a new franchise in the depressed atmosphere, Bolden faced a daunting task in finding and maintaining a fan base.[31]

Prior to the start of the 1933, Bolden skillfully used the black press to build anticipation and support for his new team. In late February, Wilson reported on another conversation he had with Bolden. According to Wilson, former Hilldale stars and other players from across the country had contacted Bolden and expressed an interest in joining the Philadelphia Stars. "Uniform makers, sporting goods houses and similar concerns" had entered into a bidding war for the Stars' business, and Bolden had spoken with owners of ballparks to schedule Stars games.[32] Though Wilson could not confirm that any player except for Lundy had agreed to join the team, he hinted that Bolden intended to sign Mackey. Wilson's column included a lengthy and ambitious pledge from Bolden: "You may [publish] ... that when the Stars take the field, they will see an experienced group of ball players most of them men who excel in their positions and under the leadership of that ace shortstop Dick Lundy, they will be able to wage even warfare with any teams in the country and by that I mean all of the colored clubs and all of the ... semi-pro outfits in this section. When they reach top form I doubt if even the major league teams will have a set-up with them."[33]

Starting in March, the *Philadelphia Tribune* assisted Bolden in his attempts to build anticipation and establish a fan base for the Stars. Randy Dixon, who once had harsh words for Bolden, welcomed his return by noting how Bolden transformed Hilldale from a sandlot team to a national champion. He lauded Bolden's roster as a "choice coterie of diamond laborers whose past exploits and present records insure [*sic*] [Bolden] of fielding an aggregation that will doff the sombrero to no rival cast."[34] That roster included Lundy, Mackey, Jud Wilson, Jake Stevens, and Dick Seay. Webster McDonald, "the plutocrat of all Negro twirlers," led the Stars' pitching staff.[35] Other pitchers on the Stars' roster included Porter Charleston and Cliff Carter. Dixon noted that Bolden could still sign other veterans—including Martin Dihigo and Eggie Dallard. Dixon quoted Bolden as asserting that he expected "to land a team which will make the city forget its baseball headaches of recent seasons."[36]

In the midst of the praise for Bolden, Ray Macey of the Darby Phantoms offered a different perspective on Bolden's return with the Stars. Macey derided Bolden for asking to remain an honorary member of the Phantoms while failing to attend weekly meetings. Sarcastically, Macey surmised that the Phantoms should remove Bolden's name and initials from the team's stationery and baseball uniforms. He also indicated that Bolden never directly informed the Phantoms that he had decided to leave the club and launch a new franchise. Macey referenced announcements made in newspapers and a letter sent by Bolden to an athletic goods store in Philadelphia. In the letter, Bolden disavowed any connection to the Phantoms and any knowledge of the club's plans for the upcoming season. Macey expressed the most disgust with the ways Bolden used his reputation and baseball knowledge to take advantage of the Phantoms' young players. The young players, all residents of Darby, idealized Bolden, also a resident of Darby, for his successful work with the Hilldale club. Bolden "expressed his thoughts, beautifully colored amid flowery scented words," convinced the young Phantoms to sacrifice their amateur status, and brought the club into the professional ranks.[37] Macey also implied that Bolden had violated an unwritten code of ethics governing professional sports and expressed concern about the Phantoms' future.[38]

Macey's denunciation represented the only piece of criticism directed at Bolden. Bolden used the black press to advertise his new franchise, and the press responded with uncritical articles. Beginning in April, the *Philadelphia Tribune* promoted the Stars' daily practice sessions at Passon Field, located at 48th and Spruce Streets, and continued to convey Bolden's belief that the Stars represented "the most colorful combination in colored baseball."[39] On the *Tribune's* sports pages, the Stars almost always bore Bolden's name. Headlines, articles, and box scores identified the team as "Ed Bolden's Philadelphia Stars" or as "Bolden's Stars." Some headlines and articles even referred to the team as the "Boldenmen," the "Boldenboys," or even simply the "Boldens."[40] Following Bolden's death, noted newspaper columnist W. Rollo Wilson claimed that he endowed the franchise with the name "Ed Bolden's Philadelphia Stars."[41] Since the Darby

Phantoms also bore Bolden's name during the 1932 season, Wilson's claim seems questionable. Additionally, official stationery from the Stars listed the team's name as "Ed Bolden's Philadelphia Stars."[42] It seems likely Bolden attached his name to the Stars for marketing purposes and in an attempt to link the new franchise with Hilldale's lofty achievements. The *Tribune's* coverage further cemented Bolden's link to the new franchise and elevated his role with the Stars above that of others, such as Gottlieb. The fact that Gottlieb booked the Stars' games and controlled many of the ballparks where the Stars played never appeared on the newspaper's sports pages during the 1933 season.

Carrying those grand expectations, the Stars finally opened their season in late April against an all-white York team from the New York-Pennsylvania League. Although the Stars split the opening day double-header, they swept through their early season schedule, playing primarily against local white semi-professional and professional teams. Their opponents included teams from Frankford, Mayfair, and Camden; they also faced teams from the Philadelphia Independent League, such as the South Phillies and the All-Phillies. The team played nearly every day of the week—mostly at nighttime under the arc lights—and they always represented the visiting team. The Stars also frequently played double-headers on either one or both days of the weekend, but a state curfew law prevented them from playing on Sunday nights. While the Stars often faced the same opponent in those double-headers, they occasionally faced two different teams or played in two different locations during the same day. The Stars' early season schedule showed Bolden's wisdom in remaining independent from the NNL and in using Gottlieb to schedule games. Bolden succeeded in giving the team positive exposure, and his talented team responded by playing well and attracting the city's interest.[43]

The Stars' early successes spurred Dixon to acknowledge the team's superiority over local white teams. In keeping with the laudatory tone of his earlier article on the Stars, Dixon saluted the "honorable" Bolden for placing a baseball team "on local green pastures that should well merit the approval of the most critical fandom."[44] Dixon, however, mentioned that he and the city's baseball fans wondered how the Stars would fare against powerful black professional teams, namely the Pittsburgh Crawfords, Homestead Grays, and New York Black Yankees. He mentioned that the Stars had scheduled an upcoming game against the Crawfords and predicted that the Stars "stand an even chance of bringing home the bacon," even though the Crawfords had also enjoyed success early in the season.[45]

Raleigh "Biz" Mackey (catcher) was a key part of the Philadelphia Stars' early seasons who played for Hilldale in the 1920s. He won championships with both of Ed Bolden's franchises and earned a reputation as one of the game's best catchers (John W. Mosley Photograph Collection, Charles L. Blockson Afro-American Collection, Temple University Libraries, Philadelphia, Pennsylvania).

Soon after that article appeared, the Stars fulfilled Dixon's prediction by defeating the Crawfords in Pittsburgh, leading the *Philadelphia Tribune* to declare that the team had "stepped in the front rank of eastern Negro baseball teams."[46] Carrying momentum from that victory, the Stars began a series with Harry Passon's Bacharach Giants, a rival black team from Philadelphia that had amassed a better percentage of games won and lost than the Stars. The Bacharachs name had been used in black baseball since 1916, and it had long been associated with Atlantic City. After the team disbanded in that city in March of 1930, however, Passon acquired the name and relaunched the franchise in Philadelphia a year later.[47] In 1932, the team, nicknamed the Bees, had garnered an impressive record, defeating nearly all the leading white teams from the local area and defeating the powerful Crawfords near the end of the season. The Bees also played their home games at Passon Field; the team made improvements at the field, installing a new grandstand and larger clubhouse and adding lights for weeknight games. In the *Philadelphia Tribune*, the Bees' general manager boasted that the improvements made Passon Field the most convenient and beautiful ballpark in the city; the reasonable admission prices allowed even the youngest fans to attend games. The Bees also promoted that they had retained the services of former Hilldale players, such as Otto Briggs, Nip Winters, and Phil Cockrell.[48]

The *Philadelphia Tribune* extensively covered the impending contest; prior to the first game, the newspaper printed a large picture of the Bees' first baseman George Carr and warned the Stars that they "gotta watch him."[49] The newspaper also reported that both teams had amassed a legion of loyal supporters and that both teams' fans had clamored for a series between the two rivals. Even though the Stars handily defeated the Bees in three games early in the season, an intense rivalry quickly developed between the two teams that lasted for the remainder of the year. For a late season contest between the Stars and the Bees, the newspaper mentioned the Bees' earlier losses and emphasized the team's desire for a chance at vindication.[50]

The Stars also entered into a bitter rivalry with the semi-professional Passon Club, another Harry Passon–owned local team. As that rivalry intensified, the *Philadelphia Tribune* tweaked the feud by declaring that the Stars' and Passons' clashes "have become bitter feuds with fans leaving the park talking about the game over and over again."[51] The newspaper proclaimed that "no club [exists] that Passon's would rather defeat than [the Stars] and the same shoe fits on the other foot."[52] Ultimately, the Stars fared well against their inner-city rivals, splitting the season series with both clubs and, more importantly, satisfying their fans with competitive and exciting baseball.

The promotional efforts from the newspaper and from Bolden succeeded in drawing numerous fans to Stars' games; the *Philadelphia Tribune* occasionally noted that the Stars played before thousands of fans or "the largest crowd of the season."[53] For their games against the Bees and the Passon Club, the Stars played in front of crowds numbering from two thousand to four thousand spectators. Starting in late July, Bolden arranged for the Stars to play home games at the old Hilldale Park. On opening day at Hilldale Park, the Stars attracted five thousand fans for a game with the Black Yankees; late in the season, a game between the Stars and Crawfords drew a standing-room-only crowd. As the football season began, the Stars quietly closed their inaugural campaign, but their success had left a positive impression with the city's fans and continued into the next year.[54]

Overall, the Stars enjoyed a successful inaugural season that stood in stark contrast to the chaotic and disappointing season for the NNL. The Stars played a regular schedule before large crowds, and the team made money during the season. McDonald boasted to the players that they had earned their eating money for the day and treated them to steak dinners after victorious games.[55] The team never lost a series throughout the season and earned praise as the "[b]est balanced Colored attraction in baseball" from *Colored Baseball and Sports Monthly*.[56] With a solid fan base and a successful inaugural season, the Stars moved ahead to their second season. For Bolden, the Stars' successful debut had helped to secure his comeback into a world he had once dominated. After several years in exile from black professional baseball, Bolden stood poised to taste the same success he had enjoyed with Hilldale in the 1920s.

CHAPTER FIVE

At the Summit, 1934

The 1934 season brought continued success for Ed Bolden and his Philadelphia Stars. After spending one season as an independent team, the Stars joined the NNL in 1934 and captured the league's championship. In addition to winning the NNL's title, the Stars participated in doubleheaders at Yankee Stadium, a new feature on the league's schedule. Those double-headers helped to introduce the black baseball world to Stuart "Slim" Jones, the Stars' phenom pitcher. As they did in 1933, the Stars played in front of large crowds and maintained a winning record throughout the season. A victory over the Chicago American Giants in the NNL championship series provided a fitting conclusion to the Stars' 1934 season.

At the same time, the 1934 season foretold problems for both Bolden and his team. Prior to the season, Bolden displayed a streak of ruthlessness when dealing with other NNL owners. He witnessed the limit of his influence when the other owners rejected a proposal he put forward at a league meeting. A great deal of controversy accompanied the Stars' victory over the Chicago American Giants. That controversy tarnished the Stars' accomplishment and sparked dissension within the NNL. The dissension among owners set an ominous tone for Bolden's, the Stars' and the NNL's future.

For Bolden, the 1934 season marked a milestone and a passage in his baseball career. The Stars' championship gave Bolden the distinct honor of leading two different teams in two different leagues to a championship. The championship also completed Bolden's comeback into black professional baseball and gave the second half of his baseball career a very promising start. Bolden also displayed some of the influence he once exerted over different leagues in the 1920s. His influence shaped the composition of the NNL in 1934 and helped secure a championship for his Stars. During the remainder of his career, however, Bolden never again reached a championship with his Stars. Bolden's Stars never dominated black baseball the way Bolden's Hilldale teams did in the 1920s. The 1934 Stars provided Bolden with his last opportunity to stand atop the black baseball world and to relive his days as a dominant force in black professional baseball in eastern states.

Ed Bolden Rejoins a League

Before Bolden could make plans for the Stars' 1934 season, he needed to mourn the untimely loss of one of the players on the team's inaugural roster. Eggie Dallard and his two-year-old son died in an automobile accident in December 1933. At the time of his death, the thirty-four-year-old Dallard had played professional baseball for thirteen seasons. In the *Pittsburgh Courier*, Bolden eulogized Dallard as "a ballplayer's ball player, the kind of fellow who was welcomed on any team."[1] He further lauded Dallard as "a mighty decent athlete" who "had the happy habit of hitting triples and doubles and singles when the big guns failed."[2]

Once he moved past that hardship, Bolden considered the biggest item on the Stars' offseason agenda—joining the NNL. Gus Greenlee wrote Bolden several times to encourage him to join the NNL, but Bolden prevaricated due to his bad experiences with leagues in the 1920s. As he told the *Pittsburgh Courier*, "Hilldale … made all of its money playing independent baseball and then went into a league and started losing money."[3] In January 1934, Bolden traveled to Pittsburgh for a meeting with Greenlee, Cumberland Posey, and other baseball officials. At the meeting, Bolden and his fellow owners discussed strategies for maximizing profits in the upcoming seasons. During the previous year, Pennsylvania's government had eliminated blue laws concerning the playing of sports on Sundays. With Sunday afternoons now open to league games in both Philadelphia and Pittsburgh, the owners could reconsider the league schedule. They resolved to leave weekday games open for league teams to schedule games against independent opponents, to avoid long trips, and to schedule league games on the weekends. The owners made preliminary plans to establish western and eastern divisions in the NNL and to include seven top-level teams in the eastern division. The Stars would represent one of those teams; despite his misgivings about league-based baseball, Bolden decided to bring his club into the NNL.[4]

Bolden did not make a graceful entrance into the NNL. At a meeting in Philadelphia in February, Bolden strongly objected to Harry Passon's application for membership in the NNL. To reduce travel costs, Greenlee and others hoped to have two Philadelphia-based franchises in the NNL, Bolden's Stars and Passon's Bacharach Giants. Other NNL owners, and sportswriter W. Rollo Wilson, believed that the Philadelphia market would patronize both teams. As Wilson noted in his column, the teams would use different ballparks and maintain alternate home schedules. Passon arrived at the meeting prepared to take all actions needed to secure league membership for his team. Bolden surprised everyone when he mounted a protest to Passon's application. He mounted that protest because he did not believe that Philadelphia could support two NNL franchises. A chastised and shocked Passon withdrew his application to avoid making enemies among the other NNL owners. Bolden then mounted a second protest, this one against the stipulation that all teams make financial deposits as a gesture of good faith to the NNL. He lost that battle since other owners refused to join the NNL unless every team made those deposits. Even though the Stars joined the NNL, Bolden's actions revealed his continued disdain for league-based baseball and the ruthlessness that lurked within his personality. He wanted to ensure his own survival, as well as his team's survival, in the often-chaotic world of black professional baseball.[5]

Despite his actions against Passon and the financial deposits, Bolden worked with his fellow owners to make plans for the NNL's second season. At a meeting held in Philadelphia's Roadside Hotel, the owners selected W. Rollo Wilson, a nationally syndicated newspaper columnist, as commissioner. Wilson, whom the *Tribune* touted as the "'Judge Landis' of colored baseball," immediately brought some stability by resolving some controversies over player trades.[6] The NNL owners also spoke with Tom Wilson to establish an arrangement with teams in the Negro Southern League. According to the proposed arrangement, the southern teams would act as farm teams for the NNL franchises. The owners made other strides toward stability. They drafted a schedule divided into two half-seasons, and the winners of the two half-seasons would meet in a post-season championship series. While the owners made those strides, the exact composition of the NNL remained unclear. The Pittsburgh Crawfords, Cleveland Red Sox, Nashville Elite Giants, Newark Dodgers, and Chicago American Giants joined the Stars as full NNL members. The Homestead Grays, Memphis Red Sox, Birmingham Black Barons and the Bees joined as associate members. The membership status of the Baltimore Black Sox stood in limbo. League owners had previously admitted the Black Sox as a full member, but the team asked for a suspension of their membership. The Black Sox's owner needed more time to ensure that he could sign players and field a team in 1934.[7]

The NNL owners' off-season moves provide insight into the reasons why Bolden would bring the Stars into the league and why he would still maintain skepticism about the health of league-based black professional baseball. Bolden and the other owners seemed genuinely interested in building a firm basis for the NNL. They selected a commissioner, made financial deposits, crafted a schedule, and established plans for a postseason championship series. At the same time, however, Bolden's actions hinted at the possibility of dissension among the owners. The lack of clarity in regards to the NNL's composition hinted at the precarious financial situation facing both the league and its teams. While Bolden appeared to harbor some doubts about the NNL, he decided to bring the Stars into the league in only their second season. His decision paid immediate dividends for the Stars.

The Season Begins

Similar to previous seasons, the *Tribune* acted like a booster for Bolden and his baseball franchise. The newspaper announced that Bolden had secured the services of Webster McDonald as the Stars' manager; he replaced Dick Lundy, who signed with another team.[8] In late March, the newspaper trumpeted that Commissioner Wilson resolved a dispute between the Buckeyes and the Stars over third baseman A.D. "Dewey" Creacy. The controversy arose because Creacy signed a contract with the Stars and then verbally agreed to manage the Red Sox. Wilson ruled in the Stars' favor because Creacy never signed a contract with Cleveland. Wilson, showing his determination to bring stability to the NNL, admonished Creacy for his actions and warned that similar future actions would result in his suspension from the league. The *Tribune* allowed the controversy to pass without further comment; it focused on Bolden's jubilation, not on the larger implications of Creacy's actions. With the addition of Creacy, the Stars' infield consisted of first baseman Jud Wilson, second baseman Dick Seay, and the shortstop platoon of Jake Stevens and Jake Dunn. The newspaper enthusiastically described that infield "as tight as a Scotch miser during a money panic."[9]

During the 1934 season, the Stars established a firm home base in West Philadelphia. In February, Bolden announced that the team had secured the P.R.R.Y.M.C.A. Park, located at 44th and Parkside Avenue in

West Philadelphia for its home games. Hilldale Park in Darby still existed and remained available for the Stars' home games. The *Tribune* cited accessibility for the Stars' fans as the prime factor in the team's decision to use a ballpark in West Philadelphia rather than in Darby. One month later, Bolden announced that the Stars had secured the use of Passon Field, located at 48th and Spruce Streets in West Philadelphia, for its NNL home games. The Stars also planned to use Passon Field for its Saturday night and Sunday games against teams not affiliated with the NNL. Passon Field underwent renovations in preparation for the Stars' games; the renovations included the installation of four thousand new seats.[10]

The Stars' opening game at Passon Field attracted five thousand spectators and set the tone for the team's successful season. With strong complete game effort from Stuart "Slim" Jones, the Stars defeated the Newark Dodgers by the score of 12 to 0. During the pregame festivities, both the Stars and the Dodgers marched to the field's flagpole. The O.V. Catto Elks Band led both teams to the flagpole, so the pregame festivities tied the Stars to one of Philadelphia's important civil rights and baseball leaders. Robert J. Nelson, one of Pennsylvania's Athletic Commissioners, threw out the first pitch. New NNL Commissioner Wilson watched the festivities and the game from the press box. In the game, Jones carried a no-hitter into the seventh inning. A single ended Jones's bid for a no-hitter, and the Dodgers added two more hits in the ninth inning. Every player in the Stars' line-up, except for Jones, garnered at least one hit. They drove the Dodgers' starter from the game in the fifth inning when they scored half of their twelve runs.[11]

Following their successful home opener, the Stars maintained a steady schedule of games against both NNL teams and teams not affiliated with the league. Near the end of May, the Stars faced the Homestead Grays in a three-game series played over two days. Even though the teams played all three games at Passon Field, the Grays represented the "home" team during the first game of the series. Before an "overflowing" crowd at the first game that "parked everywhere except on the home plate," the Stars lost the first two games by one-run scores.[12] The Stars fared better against Nashville, Cleveland, and the Crawfords; in a three-game rematch against the Grays, they won two games and tied the third. The Stars' success against NNL teams elevated them to second place in the league for the first half of the 1934 season.[13] The Stars also competed against white teams. In Newark, New Jersey, the Stars split a double-header against a team based in Meadowbrook. The Meadowbrook team featured an infielder who had previously played for the Philadelphia Phillies.[14] In an unusual double-header, the Stars faced the Crawfords in the Phillies' ballpark at Broad Street and Lehigh Avenue. For the second game, the winner of the Stars-Crawfords game faced the Philadelphia League All-Stars.[15] The All-Stars' roster included the best white players from non–Major League teams based in the Philadelphia area. Five thousand "rabid" fans watched the double-header; the Stars defeated the Crawfords and then faced defeat against the All-Stars.[16]

In the Shadow of Racial Tensions

The Stars' success in the NNL and their competitions against white teams came against a backdrop of growing racial tensions in Philadelphia. In July, police arrested three young white men for attacking a black man while he walked along a highway in West Philadelphia. The victim, identified in the *Tribune* as General Jones, spent several days recovering from his injuries in Misericordia Hospital. As outrage over that incident simmered, police released a white man whom they had arrested at the Haddington Recreation Center. Police had arrested the man, identified as forty-two-year-old Otto Wigren, after spectators at a basketball game witnessed him annoying a black girl. Spectators beat him; workers at the center rescued Wigren from the spectators, and he hid in an office until the police arrived. Before the police arrived, angry spectators descended upon the office and threatened to further escalate the situation. In a statement to the *Tribune*, a police captain downplayed the seriousness of both situations and regarded them as normal aspects of the relationships between white and black residents in West Philadelphia.[17]

In early August, the focal point of tensions between white and black Philadelphians shifted to North Philadelphia. Tensions first started to flare after Edward Morton, a Jewish merchant in North Philadelphia, assaulted Lucille Suber, a pregnant black women and a customer at his store. Black Philadelphians responded to the attack by threatening to boycott all Jewish businesses. The boycott never materialized, but police responded to attacks upon Jewish-owned businesses along Ridge Avenue. Those businesses suffered damage in the form of smashed windows and looted merchandise. A former member of a gang called the Forty Thieves told the *Tribune* that members of the gang helped to organize the attacks on Ridge Avenue's businesses. Gang members had a truck filled with bricks; as the truck moved along the road, people on the truck threw bricks at the businesses. Another group of people on the ground looted the businesses.

Police started making arrests after someone threw a bottle at an officer; the bottle hit the officer on the head and knocked him off his motorcycle. After several waves of arrests, the streets cleared, and the rioting ended.[18]

The simmering tensions between black and white Philadelphians came as Bolden, along with the rest of the NNL, maintained partnerships with white Jewish businessmen. NNL teams, including the Stars, used white Jewish booking agents to schedule their nonleague games since most of the teams did not own their home ballparks. The reliance upon white Jewish booking agents would stir debate within the NNL in future seasons. Bolden's partnership with Ed Gottlieb, a white Jewish booking agent from Philadelphia, went beyond scheduling games and securing ballparks. Gottlieb owned fifty percent of the Stars; Bolden and Gottlieb divided the team's profits, but Bolden remained the public face of the franchise. His name and designation as team owner remained on the Stars' official stationery. Bolden continued to recruit players, to remain in contact with the *Tribune*, and to complete administrative tasks. The partnership suited both men and remained in effect until the Stars ceased operations in 1953.[19]

Compared to past coverage pertaining to the involvement of white businessmen in black baseball, the *Tribune* adopted a different attitude toward the involvement of Gottlieb, Strong and Passon in the NNL. During Bolden's final days with Hilldale, the *Tribune* harshly criticized him for using white umpires and for planning to form a new franchise with Passon. The *Tribune*, however, never reported on the partnership between Bolden and Gottlieb. It continued to use Bolden's name in articles on the Stars, thereby giving the impression that he remained the Stars' sole owner. It merely mentioned, without editorial comment, the presence of Gottlieb and Nat Strong at NNL meetings. It also devoted space on its sports pages to covering the Passon-owned Bacharach Giants, a team that joined the NNL in the middle of the 1934 season. The *Tribune*, therefore, appeared to accept the involvement of white businessmen as part of the reality facing black professional baseball in the 1930s.[20]

Slim Jones and the Second Half

Despite some setbacks, the NNL enjoyed a modestly successful 1934 season. The Cleveland franchise withdrew from league play during the second half of the season, and the Nashville team had zero home games when the league released the second half schedule. A similar fate undermined the Baltimore Black Sox. The team did not play all of the thirteen home games in its second half schedule because other league teams regarded Baltimore as an unprofitable location for ball games. With their on-field success and drawing power at Passon Field, the Stars emerged as an important franchise for the NNL and contributed to the league's two great successes in 1934—the East-West Game and four-team double-headers at Yankee Stadium. The second annual East-West Game at Chicago's Comiskey Park drew twenty-five thousand spectators. Large crowds also greeted the Stars and other NNL teams at Yankee Stadium. In both the East-West Game and the Yankee Stadium double-headers, the Stars' phenom pitcher Stuart "Slim" Jones dazzled crowds and showed he could compete against the league's top pitchers.[21]

Throughout the 1934 season, Jones emerged as a top pitcher on the Stars' staff. Born in Baltimore in May 1913, Slim Jones represented the tallest player in the NNL. He earned his nickname "Slim" because he stood at six feet six inches tall and weighed only one hundred and eighty-five pounds. He joined the Stars at the start of the 1934 season. Previously, Jones spent an unproductive 1932 season with the Baltimore Elite Giants. In 1933, Jones spent the season with Tex Burnett in Puerto Rico, and he notched two hundred and ten strikeouts during Puerto Rico's fall season. His performance in Puerto Rico won him a spot on the Stars' staff, and Jones showed he belonged in the NNL. His near no-hitter in the Stars' home opener set the tone for the rest of his successful season. The Stars turned to Jones when facing tough competition—including the city rivals Bacharach Giants, the Chicago American Giants, and the Pittsburgh Crawfords. In the first game of a five-game series against the Bacharach Giants, Jones allowed one hit, faced only twenty-nine batters, and notched nine strikeouts. In the fourth game of the series, Jones pitched another shutout, limiting the Bacharach Giants to six hits. Jones showed his talents even in losing efforts, particularly in a late season game against the Craw-fords at Phillies Park. He struck out eight batters, but he could not over-power the legendary Josh Gibson. Gibson scored four runs, collected three RBIs, and hit two home runs over the fence on Broad Street.[22]

The highlights of Jones's stellar season game in the East-West Game and in the four-team double-headers at Yankee Stadium. Jones combined with two other pitchers on the East team, including Leroy "Satchel" Paige, one a 1–0 shutout of the West team.[23] A few weeks later, Jones and Paige faced off in the first of the Yankee Stadium double-headers. The double-header, held to benefit Sergeant George W. Curley and John W. Duncan, featured the American Giants and the Black Yankees in the first game and the Stars and the Crawfords in the second game.[24] The Stars-Crawfords game ended in a 1–1 tie after nine innings; darkness prevented the game from moving to extra innings. Both pitchers completed similar performances. Paige allowed six hits and notched twelve strikeouts; Jones allowed three hits and notched nine strikeouts. The *Tribune*'s Ed Harris praised Paige and Jones and noted that the event attracted many white spectators. Harris also wrote that both games featured playing "fit for the big leagues" and that the high attendance disproved the notion "that Negro baseball isn't worth a dime."[25] Three weeks later, Paige and the Crawfords triumphed over Jones and the Stars in a rematch at another Yankee Stadium four-team double-header. The second double-header attracted another large crowd to Yankee Stadium, and the crowd cheered for Jones in the losing effort.[26]

Onward to the Tainted Championship

The Stars' success propelled them ahead of other local black teams, including their rivals the Bacharach Giants. Despite Bolden's previous refusal to support the Bacharach Giants' application for league membership, the Stars and the Bacharach Giants rekindled their rivalry with a five-game series in August. According to the *Tribune*, Bolden and Passon made a wager on the outcome of the series. Gottlieb, Bolden's business partner and Passon's longtime friend, served as the stakeholder of the bet. An unidentified "well-known downtown sportsman" donated a trophy for the winner of the city championship.[27] The Stars easily won the series behind solid pitching from Jones and pitcher-manager Webster McDonald. Strong battings from Jud Wilson, Jake Stevens, and Jake Dunn also contributed to the Stars' victories.[28]

More importantly, the Stars' success elevated the team to first place in the second half of the NNL season and secured the team a spot in the league's playoffs. The Stars faced the American Giants, the winners of the NNL season's first half, to determine the league champion. The series opened in Passon Field, shifted to the American Giants' field in Chicago for the next three games, and then concluded back in Passon Field. Early in the series, the Stars' championship hopes appeared to diminish as they dropped three of the first four games. The Stars, however, made an amazing comeback and won the series in eight games. In the eighth game, Jones pitched a shutout and contributed at the plate. His seventh-inning double drove in the Stars' second run and provided him with some insurance for the final two innings.[29]

Instead of representing a moment of great triumph for the NNL, the championship series underscored the league's precarious position. The series went to an eighth game because game seven ended in a tie. Game seven fell on a Sunday, and Pennsylvania maintained a curfew of six in the evening for baseball games played on Sundays. That extension, however, represented a comparatively minor issue for the NNL. In the middle of the series, both the Stars and the American Giants competed in games unrelated to the ongoing series. The Stars swept a Sunday afternoon double-header against the Black Yankees at Passon Field; the games attracted three thousand spectators. The American Giants faced the Black Yankees in Yankee Stadium in the second of the four-team double-headers. The other game of that double-header featured the rematch between Jones and Paige. Twenty-five thousand fans attended the second Yankee Stadium double-header, and that figure helps to explain why the Stars and the American Giants halted their championship series. Four-team double-headers at Yankee Stadium boosted the NNL's profile and finances. More importantly, the double-headers and other well-attended games against league teams could entice Nat Strong to include his Black Yankees in the NNL. With the Black Yankees, the NNL would have a solid franchise in New York City and would count the powerful Strong among the league's owners.[30]

A slew of on-field controversies tainted the championship series and undermined both the league's and particularly Bolden's achievement. The on-field problems started in game six when David Malarcher, the American Giants' field manager, protested the game's outcome to Commissioner Wilson. Malarcher protested the game, which the Stars won, since the umpires had allowed Stars third baseman Jud Wilson and catcher Emile Brooks to remain in the game after they physically attacked the umpires in two separate incidents. In an early morning meeting, Bolden and Gottlieb strenuously pleaded with the commissioner to allow Wilson and Brooks to play in game seven. Bolden drew the ire of the American Giants' owner Robert A. Cole by threatening to pull the Stars from the series if the commissioner suspended any of his players. Bolden reportedly told Wilson that the Stars would not play if "50 or 50,000 people were in the park."[31] Commissioner Wilson denied Malarcher's protest and refrained from issuing any kind of punishment against the Stars' players.

The problems continued in game seven, the game that ended in a tie due to Pennsylvania's Sunday curfew law. "Mule" Suttles, the American Giants' left fielder, hit one of the umpires in the head with his bat to protest a called third strike. The umpire ejected Suttles, and a riot nearly erupted on the field. Game eight brought more protests from both the Stars and the American Giants. The Giants disputed an umpire's call at home plate. The Stars argued that the Giants used a player under contract with another NNL franchise.[32]

The ugly championship series garnered critical commentary in the *Tribune*. The only positive coverage of the Stars' championship came in the form of a team picture and an accompanying headline announcing the team's victory. Articles on the series mentioned the on-field controversies, and sportswriter Ed Harris openly showed his disgust with the players and the umpires. Harris decried that the "two sorry incidents" in game six set "[u]nhappy precedents" and fomented "out-and-out diamond lawlessness."[33] He regarded Jud Wilson's and Emile Brooks's actions as "illegal" and "unfair to their teammates and to the fans that came to the game."[34] Harris further criticized Wilson and Brooks for forgetting "it was a championship game, that their services were valuable to the teams, [and] that spectators had paid to see a baseball game and not a court-room [*sic*] debate or a prize fight."[35] He both expressed sympathy for and criticized the umpires in game six. While acknowledging umpires' decisions almost always attract criticism, Harris chastised them for not ejecting Wilson and Brooks. According to Harris, their actions set "unfortunate precedents" and gave Malarcher ammunition for filing a protest to the league commissioner.[36]

In subsequent columns on the NNL and the controversy-filled series, Harris hinted at larger problems due to erupt within the league. Harris predicted "plenty of fireworks" when the NNL owners gathered to plan for the next season.[37] He reported on fears that teams may withdraw from the league or demand more concessions, and the possibility that the NNL would not operate in 1935.[38] At a meeting in Pittsburgh, the American Giants owner Robert Cole refused to sign paychecks until all league members showed up at the meeting. Only the Crawfords' Gus Greenlee and Cumberland Posey of the Grays, an associate NNL member, attended the meeting. Some of the unsigned paychecks included a check for three hundred dollars due to Commissioner Wilson. Since he ruled against the American Giants in the series, Wilson publicly called Cole's actions spiteful.[39] Harris noted Cole helped to elect Wilson and should abide by his decisions. He warned that such selfishness on the part of Cole and other league owners threatened to destroy the NNL. Harris reiterated his point about selfishness in another column that reported on growing opposition to Wilson within the league. He again predicted a heated atmosphere when the NNL owners met to plan the 1935 season.[40]

The Stars' controversy-filled championship cast a pall over the NNL and obscured Bolden's achievement. Overall, the 1934 season represented a successful season for the NNL. The league staged another successful East-West Classic in Chicago, played two well-attended four-team double-headers at Yankee Stadium, and crowned a champion. Additionally, the NNL retained most of its members, and some NNL teams generated profits. Bolden completed a remarkable career comeback. He led another team in another league to a championship, an unprecedented feat within black professional baseball. Bolden also made an enduring partnership with Gottlieb that helped provide his franchise with financial stability. While the NNL's future seemed treacherous, the future for Bolden's Stars seemed bright. The team had a strong young pitcher in Jones, a collection of talented position players, and a capable leader in Webster McDonald.

Sadly, the Stars never again captured a championship. Over the next several seasons, the Stars faced a series of setbacks that mirrored the NNL's struggles to survive in the face of both internal and external obstacles.[41]

Chapter Six

Conflict All Around, 1935–1939

Ed Bolden and the Philadelphia Stars had little time to savor their championship victory over the Chicago American Giants. In early 1935, an owners' meeting shifted the balance of power within the NNL. W. Rollo Wilson lost his job as the league's commissioner, likely due to anger over his handling of controversies in the 1934 championship series. His replacement, Ferdinand Q. Morton, came from New York City. The league also admitted three franchises based near or in New York City—the Brooklyn Eagles, the Newark Dodgers, and the New York Cubans. With the admittance of the Brooklyn Eagles, the power couple of Abe and Effa Manley entered the NNL. The Eagles played one season in Brooklyn before moving to Newark and emerging as one of the NNL's premier franchises. Bolden and his Stars existed mostly in the shadows of the Eagles and the other NNL teams that dominated the league in the late 1930s. The Stars' championship in 1934 did not pave the way for Bolden to dominate the NNL the way he had dominated leagues in the 1920s. Instead, the Stars' championship ushered in a period of mediocrity as Bolden continually tried, and failed, to recapture the magic of his team's 1934 season.

While the Stars went through a string of mediocre seasons, Bolden and Ed Gottlieb settled into a comfortable partnership. Bolden handled all of the player personnel issues with the Stars and continued to work with the local newspapers, particularly the *Philadelphia Tribune*, to market his franchise. Gottlieb focused on financial issues and, along with Bolden, occasionally tussled with other NNL owners. Bolden's dissatisfaction with his own team frequently seeped onto the pages of both the *Tribune* and the *Philadelphia Independent*, another black weekly newspaper that devoted coverage to the Stars. At one point, Bolden seemed prepared to leave the NNL and to return his Stars to independent status. He never carried out his threat, and the Stars remained part of the league as the country moved into a new decade.

The battles that Bolden and Gottlieb faced characterized the Stars' conflict-filled existence during the late 1930s. Many stories concerning the Stars in both the *Tribune* and the *Independent* recounted Bolden's dissatisfaction with his players and his unsubtle threats to make changes to the roster. Both Bolden and Gottlieb engaged in disagreements, publicly and privately, with other NNL officials over finances, players, and schedules. Starting in 1937, the appearance of the Negro American League (NAL) offered additional challenges for Bolden and his fellow NNL owners. At the same time, the lure of leagues in Central and South America threatened the very existence of black professional baseball in the United States. Through all of those conflicts, Bolden showed the same ruthlessness he displayed in the wake of his nervous breakdown in the late 1920s. He made changes to the Stars roster when players did not fulfill his high expectations, and he annoyed other NNL officials when he felt their actions harmed the franchise that bore his name.

The 1934 Championship Fallout

For Bolden, the 1935 season started with promising notes. In February, Randy Dixon revealed Bolden's intention to sign an unnamed top-level pitcher to the Stars' staff. Dixon, likely with Bolden's backing, offered tantalizing clues about the unnamed pitcher's identity. He hailed from New England, had amassed an impressive record in semipro baseball, and had even attracted the interest of Major League clubs. During that same month, the sports pages of both the *Tribune* and the *Philadelphia Independent* carried stories about a productive NNL owners' meeting held in New York City. At that meeting, the owners reached decisions on several key items, including decision on building a league treasury and refining the umpire-hiring process. Bolden sat on a committee that focused on the umpire issue; Alex Pompez and Cumberland Posey joined him on that committee. The three men established a process that required umpires to make formal applications to the league secretary. From those applications, the NNL owners would select eight umpires at their next meeting. The report from Bolden's committee further outlined specific duties for the umpires. It gave the chief umpire at each league game the responsibility of reporting the game's box score to the league secretary. Umpires who neglected that duty faced a fine of $500.[1]

The harmony present at the first NNL owners' meeting of 1935 belied lingering tensions stemming from the controversial 1934 championship series. Prior to the NNL owners' meeting held in Philadelphia in 1935, the *Philadelphia Independent*'s sports page correctly predicted a fight over Commissioner W. Rollo Wilson. Due to his decisions in the 1934 series, Wilson faced opposition from the Chicago American Giants' R.A. Cole. Posey joined Cole in his opposition to Wilson; on the other side, Bolden, Harry Passon, and Gus Greenlee supported the incumbent commissioner. As predicted, the owners battled over Wilson's job when they met in March and replaced him with Ferdinand Q. Morton, a Civil Service commissioner from New York City who lacked any baseball experience. Though Greenlee had initially supported Wilson, he threw his support behind Morton and ultimately doomed Wilson. While Morton lacked baseball experience, he had the support of owners from new franchises welcomed into the league. Like Morton, two of the new franchises hailed from New York City; the third new franchise hailed from Newark, New Jersey. Morton's election, along with the admission of new franchises, symbolized the start of a new era for the NNL.[2]

In addition to selecting a new commissioner, the NNL owners welcomed new franchises and bid farewell to one franchise. The three new franchises—the New York Cubans, Brooklyn Eagles, and Newark Dodgers—infused the NNL with new leadership. Alex Pompez, who had worked with Bolden on the umpire issue, owned the Cubans. Abe and Effa Manley, who would emerge as a force within the NNL, operated the Eagles. That new leadership immediately made its presence known by supporting Morton over Wilson in the commissioner's election. Their arrival coincided with the departure of Harry Passon and his Bacharach Giants from the NNL. Bolden and his Stars remained the only Philadelphia-based team in the league. With Wilson's ouster, none of the league's leadership came from Philadelphia. Power within the NNL centered on Pittsburgh with league chairman Greenlee and in New York City with Commissioner Morton and the three new franchises.[3]

The *Tribune*'s Ed Harris regarded the proceedings with thinly-veiled contempt and bemusement. Harris noted that the owners allegedly voted unanimously for Morton and wondered what happened to sway Bolden's vote away from Wilson. He concluded that, despite Bolden's vote for Morton, the move to oust Wilson represented a move to take power away from Bolden and the Philadelphia market. While Harris refrained from criticizing Morton's abilities, he predicted a brief and unsuccessful tenure for him as the NNL's commissioner. As Harris reasoned, Morton would likely make a decision that rankled at least one of the NNL owners, and that decision would likely lead to his ouster from the commissioner's office. He lamented that the NNL needed a commissioner in the mold of Kenesaw Mountain Landis, someone who commanded respect from the owners and who knew how to operate a successful baseball league. Instead, it appeared to Harris as if "the league [were] working for the owners, and not the owners for the league."[4]

Ironically, the owners' actions came on the heels of a successful season for the NNL. While the championship series had its fair share of controversies, the 1934 regular season provided some reasons for the owners to feel optimistic about the 1935 season. As league secretary John L. Clark noted, the NNL enjoyed "almost unlimited newspaper publicity," particularly in regards to the annual East-West game.[5] The game attracted a crowd of twenty thousand fans, and the NNL netted $1000. The NNL saw similar gains from the four-team double-headers held in Yankee Stadium, double-headers that prominently featured Slim Jones and the rest of the Philadelphia Stars. Cities like Philadelphia and Pittsburgh demonstrated their value to the league; according to Clark, Philadelphia proved its position as the best "constantly good" city within the NNL.[6] Other cities that boasted NNL teams, or that represented possible expansion sites for the NNL, also demonstrated their value to the NNL and to the promotion of black professional baseball. Due to all of those factors and the promise of continued support from the black press, the outlook for the 1935 season seemed promising.[7]

Bolden's Stars in 1935

The 1935 season marked Bolden's twenty-fifth season in black professional baseball. At the end of the season, a laudatory article in the *Philadelphia Independent* reviewed his twenty-five seasons. Randy Dixon, the article's author, claimed that in "the realm of Negro baseball, no name shines forth with more lustre than that of Ed Bolden."[8] He praised Bolden's genius for assembling the great Hilldale teams and "one of the most colorful and most polished clubs of all time," the 1934 Philadelphia Stars.[9] Dixon also noted that Bolden maintained his full-time job with the Philadelphia Post Office and achieved perfect scores on his examinations. Dixon, furthermore, noted Bolden's advocacy for clean and fair playing in black professional baseball. To Dixon, Bolden represented "a conspicuous representative of talents possessed by sepia diamondeers" and as someone who defended black players "as players equal if not superior to any others in any league, anywhere."[10]

As he entered his twenty-fifth year in black professional baseball, Bolden himself encapsulated both the promise of the 1935 season and the discord threatening the NNL's existence. Shortly after the off-season meetings concluded, Bolden fell ill and spent time at a local hospital. The *Philadelphia Independent* reported that Bolden suffered from a stomach ailment and a "general rundown condition."[11] A headline across the top of the sports page claimed that Bolden had suffered another nervous breakdown. Despite his illness, Bolden felt well enough to speak to one of the sportswriters by telephone and provide him an optimistic update about the Stars' 1935 season. He confidently predicted that the Stars would enjoy a fast start and would benefit from the contributions of both their new players and their veterans. While Bolden lamented the early start to the regular season, he seemed certain that the Stars would have sufficient time to train before opening day.[12] One week later, Bolden again embodied both the promise and the underlying tension associated with the NNL. In another interview with the *Philadelphia Independent*, Bolden accused the NNL of engaging in unspecified "filthy politics."[13] At the same time, however, Bolden expressed optimism about the Stars' prospects for the upcoming 1935 season. He also used the opportunity to depict himself as a principled leader interested only in quality baseball: "[The NNL's filthy politics] makes me all the more determined to give Philadelphia a perfect ball park, with a classy championship team performing and conducting themselves in such a manner that fans will be proud and always enjoy a thrill."[14]

As Bolden predicted, the Stars enjoyed a fast start to their 1935 regular season. With star pitcher Slim Jones on the mound, the Stars defeated a non–NNL opponent from Wentz-Olney in their opening game. In addition to Jones, the Stars' roster included familiar names like Dewey Creacy, Porter Charleston, Dick Seay, Jake Stevens, Jud Wilson, and Bizz Mackey. Webster McDonald again served as the team's field manager. Following their victory over the Wentz-Olney team, the Stars collected victories against other non-league foes before opening the NNL season in Pittsburgh against the Homestead Grays. The Stars and Grays split their games, and the Stars then returned to Philadelphia for their home opener against the Brooklyn Eagles. Instead of using Passon Field at 48th and Spruce, the Stars hosted their opener at the P.R.R.Y.M.C.A. field located at 44th and Parkside in West Philadelphia. Known in both of the local black newspapers as Bolden Bowl, the field would serve as the Stars' home for the next twelve seasons. Prior to the game, the O.V. Catto Elks Band paraded around the field, and the Stars raised a banner commemorating their 1934 title. Austin Norris, Pennsylvania's Deputy Attorney-General, tossed the ceremonial first pitch. After those festivities, four thousand fans watched the Stars continue their promising start by defeating the Eagles.[15]

Following their promising start, the Stars endured a turbulent season and missed the opportunity to defend their NNL title. In June, a losing streak awakened Bolden's ruthlessness, the same kind of ruthlessness that he displayed during his final years with Hilldale. Speaking to Randy Dixon in the *Philadelphia Independent*, Bolden outlined his plans to drastically alter the Stars' roster by making trades. Bolden provided extensive details about his trade plans and justified his actions by describing the short-comings of the players currently on the Stars' roster. By detailing his plans in a public forum, Bolden may have wanted to use the newspaper to jolt his team into playing better baseball. His plans did not materialize since other owners demanded players Bolden wanted to keep on the Stars' roster. During the second half of the season, the Stars briefly enjoyed the NNL's best record, but they faltered near the end of the season and missed the opportunity to capture the second-half title. The Stars' flirtation with first place helped to secure several spots on the East team in the annual East-West Game. McDonald enjoyed the honor of managing the team. Slim Jones, Dewey Creacy, Jake Stevens, Biz Mackey, Jud Wilson, Jake Stevens, and Dick Seay joined McDonald on the East squad.[16]

The Stars' improved play during the second half of the season and securing of several spots on the East team obscured deeper fissures. Iron-ically, Slim Jones secured a spot on the East team at the same time as he faced a suspension from the Stars. Jones reportedly had an injured shoul-der, and he evidently did not take the proper steps to recover from the injury. Bolden stopped Jones's salary and suspended him from the Stars for his "failure to attain proper physical condition."[17] Two other pitchers, Paul Carter and Rocky Ellis, faced fines of $5.00 and $10.00 respectively for "absence from the club during working hours without permission."[18] Instead of celebrating the high number of Stars on the East team's roster, Bolden seemed annoyed at the loss of talent. He canceled the Stars' NNL games scheduled at Bolden Bowl during the same weekend as the East-West Game. Bolden also asked NNL President Greenlee to limit the num-ber of Stars players on the East team to four and to fill the remaining spots with players from other NNL teams.[19] At the same time, Bolden again used the *Philadelphia Independent* to voice displeasure with his roster even while acknowledging that his team had amassed a winning record. As he had earlier in the season, Bolden likely used the newspaper to threaten his players into improving their on-field contributions. He issued the very unsubtle threat: "[T]he next six or seven weeks will determine just what men will be retained and just what others will walk the plank."[20]

Bolden also used the local sports pages to vent his frustration about issues involving the NNL's management. Late in the 1935 season, a team spokesman announced that the "Chief is sick and tired of losing money going on road trips to Pittsburgh, Chicago, and other places where it is impossible to fill in the open dates playing independent teams."[21] Bolden asserted that the NNL covered too much territory and carried too many teams for the number of days reserved for league competition. He also complained that a small group of owners controlled league affairs and that a double standard existed for the punishment of owners who flaunted league rules. Furthermore, while the Stars lost money on their road trips, other league teams made money by playing in the Philadelphia area, the best semi-professional market in the country. Bolden made a final demand—since the Stars paid more money into the league treasury than any other team, Philadelphia should host the next East-West game.[22]

The laudatory article commemorating Bolden's twenty-fifth season accurately captured his impressive contributions to black professional baseball. The article, however, obscured an important fact concerning Bolden's determination to uphold high standards on and off the baseball diamond. When Bolden sensed that his players had not lived up to his high expectations for them, he used his close relationships with the local black press to assert his authority and threaten to make changes to his roster. Bolden also bristled when he felt that he faced unfair treatment from the NNL. His ruthlessness in dealing with underperforming players and reaction against perceived slights from the NNL manifested themselves as new personalities and rivals emerged in black professional baseball.

Black Baseball and the Numbers

The NNL's expansion in 1935 brought into the league owners with backgrounds dissimilar from Bolden's background. While Bolden maintained full-time employment at the respectable Philadelphia Post Office, many of his fellow NNL owners maintained connections to less respectable business enterprises, specifically the numbers lottery, a form of gambling popular among African American communities in urban areas. For as little as a nickel, individuals gambled on hitting a lucky combination of three numbers and winning a payoff of six hundred to one. Since the true odds of winning stood at nine hundred ninety-nine to one, considerable profits awaited a resourceful and reliable people who could oversee the operation. Reportedly, the Cubans' Alex Pompez grossed as much as $7,000 to $8,000 a day from his gambling organization, and Gus Greenlee's peak income reached $20,000 to $25,000 per day. Abe Manley operated the numbers game in several New Jersey cities, and Rufus Jackson bankrolled Cum Posey's Homestead Grays with his gambling profits. Tom Wilson, owner of the Nashville and later Baltimore Elite Giants, also participated in the numbers game. Neither Bolden or Ed Gottlieb, Bolden's behind-the-scenes partner, had any known connections to the numbers lottery in Philadelphia.[23]

Due to the ongoing Great Depression, the numbers lottery offered a financial lifeline to many of the men who ran the NNL. President Franklin Roosevelt's New Deal policies had done little to ameliorate the poor economic conditions ravaging African American communities in urban areas. With their earnings from the numbers lottery, men like Gottlieb, Pompez, and Manley had the financial means to bankroll black professional baseball franchises. They also could provide employment for members of their respective communities and, in their own ways, emerged as community benefactors. In addition to owning the Crawfords and the Crawford Grill, Greenlee worked as a boxing promoter, maintained other legal businesses, and participated in local politics in Pittsburgh. Greenlee, furthermore, used his earnings from the numbers lottery to support businesses within Pittsburgh's African American community; those businesses included the *Pittsburgh Courier*. His connections to others running illegal businesses gave him the financial resources needed to build a ballpark, Greenlee Field, for his Crawfords. That ballpark gave Greenlee the foothold necessary to revive the NNL and to serve as its leader.[24]

The presence of the numbers lottery starkly highlighted the financial reality facing the NNL in the 1930s. Team owners could not build a corporation akin to Bolden's Hilldale Baseball Corporation; they turned to the numbers lottery as well as white capital in order to remain in business. The funds Greenlee used to build his ballpark came from white businessmen, not African American businessmen, in Pittsburgh. To please his white financial backers, Greenlee used white employees, and not black employees, at Greenlee Field. Across the state, Bolden never attempted to rebuild an African American corporation, akin to the Hilldale Corporation, to promote the Stars. Instead, he worked with Gottlieb, who had business interests with Harry Passon and other white entrepreneurs in Philadelphia. Through Gottlieb, the Stars secured their home ballparks in West Philadelphia and games against local teams.[25]

Even with the presence of the numbers lottery and the involvement of white booking agents, the Stars and other NNL teams faced the threat of financial disaster. That looming threat likely added to a sense of competitiveness among Bolden and his fellow NNL owners as they sought to obtain every available advantage to make money through their teams. That sense of competitiveness heightened the need for a strong leader to maintain order within the NNL, but Ferdinand Morton lacked the leadership skills necessary to bring order to the league. In the *Philadelphia Independent*, Dixon likened the commissioner to the vice-president, a man with a "big sounding title that means nothing."[26] He lamented that Morton had failed to popularize the NNL and questioned his judgment in a controversy involving former Star Dick Lundy. Morton approved a trade sending Lundy to Pompez's New York Cubans even though a separate deal had Lundy going to the Brooklyn Eagles. As Dixon reasoned, Pompez's connections to Nat Strong, a powerful booking agent in New York City, compelled Morton to favor the Cubans at the expense of the Brooklyn franchise. To Dixon, Morton's actions demonstrated that powerful booking agents and owners ran the NNL. He further lamented that the NNL's expansion into New York City had failed to improve the league's financial situation. Dixon concluded that Philadelphia remained the "backbone" of the NNL and that the league would remain dependent upon white booking agents like Gottlieb as long as it lacked an innovative leader.[27]

The Conflict Deepens

As the 1936 season dawned, the NNL underwent a shift in geography and in leadership. The withdrawal of the Chicago American Giants reshaped the NNL's borders and ended its reach into the upper Midwest. Additionally, the Manleys returned the Brooklyn franchise to the league once they purchased the Newark franchise and renamed it the Newark Eagles. As part of the deal, the Manleys had control over players from both the old Brooklyn and Newark franchises. The move came with some controversy as Bolden publicly objected to the Manleys' purchase of the Newark franchise and of their ability to retain players from both franchises. Bolden, however, directly benefited from a change in the NNL's leadership when he won election as the league's new president. He replaced league founder Greenlee, who resigned his position prior to an owners' meeting in March 1936. Though he held a league office, Bolden retained ownership of the Stars and remained in charge of personnel decisions. Instead of commenting upon his leadership of the NNL, Bolden again used his connections with the black press to broadcast his intentions for the Stars and his determination to build a winning team.[28]

Bolden's elevation to the NNL's presidency failed to quench a sour mood accompanying the impending 1936 season. Dixon captured that mood in several of his columns, and he claimed to have fan-written letters full of complaints about the NNL. He lamented the lack of action on the part of NNL owners to investigate the league's finances and to operate as a genuine league. Prior to the start of the season, NNL Secretary John Clark echoed Dixon's words when he issued stern public warnings to the owners, managers, and players. Clark called upon the owners to act in a more disciplined manner and to uphold their pledges; for the managers and players, Clark urged them to watch their behavior on the baseball diamond. He also called upon the teams to maintain efficient scorekeepers and to work with the black press in order to share accurate information with the league's fandom. Clark, furthermore, urged teams to help develop umpires, maintain good field conditions, hire professional staff for their home ballparks, and adhere to strict rules governing player behavior.[29]

While Bolden had oversight over the NNL, he seemed to devote most of his focus to building a championship-caliber Stars team. He finally carried out his threats from the previous season by making trades and other transactions designed to overhaul the team's roster. As a result of his machinations, new faces like Norman "Turkey" Stearns, Larry Brown, Roy Parnell, Bill Yancey, and Henry Miller joined the franchise. Bolden sent Dick Seay to the Crawfords in a trade that yielded nothing for the Stars as the ex-Crawfords did not report to their new team. Former ace pitcher Slim Jones presented another problem for Bolden as he again needed time to get into top physical shape. Instead of training in the South, the Stars held their spring training sessions at a Y.M.C.A. in southwest Philadelphia, near the site of Bolden Bowl. On the eve of the 1936 season opener, Bolden invited reporters to the Y.M.C.A. and used the opportunity to deliver a stern lecture to his players. Through his lecture, Bolden established his high expectations for the Stars' players both on and off of the field and his determination to release underproducing players.[30]

During the first half of the 1936 season, Bolden's efforts to remake the Stars paid off as his team surged to first place in the NNL. The Stars set the pace for their first-half success by sweeping their opening series at Bolden Bowl over the Homestead Grays. Opening Day at Bolden Bowl again featured a parade led by the O.V. Catto Elks Band and a dignitary, Representative Hobson R. Reynolds, tossing the ceremonial first pitch. The Stars' surge did not come without controversy as complaints about the umpires and on-field behavior again filled newspaper columns. In June, the Stars faded and lost their first-place position. The first half of the NNL season ended without an official winner; both the Stars and the Elite Giants had claims to the title, but they needed to play additional games in order to determine a champion. Rules drafted at the start of the 1936 season mandated that league teams play each other at least five times during each half of the season. Since that did not happen during the first half of the season, the league officially did not award the title to either team. The league directed the Stars to play the Cubans and the Elite Giants to play the Stars twice during their next visit to Philadelphia. Those rules meant that the first-half title remained undecided as the second half of

The Philadelphia Stars' home openers began with elaborate pre-game ceremonies. Those ceremonies typically included a marching band, like the one featured in this photograph, from the local Otto V. Catto Elks organization (John W. Mosley Photograph Collection, Charles L. Blockson Afro-American Collection, Temple University Libraries, Philadelphia, Pennsylvania).

Pre-game ceremonies marked the Philadelphia Stars' home openers. Local dignitaries like Hobson Reynolds, pictured at left with Bolden and an unidentified man in uniform, tossed the ceremonial first pitch as part of the opening day festivities (John W. Mosley Photograph Collection, Charles L. Blockson Afro-American Collection, Temple University Libraries, Philadelphia, Pennsylvania).

the season commenced. The lingering dispute about the first-half title opened fissures within the NNL and nearly wrecked the league.[31]

Much of the controversy over the first-half title played out on the sports pages of black newspapers. In July, the league published official first-half standings that showed the Elite Giants in first place with a record of 14–10. The Stars stood in second place with a record of 15–12. The two teams, however, had not played the two games that NNL rules demanded they play. Though the Elite Giants' manager Jim Tayler and owner Tom Wilson supported the standings, Bolden publicly objected and accused the two men of avoiding the two needed games against the Stars. Bolden also noted that he did not exercise his power as NNL president to compel the Elite Giants to play the two missing games due to his ownership of the Stars. He did caution that he would have exercised that power had the controversy involved another team. In his newspaper column, Posey threw his support behind Bolden and, like Bolden, placed most of the blame for the situation on NNL Secretary John Clark. Bolden questioned Clark's approval of the official NNL standings, and Posey wondered if Clark's connections to Greenlee's Crawfords swayed his judgment. Posey also lauded Bolden as the best of the NNL's terrible officials and reasoned that the league needed officials who lacked connections to teams. Bolden's position as NNL president placed him in an awkward position; Wilson, the owner of the Elite Giants, also served as the NNL's treasurer.[32]

Ultimately, it did not matter which team officially captured the first half title since the NNL failed to stage a postseason championship in 1936. The Stars and the Elite Giants did finally stage their two games; the Elite Giants won, putting them in position to meet the second-half winners, the Crawfords, for the NNL title. The two teams played what appeared to mark the opening game of the championship series at Bolden Bowl in late September. Many of the players for those teams, however, did not participate in the game at Bolden Bowl. Instead, they participated in a tournament in Denver, prompting the NNL to simply cancel the league championship. Around the time of the canceled championship, Greenlee's Crawfords faced accusations that they associated with gamblers and deliberately threw a game against a semi-pro team in New York City. Both the canceled championship series and the gambling accusations brought the 1936 season to a messy conclusion and added fuel to the criticisms the NNL faced from black sportswriters.[33]

Columns from the *Tribune*'s Ed Harris and the *Independent*'s Randy Dixon captured the frustration facing the NNL on the heels of the canceled championship series. Harris called the canceled series a "sorry ending to a sorry season" and "the latest of the many arbitrary actions that have hampered the growth and development of the National Association."[34] Harris also directed his ire at Commissioner Morton for allowing the first-half title dispute to linger and at the owners for their selfish behavior. He predicted that the owners' selfishness would erode fan support of the NNL and make the league an unprofitable business. Harris also asserted that if the owners refused to operate as a league, then they should abandon the league structure, operate as independent franchises, and wait for the right people to rebuild the league structure.[35] Dixon expressed similar sentiments. He blamed the NNL for duping Philadelphia baseball fans into patronizing the alleged first game of the championship series. Similar to Harris, Dixon accused the owners of engaging in selfish behavior and regarded the NNL as having little value.[36]

In his capacity as NNL President, Bolden felt compelled to respond to criticisms directed at the league. After initially expressing surprise at the cancellation of the championship series, Bolden then asserted that the league did not need to complete a postseason series if "it does not pay financially."[37] Bolden further asserted that local interest in the competing teams' hometowns determined the success of postseason series and that he had worked tirelessly to promote the success of league baseball. He noted the high attendance figures at four-team double-headers at Yankee Stadium and at other NNL games held in Major League ballparks. Bolden also downplayed the charges of cheating against the Crawfords, alleging that a member of the defeated team made the accusations as a way of avenging their defeat. He concluded his column by defending the actions of his sincere fellow owners who had purchased streamlined buses and paid top salaries for talented players. Contrary to the claims of the sportswriters, the NNL did not need new leadership. The NNL had enough good leaders who could make the organization work.[38]

Following Bolden's defense of the NNL, league Secretary Clark also responded to criticisms leveled against the organization. Clark asserted that the NNL would operate in 1937; five owners had already pledged to join the NNL, and league officials had reached out to the two clubs that had yet to respond, the Grays and the Cubans. He also asserted that the NNL had postponed, not canceled, the postseason series between the Elite Giants and the Crawfords. According to Clark, the Elite Giants and the Crawfords could stage the championship series in the South during the late winter or early spring of 1937. Clark saw the postponed championship as a benefit to the entire league since it would force both the two competing teams, as well as the other NNL teams, to increase their training and open the 1937 season in top form. To counter criticisms about the NNL's profitability, Clark noted that the league had come close to turning a profit in the 1936 season. He blamed bad weather in August for turning profits into deficits. Clark concluded by optimistically looking forward to the 1937 season, to continued patronage of NNL games, and to potentially new sources of revenue for the league.[39]

With their columns, both Bolden and Clark sought to contain the damage caused by the 1936 season's messy conclusion. The lingering dispute over the first-half title and the canceled championship series revealed the lack of control Commissioner Morton held over the NNL. He did not assert the authority to force the Elite Giants and Stars to play their remaining games, nor could he compel the players on the winning teams to play in the postseason series. The fact that both Bolden and Wilson held positions within the NNL's leadership and owned teams involved in the dispute further compounded the problem facing Commissioner Morton. Both

Bolden and Clark optimistically looked forward to the 1937 season, but that season would heap additional troubles upon the NNL. In 1936, the NNL's troubles came from internal sources. In 1937, the NNL's troubles expanded as both internal and external factors shook the league's foundation and increased the sense of competitiveness among the league's owners.

New Leagues, New Troubles

During the early months of 1937, the NNL again underwent changes in leadership and witnessed some discontent among the owners. Clark resigned his position as NNL secretary in order to spend more time with the Crawfords; Greenlee needed more help running the franchise, since he managed boxer John Henry Lewis. Abe Manley won election as NNL treasurer, while Morton retained his role as the NNL commissioner. Bolden did not win reelection to his post as NNL president; the owners initially chose Leonard Williams, a Pittsburgh resident and former official in Rube Foster's old NNL, as the new president. Williams, however, declined the role, and the owners subsequently chose Greenlee to again serve as the president. Bolden's surprising ouster spurred the *Independent*'s sports page to declare the existence of a conspiracy against Bolden and Philadelphia brewing within the NNL. As that drama played out, Effa Manley voiced her disapproval of the ways the league conducted its business. The 1936 champion remained uncrowned, as the Elite Giants and Crawfords never played the supposedly postponed championship series. Overall, the NNL seemed again poised to endure another tumultuous season under the guidance of a weak commissioner and subjective officials who owned teams within the league.[40]

In the Midwest, a far more potent threat to the NNL emerged when eight clubs formed the Negro American League (NAL). The Chicago American Giants, formerly of the NNL, represented one of those eight clubs. The remaining NAL members included the Kansas City Monarchs, Cincinnati Tigers, Memphis Red Sox, Detroit Stars, Birmingham Black Barons, Indianapolis Athletics, and St. Louis Stars. Like the NNL, teams in the NAL adopted a split-season schedule and relied upon white booking agents to schedule their games. Almost immediately, disputes arose between the two leagues in regard to player contracts. NAL owners contended that several players, most notably Turkey Stearns, participated in the NNL in 1936 despite the fact that they had contracts with their teams.

While the NAL owners pressed their claims, Bolden and other NNL owners insisted they could sign the disputed players since none of them had contracts with a league team. NNL rules did not require the owners to respect contracts players signed with independent teams. NAL owners understandably rejected that premise, but they too had players whom NNL owners claimed belong to their franchises. As the season approached, officials from both leagues worked to resolve the player disputes and to develop an agreement by which owners from one league respected the contracts involving teams from the opposing league.[41]

While the NNL and the NAL worked through their differences, Rafael Trujillo of the Dominican Republic laid the foundation for a far more devastating threat to both leagues. Trujillo had ruled the Dominican Republic since

In 1937, Roy Parnell and other top Negro League players jumped their contracts and joined Ciudad Trujillo in the Dominican Republic. Like other contract jumpers, Parnell returned to his Negro League team, the Philadelphia Stars, without facing any punishment for his actions. Overall, Parnell played with the Philadelphia Stars for eight seasons (John W. Mosley Photograph Collection, Charles L. Blockson Afro-American Collection, Temple University Libraries, Philadelphia, Pennsylvania).

1931, and he sought to assemble a baseball team as a way to increase his popularity. He successfully enticed Negro League talent to jump their contracts and join his team, known as Ciudad Trujillo. The players who joined Ciudad Trujillo included several Crawfords, most notably pitcher Satchel Paige and outfielder Sam Bankhead, and one member of the Stars, Roy Parnell. Like their Major League counterparts, Negro League players had participated in winter leagues in the Caribbean and South America. Unlike their Major League counterparts, Negro League players did not fear repercussions from a commissioner if they jumped their contracts. Kenesaw Mountain Landis, the Major League commissioner, threatened lifetime bans to contract jumpers. Neither the NNL nor the NAL had an authority with that kind of power or respect. Trujillo's willingness to pay higher salaries acted as a further enticement for Negro League players, and both leagues faced a problem they could not easily resolve.[42]

Initially, Bolden and other NNL owners acted decisively to assert their authority and prevent further contract jumping. Bolden, other owners from the NNL, and the NAL president sought to develop an agreement with the Dominican Republic that would permit their players to participate in leagues in the island nation during the winter months. In the meantime, the contract jumpers faced bans once they returned to the United States. The bans did not trouble the contract jumpers, as they formed a traveling independent team and went on a tour throughout the United States. Instead of remaining firm, NNL officials sought to capitalize on the banned players' popularity, particularly since teams composed of replacement players drew smaller crowds. Gottlieb booked a contest between them and the NNL all-stars at the 44th and Parkside field, and the blacklisted players won the game before a near-capacity crowd. Writing in the *Philadelphia Independent*, Earl Barnes alleged that Greenlee and a white boxing promoter backed the outlaw team and made money for its appearances. Due to that alleged connection, Barnes raised important questions about Greenlee's priorities and fitness to serve as the NNL's president.[43]

As the NNL made a feeble response to the contract jumpers, the league made an equally feeble attempt to eliminate bad on-field behavior from players, managers, and even owners. Greenlee promised the umpires that they would have the full support of league officials and urged them to uphold the NNL's rules governing on-field behavior. NNL rules prohibited owners from entering the field and arguing with umpires, yet owners engaged in that behavior when umpires made disputed calls. Greenlee also threatened suspensions against rowdy players, but his threats did not seem potent enough to deter the behavior that had marred the 1937 season. In June, members of the Black Yankees assaulted an umpire in his dressing room following a game against the Stars. Another umpire endured a similar beating from members of the Elite Giants, also following a game against the Stars. Oscar Charleston, former player and manager of the Crawfords, assaulted an umpire who had made a call against his team. In other cases, players threw objects into the stands and hurt spectators. The rowdyism added to the NNL's woes and demonstrated the lack of strong, respected leadership from either the commissioner or league president.[44]

Due to the woes facing the NNL, Greenlee faced questions about his continued leadership over the league he founded. Posey used his column in the *Pittsburgh Courier* to take the claims Earl Barnes raised in his *Independent* column one step further and call upon Greenlee to resign his post as league president. According to Posey, Greenlee's other commitments made him "too busy to attend to league business in a satisfactory manner," and, consequently, "all the members of the league are suffering accordingly."[45] He cited poor discipline as the most glaring manifestation of Greenlee's neglect of his league duties. Posey demanded answers from Greenlee concerning the consequences players faced once umpires removed them from games due to poor on-field behavior. To Posey, Greenlee's weakness on that issue supported his contention that Greenlee lacked sufficient interest in the NNL's welfare, remained aloof from the problems plaguing the league, and needed to resign his position for the good of the NNL.[46]

Greenlee rejected Posey's call for his resignation and desperately sought to assert his authority over the NNL. In September, Greenlee spoke against the proposed World Series planned between the winners of the NNL and NAL. Through his diatribe, Greenlee addressed other issues concerning his leadership of the NNL and his alleged affiliation with players who had jumped their contracts. According to Greenlee, the Manleys, Posey, and Rufus Jackson of the Grays had made arrangements for a World Series without first seeking his approval. Greenlee, therefore, accused those individuals of usurping his office and issued warnings about continued usurpations in the 1938 season. Greenlee, furthermore, declared his intentions to remain active within the NNL and blamed others, namely Effa Manley, for working to undermine the league structure. He concluded by noting the thousands of dollars he had spent on his team as well as his team's ballpark and predicting a reorganization of the league in 1938.[47]

Greenlee's diatribe represented his desperate attempt to reassert authority over owners who no longer seemed to respect his leadership.

The Crawfords suffered the most from Ciudad Trujillo, and the franchise never recovered. Greenlee also never recovered, and he soon relinquished the presidency to the Elite Giants' Tom Wilson. Greenlee's diatribe also revealed a certain level of hypocrisy present within the NNL. While he claimed to have no connections to the outlawed players, he wrote a letter, possibly to Abe Manley, promoting a game involving them and NNL stars at Yankee Stadium. Greenlee jokingly referred to the contest as a war, enclosed tickets to the game, and made references to an armistice commencing on September 26. Similar to others involved with the NNL, Greenlee prioritized financial gains over adhering to league rules. His actions helped to destabilize the NNL and to heighten the sense of chaos and competition among the owners.[48]

The Mediocre Stars

While the league structure crumbled around them, Bolden's Stars plodded through a mediocre 1937 season. Bolden again made changes to the Stars roster, and Jud Wilson assumed the managerial duties from Webster McDonald. Wilson had the capability to serve as a good manager, but he still possessed the fiery temper that nearly led to his suspension during the 1934 championship series. At one point, Wilson argued so fiercely with an umpire that he pulled the umpire's mask off of his head and broke one of the straps on the mask.[49] The highlight of the Stars' season came when the team suffered a dangerous yet non-fatal bus crash on a trip to face the Crawfords. Wilson sustained the worst injury with a broken rib; most of the players suffered from minor injuries and shock. The Stars continued their road trip, played a double-header against the Crawfords, and actually went on a winning streak. They showed more enthusiasm than they had showed in the past two years, won with exciting late-inning rallies, and earned accolades from their fans. In the *Tribune*, Randy Dixon jokingly said that the Stars needed to endure more bus wrecks and praised manager Wilson as an unsung hero since he "just stuck out his chest and the bus landed on it."[50] As Dixon predicted, the Stars' winning streak turned out to "be a flash in the pan," and the team never contended for a postseason berth.[51]

Bolden again made changes to his roster for the 1938 season, but those changes failed to bring another pennant to Philadelphia. In order to acquire top players from the Crawfords, Bolden had to part with his promising rookie Gene Benson. The players Bolden acquired—Phil

Perkins, Pat Patterson, and Ernest Carter—had jumped their contracts and played for both Ciudad Trujillo and the popular traveling team of NNL outlaws. The NNL had formally forgiven those players, yet Bolden had announced his intentions to sign outlawed players before the league took that action. He added four other former outlaws to a roster that included Slim Jones, Webster McDonald, Dewey Creacy, and Wilson. With those players under contract, and with Slim Jones seemingly recovered from his injuries, Bolden confidently predicted a pennant for his Stars. The Stars enjoyed a promising start to the season, and remained in contention for the league lead during both halves of the season. The Stars, however, did not capture either of the half-season titles and again remained shut out of a postseason berth. Injuries to key players hurt the Stars; the team also had the misfortune of facing a powerful Grays squad, the team that won the 1938 championship.[52]

In the local black press, stories praising the improved Stars appeared interspersed with stories on controversies with umpires and on other issues troubling the NNL. At least twice, the NNL failed to assign an umpire to a game at the Stars' 44th and Parkside field. When the league assigned a white umpire to a Stars home game, both mangers rejected the umpire on account of his drunkenness. In Chicago, umpires formed a union in the hopes of forcing the NAL to address physical attacks from players and managers. Writing in the *Independent*, Earl Barnes complained about the NNL's secrecy concerning these problems and the seeming lack of leadership from any league officials. He also called for a "true" World Series pitting the winner of the NNL against the winner of the NAL. In the *Tribune*, Randy Dixon seconded Barnes' complaints about the NNL's operations and urged the fans to voice their displeasure by staying home. He also wrote about the troubling rumors that several Stars players intended to jump their contracts and join Satchel Paige in Venezuela. Dixon blamed the rumors on the owners who had forgiven the contract jumpers and, therefore, exposed themselves to additional threats from teams outside of the United States. The Stars did lose one player, pitcher Tommie Thompson, to the contract-jumping phenomenon. His loss weakened the pitching staff and likely kept the Stars from a title.[53]

For the most part, stories concerning the Stars in the local black press conveyed both the writers' and the fans' pleasure with the 1938 season. Dixon noted that fans who had previously attended Stars games to root for the Crawfords had become "extreme in their partisanship for the Boldenites."[54] He took the time to praise each player on the Stars' roster and noted that even oft-injured Slim Jones contributed as a pinch-hitter and replacement first baseman.[55] Ed Harris praised the leadership of Wilson, who had softened his fiery temper and set a standard of high behavior for his players.[56] Late in the season, Harris composed a lengthy poem to the Stars' manager that began with:

> Who is this, ambling to the plate
> Bow legs a'rocking side to side?
> It's mighty Jud, our heart's delight,
> To take a crack at the horsehide.[57]

In November 1938, a sad story appeared in the *Independent* concerning the former ace Slim Jones. The troubled pitcher died at the young age of 25 in his hometown of Baltimore, Maryland. According to the story, Jones died from double pneumonia; it did not provide additional details concerning the causes of Jones's untimely death. The story did briefly review Jones's dip in performance during the previous seasons. Jones, a left-handed pitcher, suffered from injuries to his left shoulder and had turned to alcohol to cope with his injuries. His growing dependence upon alcohol likely contributed to the decline in his performance and to his death. Jones's early death represented a sad ending for a promising pitcher who had matched the great Satchel Paige and had enthralled fans at Yankee Stadium. His death also left a hole in the Stars' roster and sadly symbolized the team's decline since its 1934 championship season.[58]

For the 1939 season, both Bolden and Gottlieb assumed prominent positions within the NNL's management. Bolden won election as NNL vice-president, and Gottlieb assumed the position of NNL secretary. The changes came in the wake of Greenlee's resignation as NNL president; Tom Wilson of the Elite Giants replaced him. Greenlee subsequently resigned his presidency of the Crawfords, and the once-dominant franchise soon disbanded. Bolden's and Gottlieb's new roles put both of them in the center of issues concerning the league's operations. In particular, Gottlieb communicated at length with Effa Manley concerning games played at Yankee Stadium, the status of the Crawfords, and publicity for NNL teams. Effa ran the Newark Eagles and, with her husband Abe serving as the NNL's treasurer, played active role in managing the league's finances. Effa pressed Gottlieb for the names of the players on the Stars' roster, but Gottlieb noted that personnel decisions belonged to Bolden. The two discussed possible plans to help Greenlee stay in business before he made the decision to leave the Crawfords. Gottlieb and Effa also discussed the assignment of and payment due to umpires, the status of the Crawfords' players, and the formation of a schedule for NNL teams. At one point, Effa advised Greenlee to send a reminder to all of the clubs asking them to send him results of their games so that he could then send the information to the black newspapers. While NNL officials often operated in their own selfish interests, the letters between Gottlieb and Effa showed that they did work to find common ground and to make the league operational.[59]

While Gottlieb worked behind the scenes on issues concerning league finances and schedules, Bolden again saw his efforts to build a winning team fail. In June, Bolden led a shake-up of his team by replacing Wilson as manger with Jake Dunn and signing a new left-handed pitcher to his staff. The Stars responded with a winning streak in early July behind strong pitching from Jim Missouri and Henry McHenry. With their winning streak, Bolden envisioned a second-half title after a disappointing fifth-place finish in the first half of the season. The Stars also boasted a strong showing from outfielder Benson, the player whom Bolden reacquired in trade soon after trading him to the Crawfords during the previous season. Near the end of the season, the Stars vaulted into second place thanks to a thirteen-game winning streak. The Stars, however, finished fourth in the NNL and ended the decade without a repeat of their 1934 championship.[60]

Appropriately, the 1930s ended with Bolden's Stars and the NNL facing the same problems that had plagued them for most of the decade. Bolden constantly tinkered with his roster, yet his Stars consistently fell short of contending for the league championship. The Stars boasted good players like Benson, McHenry, Wilson, and McDonald, but they either suffered key injuries or encountered more talented teams like the Grays, Crawfords, and Eagles. Since the start of the 1938 season, the NNL had operated without a commissioner. Since Morton had failed to provide the NNL with the leadership it desperately needed, the move to abolish the commissioner's office had little practical impact upon the NNL's operations. The move did mean that all NNL officials had interests in league teams and could not provide objective responses to issues plaguing the league. Bolden, Gottlieb, and other NNL officials had no idea about the challenges awaiting them in the new decade. Some of those challenges stemmed from issues that rose in the 1930s. Other challenges arose from another world war that altered the world's landscape and that ushered in a change that ultimately doomed black professional baseball.[61]

CHAPTER SEVEN

The War, 1940–1945

The 1940s marked the fourth decade of Ed Bolden's involvement in black professional baseball, and the decade represented the most trying time of Bolden's long career. As he had in previous decades, Bolden confronted obstacles and remained focused on his goal of building a winning baseball team within the Philadelphia market. The 1940s, however, presented Bolden with a set of obstacles both similar to and different from the ones he had encountered in previous decades. Since neither the NNL or NAL had effectively dealt with contract jumpers, that problem continued to plague Bolden and other league owners. Another overseas threat to the stability of black professional baseball emerged when the United States entered World War II in 1941. Bolden and other owners lost players to the armed services, but World War II had a far more significant impact upon black professional baseball. The war spawned the Double Victory Campaign, a campaign to fight against racism overseas and in the United States. That campaign breathed life into a movement that had remained in its infancy during the 1930s—the movement to reintegrate Major League Baseball.

Even though the movement involved their players, Bolden and other NNL and NAL owners remained largely unresponsive to the possibility of an integrated Major League. Black sportswriters, not team owners or league officials, led the movement and worked with Major League officials to secure tryouts for black players. Bolden issued only one comment about the movement; he and other owners focused on making their own teams profitable and successful. In their efforts to achieve profits and success, Bolden and other owners often followed the same behaviors that characterized their actions in the 1930s. They also increasingly relied upon Major League ballparks to stage their games. Starting in 1943, Bolden and the Stars played at Shibe Park, a ballpark that already served as the home for the Philadelphia Phillies and Athletics. The heightened use of Major

League ballparks provided some short-term gains for the Stars and other Negro League teams, yet it weakened those franchise in the long term and represented a factor in their ultimate demise.

Before that time arrived, Bolden remained an active owner and official in the NNL. He communicated directly with players, battled with his fellow owners, and remained committed to building a successful team. His associate Ed Gottlieb also remained committed to aiding the Stars and battled with owners, in particular Effa Manley, over issues concerning the NNL's management. Bolden had used the World War I era to transform his amateur Hilldale team into one of the top black professional baseball teams in the nation. He did not have the same opportunity to make such a transformation with his Stars during the World War II era, but he did try to recapture the glory of an earlier era.

Philadelphia vs. Newark

In early 1940, both Bolden and Gottlieb found themselves the target of Effa Manley. Effa led a campaign to install William Hastie, dean of Howard University, as commissioner for both the NNL and the NAL. She also directed an attack on Gottlieb, arguing that "the league should be run by colored for colored," and claiming he charged an unfairly high fee for booking games at Yankee Stadium.[1] Since the 1935 season, the NNL had sponsored four-team double-headers on Sundays in Yankee Stadium that consistently attracted over ten thousand fans and delivered much-needed revenue to the league's coffers. Due to their association with Gottlieb, the Stars regularly appeared in those double-headers, and other NNL owners wanted greater shares of the attractive Yankee Stadium dates. Jim Semler and Alex Pompez joined Effa's attack on Gottlieb since they viewed Yankee Stadium as part of their territory and wanted more control over the stadium's promotions. As a further effort to decrease Philadelphia's power within the NNL and to increase the New York area's influence, Effa nominated Dr. C.B. Powell of Harlem for league president and attempted to oust Bolden as vice-president.[2]

A letter from Effa to William Hastie provides additional insight into her motivations. In her letter, Effa expressed her enthusiasm and her hope for Hastie to accept the commissioner's position. As she explained to Hastie, the commissioner would have a limited role in league affairs, a role more limited than the one they had discussed at a previous time. In her plan, the commissioner would "only be called on to settle disputes between players and owners, and owners and owners, and things of this kind."[3] She further explained to Hastie that she and unnamed others within the NNL wanted a businessman to serve as the league's president. Pointedly, Effa and her allies wanted a "non member" businessman, someone without any ties to any teams within the NNL.[4] To emphasize the pressing need for a commissioner, Effa informed Hastie about conflicts among owners that only a commissioner could resolve. She concluded by asking for a time when they could meet to further discussion the commissioner's role.[5]

Effa's plans did not succeed. After a series of heated discussions, the NNL owners reached a tense compromise that allowed Wilson and Bolden to retain their positions as president and vice-president and that gave the Black Yankees more dates at Yankee Stadium. Cum Posey defended Gottlieb's role as the league's top booking agent, pointing out that Gottlieb had used his influence to cut the fee Negro league clubs paid to rent Yankee Stadium from over three thousand dollars to one thousand dollars per game. As a result, Gottlieb had saved the league around ten thousand dollars in 1939; additionally, while Gottlieb had collected eleven hundred dollars in booking fees for those Yankee Stadium dates, league teams reaped about sixteen thousand dollars in profit. By contrast, when Jim Semler tried to circumvent Gottlieb and promoted three Negro league double-headers at Randall's Island Stadium on the East River, the profits totaled twelve dollars per team. Furthermore, Gottlieb had secured baseball supplies on convenient credit terms for league teams through his association with Harry Passon, a sporting goods merchant from Philadelphia. Despite that support, Gottlieb agreed to allow the owners to hire a new promoter after the 1940 season; the owners, however, never chose a replacement, and Gottlieb continued to book league games at Yankee Stadium.[6]

The friction between Effa, Bolden, and Gottlieb boiled over from letters exchanged between Effa and Gottlieb during the 1939 season. Those letters exposed friction between the two over fees due to teams and to Gottlieb for booking games. In one letter sent in September 1939, Gottlieb made suggestions to Effa concerning the percentage of the promotional dues teams should receive for games he booked in Newark, Philadelphia, and Baltimore. He suggested that each club receive one-fourth credit; if Effa followed Gottlieb's suggestion, her Newark Eagles would receive approximately six dollars from the promotional dues for those games. Other letters exchanged between the two revealed that Gottlieb booked games for the Eagles at ballparks he controlled and that he did not collect booking fees from the Stars. In an October 1939 letter to Effa, Gottlieb referred to discrepancies between the amounts they had figured the league owed him for booking games. Gottlieb admitted to a computing error and sent Effa a check for money he owed the league, minus one dollar he earned for booking an Eagles game.[7]

Letters between Gottlieb and Effa exposed additional friction between them concerning other league affairs. In December 1939, Gottlieb wrote Effa concerning a meeting in Chicago involving the NNL and the NAL. Gottlieb advised against sending multiple NNL officials to the meeting, believing that NNL President Tom Wilson alone could represent the league's interests. He wanted to use the upcoming meeting to assert the NNL's dominance as the "major" Negro League and to push the NAL into "fall[ing] in line" with the NNL's plans.[8] Gottlieb lamented that "[t]he way we are handling it makes it appear as if they are the leading organization and we need them to show us the way."[9] Gottlieb, furthermore, asserted his opposition to taking any action on the issue of a commissioner at the upcoming meeting in Chicago. He insisted, "Under no conditions will I agree to allow the Philadelphia vote to be given in the choice of a Commissioner at any other meeting before the Negro National League gets together."[10] Effa did attend that meeting and used it to launch her ill-fated move against Bolden and Gottlieb.

Tension between Effa and Gottlieb seethed through letters exchanged between the two later in 1940. In August, Gottlieb wrote to Effa asking why the Stars did not receive the $250 guaranteed to them for games played in Newark on August 4. Based upon his letter, it appeared as if Effa withheld the money in response to unfair treatment she believed the Eagles received when they played in Philadelphia on July 4. To Gottlieb, the events of July 4 had no bearing on the games played in Newark one month later. As he explained, a rainstorm greeted both the Stars and the Eagles when they arrived for their scheduled July 4 game. He further explained, "The proposition was put up to Abe Manley, that we were willing to play, providing he would gamble with us, in spite of the rain, and your husband agreed to play 50–50 after expenses, feeling that anything gotten under the weather conditions would be better than nothing."[11] Gottlieb noted that good weather greeted the teams when they met in Newark on August 4; the games simply did not draw a large crowds, but NNL rules stipulated that teams receive a certain amount on Sunday games. He reminded Effa about the guarantee, $150, due to Stars for a game scheduled for that evening and inquired about booking fees as well as a possible alteration to the NNL schedule.[12]

The tension between Effa and Gottlieb reflected a larger unease about the place of white Jewish booking agents in black professional baseball. Agents like Gottlieb played a vital role in both the NNL and the NAL, yet their presence highlighted the fragility of black professional baseball. Teams typically did not own their home ballparks, and they needed to play games against non-league foes in order to make profits. For those reasons, the Stars and other teams needed the assistance of agents like Gottlieb, and agents like Gottlieb expected some compensation for their efforts. Bolden had long since made peace with the role of white booking agents in black professional baseball, and he had worked with Gottlieb since the Stars' inaugural season. Gottlieb's presence, as well as the presence of other booking agents, irked Effa, yet the NNL could not function without a booking agent.

Contract Jumpers Strike Again

After successfully securing his role as NNL vice-president, Bolden faced more bad news while he sought to build his 1940 roster. Six of his players from the 1939 Stars team—including Henry McHenry, Pat Patterson, Roy Parnell, and Gene Benson— announced their intentions to play with their winter teams unless Bolden met their contract

Eugene "Gene" Benson spent his childhood in Philadelphia and debuted with his hometown NNL team in 1937. He spent part of the 1938 season with the Crawfords before returning to the Stars in 1939 (John W. Mosley Photograph Collection, Charles L. Blockson Afro-American Collection, Temple University Libraries, Philadelphia, Pennsylvania).

demands. Like many Negro League players, the Stars players who balked at returning for the 1940 season played winter baseball in Mexico, the Caribbean, or South America. According to a report in the *Philadelphia Independent*, McHenry believed that he had earned a higher salary from Bolden due to his strong performance in the 1939 season. McHenry and others sought to use offers from owners in Mexican or South American leagues as leverage with owners like Bolden. Though Bolden later signed several of the players who had threatened to stay with their winter clubs, McHenry remained a holdout. Bolden's signings also failed to quench the rumors that the players intended to jump their contracts and to leave the Stars bereft of talent.[13]

The articles in the local black press hinted at Bolden's virtual powerlessness to prevent his players from jumping their contracts and joining teams south of the American border. By the 1940s, the Caribbean had an established baseball world consisting of leagues in Panama, Venezuela, Cuba, Puerto Rico, the Dominican Republic, and Mexico. Negro league players had regularly participated in the Caribbean winter leagues, but the players had begun to stay for the summer leagues in response to the lure of higher salaries and freedom from segregation. In Mexico, multimillionaire Jorge Pasquel attempted to strengthen his country's league by stocking Mexican teams with a nucleus of Negro league stars and then adding a smattering of white major leaguers. Pasquel, an important financial backer of Mexican President Aleman, hoped to spark nationalistic pride by proving that the Mexican league stood equal to the major leagues and that Mexico stood equal to the United States.[14]

Although the Mexican league existed prior to 1940, the participation of Americans promised a significant strengthening of the six-team summer league. With promises of fabulous salaries, Pasquel attracted the services of Josh Gibson, Ray Dandridge, and other top Negro league talent; with a nucleus of Negro leaguers in Mexico, the recruiting process grew easier and more successful. The major league moguls viewed Pasquel's scheme with uneasiness, knowing that he had strong baseball contacts and, as Mexico's largest liquor importer, the money to support his ambitions. When rumors surfaced in 1946 that Pasquel wanted the likes of Ted Williams, Joe DiMaggio, and Stan Musial, the major leagues squelched Pasquel's plans by issuing a five-year ban on any players who went to the Mexican league. By contrast, the Negro league owners lacked that power since Pasquel vowed to double or triple the black players' salaries, and since black players possessed little loyalty for their owners. Additionally, black players in Mexico enjoyed accolades from the country's baseball fans, received on-the-spot bonuses for tremendous plays, and remained free from degrading segregation statutes.[15]

In August 1941, the *Philadelphia Tribune* published a report on the Mexican league that outlined the difficulties Bolden and other owners faced in trying to prevent contract jumpers. By participating in the Mexican league, black players earned far more money than they earned in the United States and avoided grueling double-headers as well as tiring bus rides between games. The Mexican owners provided railroad fare for the players and their wives, gave the players comfortable housing, and ensured that ill players received proper medical care. Furthermore, the players enjoyed participating in a real league—each team owned their home ballparks, played an equal number of league games, and never played exhibition games against other league teams during the regular season.[16]

The powerlessness confronting Bolden reflected a larger powerlessness that pervaded both the NNL and the NAL. In April 1940, Effa wrote to both J.B. Martin, NAL president, and Tom Wilson, NNL president, concerning the prevalence of contract jumping in their two leagues. To press her case, Effa noted that the leagues in the Caribbean, Mexico, and South America only wanted seasoned players, players who had received a great deal of money and publicity from Negro League owners. She understandably wanted Martin and Wilson to press for compensation from owners in the Caribbean, Mexican, and South American leagues who signed Negro League players. If neither Martin nor Wilson took the lead in this situation, Effa stated her intentions to press her case individually with the owners who signed her players. She assured both men that she had no intention of dictating to them how to perform their jobs, but she could not sit "idly by any longer and not put forth an effort to protect" her investments in her ballplayers.[17] Neither Martin nor Wilson took the lead in preventing contract jumping, and Effa wrote another letter to Martin at the end of the season. Her second letter had a greater sense of desperation and frustration, two feelings that other owners likely shared. She disgustedly referred to the NAL and NNL as "high class farms" for the leagues south of the American border.[18] Effa also proposed a plan for the teams to devote money to hire a lawyer, "who is a race man and interested in Negro baseball," to press the leagues' claims.[19]

The atmosphere of contract jumping remained with Bolden's Stars as they plodded through a mostly disappointing 1940 season. The Stars finished with a losing record against NNL foes; McHenry, Benson, and local product Mahlon Duckett represented a few of the bright spots in an otherwise somber season. Neither McHenry nor Benson followed through on their earlier threats to play with teams in Latin America. McHenry's and Benson's feats landed them spots on the East team during the annual East-West Game. McHenry won fifteen games and tossed eleven complete games; Benson batted over .300 and earned a spot among the league's top centerfielders. Duckett, an eighteen-year-old rookie from Overbrook High School, showed promise while playing a mostly utility role on the Stars' roster. He came to the Stars' attention while playing for a local team, the Wayne Black Hawks, and allegedly amassing a batting average of .342. Jake Dunn, the Stars' manager, gave Duckett a tryout at the 44th and Parkside field, and Bolden signed him after the successful tryout.[20]

McHenry's, Benson's, and Duckett's seasons overshadowed underwhelming performances from other Stars players, and Bolden again made in-season changes to his roster. Bolden's first change came in early June when he reappointed Jake Dunn to serve as the team's field manager. Dunn had supplanted Jud Wilson during the previous season, and the Stars had responded with a thirteen-game winning streak. When he resumed his role as field manager, he replaced Roy Parnell, who had replaced Dunn when Dunn stated his intentions to play in Mexico. Similar to

"Sad" Sam Thompson, a right-handed pitcher, spent five seasons with the Philadelphia Stars. He remained with the team as it experienced disappointment in the 1936 season, endured the threat of contract jumpers in the late 1930s, and struggled to relive the glory of its earlier seasons (John W. Mosley Photograph Collection, Charles L. Blockson Afro-American Collection, Temple University Libraries, Philadelphia, Pennsylvania).

McHenry and Benson, Dunn did not follow through on his threat to play outside of the United States. Parnell remained with the team and played in the outfield. Later in the season, Bolden initiated another shake-up when he released three players—Charlie Hayes, Darius Bea, and Sammy Thompson. Though Bea had played well for the Stars, he refused to quit his full-time job, and his job limited him to playing on weekends and prevented him from joining the Stars on long road trips. Bolden dismissed Thompson due to substandard play, while Duckett gave Bolden the freedom to dismiss Hayes.[21]

With McHenry, Benson, and Dunn rejecting offers to play outside of the United States, the contract-jumping phenomenon had a slight impact upon Bolden's Stars in 1940. Bolden lost at least two players, Ches Williams and Curtis Harris, but his top players remained with the Stars. Williams seemed content to both play with and manage a team in Mexico, but Harris and other players sought to return to the NNL or NAL teams in late July. Their return presented a problem for Bolden and other NNL owners since they had agreed to impose a three-year ban on contract jumpers. While some owners seemed willing to evade that rule, Bolden seemed determined to uphold the three-year ban. In August, Bolden blocked the Stars from taking the field in a game against the Brooklyn Royals due to the presence of two blacklisted players, Charles Roberts and Ray Dandrige. Roberts had jumped his contract with the Elite Giants, while Dandridge jumped his contract with the Newark Eagles. The Royals did not belong to the NNL and could use the players in games against independent teams. Bolden protested due to the fact that the game took place at 44th and Parkside, an NNL ballpark. The owner, field manager, and players from the Royals protested Bolden's demands, but Bolden prevailed. Roberts and Dandrige left the field, changed out of their uniforms, watched the game from the stands, and voiced their displeasure with Bolden. The Stars won the game 3–1.[22]

After a quiet offseason, Bolden's displeasure with the NNL surfaced. In January, the *Philadelphia Independent* reported on Bolden's displeasure with the NNL. He claimed that representatives from NNL and NAL clubs met recently in Baltimore, but an invitation never went to the Stars. A furious Bolden announced his intentions to ask magistrates Edward W. Henry and James H. Raney and attorney Raymond Pace Alexander to investigate the NNL's operations. He made claims about irregularities in the league's finances and in the four-team double-headers held at Yankee Stadium. Despite Bolden's claim about the lack of an invitation, a representative from the Stars did attend the meeting in Baltimore—Gottlieb.

At the meeting, Gottlieb ceded to the Manleys' requests for more games for the Eagles at Yankee Stadium. The two leagues also agreed to try a joint regular season schedule. Nothing came of Bolden's threats, and both he and Gottlieb represented the Stars at the next joint NNL-NAL meeting held in Chicago in March 1941. At that meeting, the owners unsurprisingly dropped the three-year ban against contract jumpers. Instead of the lengthy bans, contract jumpers faced meager fines of $100 that they had to pay by May 1. Due to that feeble action, Bolden and other owners ensured that contract jumping would continue to plague their teams.[23]

For Bolden, contract jumping ruined a promising season for his Stars. Bolden expressed optimism since his top players from the 1940 team—including McHenry, Benson, and Duckett—agreed to return to the Stars. He also solicited promises from Pat Patterson and Chet Brewer, two talented players who had jumped their contracts during the previous season. While most of their counterparts conducted training exercises in the South, the Stars spent most of their

Chet Brewer's pitching career in the Negro Leagues spanned three decades and involved stints with the Kansas City Monarchs, the New York Cubans, and the Pittsburgh Crawfords. He played for the Stars for part of the 1941 season (John W. Mosley Photograph Collection, Charles L. Blockson Afro-American Collection, Temple University Libraries, Philadelphia, Pennsylvania).

spring training at their 44th and Parkside home. Bolden lost Dunn, the incumbent field manager, to the United States Army. As his replacement, Bolden secured the services of legendary player Oscar Charleston. Similar to the previous season, Charleston replaced Parnell, who seemed unable to handle the double duties of playing and managing the team. With Charleston at the helm of his team, Bolden initiated yet another shake-up of his roster. One of his moves, releasing second baseman Dan Campbell, brought a protest from some of the Stars' veteran players. Bolden's plans, however, amounted to nothing when Patterson and Benson jumped their contracts in late June. The players' decisions seemed to vex Bolden, since he had granted both Patterson and Benson salary advances prior to the start of the 1941 season. Without those players, the Stars amassed another losing record against NNL foes. While a story in the *Philadelphia Independent* hinted at a decline in the allure of baseball in Latin America, the threat of contract jumping seemed likely to remain an obstacle for Bolden and other NNL owners in future seasons. The threat of contract jumping added to the stresses that Bolden faced as he worked to balance his full-time job with his multiple responsibilities to the Stars.[24]

A Man of Many Duties

As Bolden entered his fourth decade working in black professional baseball, he maintained many of the same habits that he had exhibited since joining Hilldale in 1910. He fulfilled multiple duties for the Stars—owner, general manager, and publicist—and continued to work at the Philadelphia Post Office. In 1944, a statement from his record at the Post Office gave him a "100 rating" and zero demerits over the previous twelve months.[25] Prior to the 1942 season, Bolden issued a press release in which he reviewed the disappointing 1941 season and made a promise for better results in the 1942 season. He listed some of the players he had signed to contracts and improvements made to the Parkside Field. Bolden's press release, however, did not fully capture all of the work he had undertaken to sign players during the offseason. Starting in October 1941, Bolden wrote letters to multiple people—including James Bell, Henry McHenry, Edward Davis, and L.C. Davis—inquiring about their own services or other players' services for the upcoming season. Those letters revealed that Bolden used his field managers to scout and solicit players. Since Bolden had replaced Oscar Charleston as the Stars' manager with Homer

Curry, he wanted to inform players of the change in managers and to ensure the players' continued interest in signing with the Stars.[26]

Letters exchanged between Bolden and McKinley "Bunny" Downs revealed an interesting relationship between different leagues within the larger umbrella of the Negro Leagues. Downs worked for the Mobile Colored Baseball Association, which sponsored the Mobile Black Shippers. The stationery he used referred to the Black Shippers as the Gulf Coast Champions. The tenor of Downs's letters to Bolden indicated that his team functioned like a minor league team for the Stars and other teams in the NNL and NAL. One of Downs's letters informed Bolden about three outfield prospects and at least two third baseman prospects on the Black Shippers. In another letter to Bolden, Downs inquired about Bolden's interest in one of his players, Norwood "Whizzer" White. Downs noted that White had beaten the Birmingham Black Barons, the Ethiopian Clowns, and all of the teams in Alabama, Florida, and Mississippi over the past two years. He tried to nudge Bolden to sign White by telling him that several other unnamed Negro League teams had attempted to sign him. Bolden responded that he intended to try to recruit White for the Stars, and he asked for Downs's advice about the amount of money he should offer White.[27]

Other letters that Bolden received and sent highlighted his role as the Stars' chief publicist and his efforts to make the Stars part of the Philadelphia community. Bolden sent season passes to distinguished people, most notably civil rights leader and judge Raymond Pace Alexander, who referred to Bolden as a "good friend."[28] Another recipient of season passes from Bolden, Eustace Gay, worked as the *Tribune*'s editor. When Bolden sent Gay the passes, he also asked the editor to take part in the Stars' Opening Day festivities in 1942. Gay declined; he asked the paper's sports editor, John Saunders, to take his place. Bolden did secure the services of the O.V. Catto Elks Lodge Band to participate in Opening Day festivities at the Parkside Field. Later in the 1942 season, he received a letter from W. Howard Still, Sr., from the Sons of Union Veterans of the Civil War. Still asked for a schedule of remaining home games since he and some of his acquaintances wanted to attend Stars games. Bolden sent a favorable reply and enclosed a schedule of the remaining home games.[29]

In addition to cultivating relationships with key social leaders and institutions, Bolden maintained amicable relationships with the local press. While Bolden had a long relationship with the *Tribune*, he also developed a relationship with the *Philadelphia Inquirer*, a white newspaper. In April 1942, Bolden received a letter from Kent Jackson, the person assigned to cover Stars games for the *Inquirer*. According to the letter, the newspaper had previously relied upon news agencies to gather information about Stars games. Jackson asked for a season pass so he could cover all Stars games at the Parkside Field; Bolden complied and later complimented Jackson on one of his articles. In August 1942, Bolden quickly responded to complaints from Leon M. Snead, president of the Press Club, concerning crowded conditions in the Parkside Field's press box. Bolden deflected Snead's offer to have the Press Club assume responsibility over the press box and promised to add seats to accommodate all reporters covering Stars games.[30]

Bolden's efforts to recruit players, maintain contacts with Philadelphia's social leaders, and cultivate strong relationships with the local press showed that he remained a visible leader of the Stars' organization. At the same time, Gottlieb maintained his active involvement with both the Stars and the rest of the NNL. According to the NNL's treasurer's report from 1941, Gottlieb collected dues for scheduling games for most of the teams belonging to the NNL and billed the league for $60 in expenses. Gottlieb and Effa Manley continued to exchange letters concerning lineups, advertising for games, and schedules for their respective teams. Since both Bolden and Gottlieb remained active leaders within the NNL, they had to confront issues that the league faced after America's entry into World War II. Those issues included the loss of players to the armed services and the looming possibility of black players in the Major Leagues.[31]

War and Disharmony

Following the Japanese attack on Pearl Harbor on December 7, 1941, Bolden and other Negro league owners pledged to put aside their differences and agreed to work together to take full advantage of the war's unifying affects on the home front. Soon after America's entry into World War II, however, an issue emerged that could undermine the harmony among the owners. John L. Clark, former NNL secretary and associate of Gus Greenlee, sent letters asking for feedback concerning Greenlee's return to the NNL. To calm any potential fears, Clark explained that Greenlee did not intend to seek any of the leadership positions within the league he founded. He also noted that Cum Posey supported Greenlee's return to the NNL. Since Posey owned Pittsburgh's remaining franchise in the NNL, Clark's note on Posey's support intimated that other owners should also support Greenlee's return. At an owners' meeting in February 1942,

Bolden and his fellow NNL moguls considered Greenlee's proposal after reelecting Wilson, Bolden, and Posey as the league's president, vice-president, and secretary-treasurer. Bolden and the others tabled Greenlee's proposal once his representatives, Mr. "Bubber" Allen and Clark, failed to respond to questions about the new iteration of the Pittsburgh Crawfords. The moved irked Greenlee, and he threatened to run an independent team and sign the best players.[32]

Greenlee's threat represented one of the notes of disharmony as Bolden and the rest of the NNL embarked upon the first wartime season. Effa again tried to get Joseph Rainey elected as the league's president and even threatened to leave the league, but Bolden and others persuaded her to remain in the NNL. While the NNL and NAL owners eventually agreed to stage a World Series between the winners of both leagues, they engaged in a prolonged disagreement over players prior to the start of the 1942 season. Their dispute centered on players from a disbanded NAL club formerly based in St. Louis. NNL owners, including Bolden, wanted access to those players; NAL owners wanted control over those players to revert to their league and, consequently, to prevent NNL owners from adding those players to their rosters. Wartime conditions forced Bolden and other owners to confront an additional obstacle in their plans for the 1942 season. The United States Navy had launched patrols in the Caribbean due to the threats of German submarines. Bolden and other owners feared that those patrols would delay or block the return of their players from their winter leagues in Puerto Rico and other areas in Latin America.[33]

As the owners dithered on the disputed players, they faced a potentially bigger problem when a new league formed under the leadership of former NAL president Major Robert R. Jackson. Known as the Negro Major Baseball League, the new circuit announced plans to have six teams—the Boston Royal Tigers, the Baltimore Black Orioles, the Detroit Black Sox, the Chicago Brown Bombers, the Cincinnati Ethiopian Clowns, and the Minneapolis Gophers. The *Philadelphia Independent* reported on a rumor of Greenlee's involvement in the new league and of upcoming raids on NNL and NAL teams. According to the report, owners in the new league intended to entice NNL and NAL players to jump their contracts by promising them higher salaries. The newspaper, however, predicted an early death for the Negro Major Baseball League because the raids would create an all-out war in black professional baseball. To support its claim, the paper referred to raids that had marred black professional baseball in the 1920s when Bolden's league arose and challenged the hegemony of Foster's league.[34]

Despite the newspaper's dire predictions, Major Jackson refrained from declaring war on the two other professional leagues, explaining that the new league merely aimed to please baseball fans with a high caliber of playing and good conduct on the field. During its brief existence, the new league failed to challenge the two established Negro leagues' supremacy; due to financial and manpower problems, the league never had a set number of franchises, since most of the clubs either withdrew or folded. In Philadelphia, a revived Hilldale Daisies team under the guidance of Webster McDonald joined the new circuit as an associate member and played their home games in a newly renovated Hilldale Park. Throughout the season, the Daisies garnered favorable attention in the *Philadelphia Tribune*, but they only averaged small crowds of one thousand fans to Hilldale Park and never threatened the Stars' fan base in Philadelphia.[35]

War and Integration

While Bolden and other owners confronted issues concerning player contracts and the new professional league, an item appeared in the *Philadelphia Independent* that unknowingly foreshadowed the ultimate end of black professional baseball. In March, the newspaper reported on a story involving Jackie Robinson, an African American three-letter athlete from UCLA, and Jimmy Dykes, field manager of the Chicago White Sox. Along with a pitcher named Nate Moreland, Robinson approached Dykes and asked for a tryout with the Chicago White Sox. At the time, both Robinson and Moreland played for the Pasadena Sox, a semi-pro team based in southern California. In response to their request for a tryout, Dykes told them, "There is no clause in the National Baseball Federation's Constitution, nor is there one in the by-laws of the major leagues which prevents Negro baseball players from participating in organized baseball."[36] Instead, Dykes opined that an unwritten law kept players like Robinson and Moreland out of the Major Leagues, and that field managers like himself lacked power to use black players. He insisted that the issue of using black players belonged with team owners and Commissioner Kenesaw Mountain Landis. Dykes also declared that he would welcome black players on the White Sox and that other managers in the Major Leagues shared his views. As the story noted, Dykes had watched Robinson play and lauded his performance. The story also lauded Robinson's reputation as a talented hitter and a top-level shortstop "equal of any shortstop in the game today."[37] The story, however, noted that Robinson expected to enter the United States Army and join the ongoing war effort against the Axis powers.[38]

In July 1942, Commissioner Landis verified Dykes's claims that no written laws bar African American players from the Major Leagues. As a result, six Major League clubs, including both the Philadelphia Athletics and Phillies, sent scouts to NNL and NAL games. Some of those scouts attended a game between the Stars and the Eagles in Buffalo. They focused on the Stars' hard-hitting first baseman Jim West, who played "with a lot of style" and was "enjoying his best season yet with the stick."[39] Scouts also went to a game between the Homestead Grays and the Kansas City Monarchs in Pittsburgh. While nothing immediately came from those scouting trips, the trips revealed an interest among some Major League clubs in signing Negro League players. They also demonstrated that an ongoing movement to bring black players to the Major Leagues had left an impact and had moved closer to success.[40]

Tellingly, the story on the Major League scouts at Negro League games did not mention any owners or other officials connected to the NNL and NAL. Those scouting trips in 1942 stemmed from articles from Wendell Smith, a sportswriter for the *Pittsburgh Courier*, not from conversations involving NNL or NAL officials. After expressing frustration with African Americans' patronage of the Major Leagues, Smith called for a movement in 1939 to challenge the unwritten rule against black players in the Major Leagues. Smith noted similarities between Nazi Germany and segregation in the United States, and then interviewed National League President Ford Frick. In the interviews, Frick blamed public opinion, the views of white players, and segregation statutes in Southern states for the lack of black players in the Major Leagues. Similar to what Commissioner Landis would do in 1942, Frick never acknowledged the existence of a written law barring black players from the Major Leagues. When Smith subsequently interviewed Major League field managers, he found almost unanimous support for the use of black players. He found a similar result in interviews with Major League players.[41]

Dykes's statements, Commissioner Landis's announcement, and the aforementioned scouting of NNL and NAL games all indicated that the movement to reintegrate Major League Baseball accelerated in 1942, America's first full year as a belligerent in World War II. Early in 1942, the *Philadelphia Tribune* engaged in the movement with a series of articles from J.A. "Artie" Lee, the Stars' secretary. In his articles, Lee traced black players' successes in contests with white major leaguers and concluded that black players possessed the talent to compete in the Major Leagues. Lee pointed out that Josh Gibson of the Homestead Grays boasted a higher batting average than either Ted Williams or Joe DiMaggio and that Satchel Paige had defeated almost every nationally known white pitcher. A few months later, the *Philadelphia Tribune*'s Jack Saunders offered a more somber outlook on the prospect of black players in the Major Leagues. Saunders asserted that despite Landis's declaration, the South would ultimately decide if black players entered the Major Leagues since many players came from that area and most teams trained in the deep South. He concluded that owners probably would refrain from signing black payers in order to avoid dissension with Southern players and to avoid problems with segregated spring training and traveling accommodations.[42]

A controversy involving William Benswanger of the Pittsburgh Pirates confirmed Saunders's pessimism and revealed the perilous nature of the campaign to reintegrate Major League Baseball. In the summer of 1942, Benswanger asked Smith to compile a list of black players who would try out for the Pittsburgh Pirates. Benswanger likely made the request because he faced pressure from the *Daily Worker*, the Communist party's newspaper, to sign black players. Smith compiled a list of four players— Willie Wells, Josh Gibson, Leon Day, and Sam Bankhead. Benswanger, however, carried through with his request, and the tryouts never happened.[43]

After those canceled tryouts, the *Philadelphia Tribune* announced that it would join with other local black newspapers and local black civic leaders to form a committee that would confer with Phillies president Gerry Nugent to urge him to sign Negro league players. While the committee members admitted that segregated traveling and housing accommodations presented obstacles to Major League integration, they decided to tackle those obstacles once they accomplished their main goal of integrating organized baseball. After the *Tribune* made its announcement, rumors circulated that two associates of Ed Gottlieb would purchase the Phillies and stock the team with Negro league talent. Bill Veeck, a master showman and innovator who co-owned (along with Charlie Grimm) the American Association's Milwaukee Brewers, reached a deal after the 1942 season with Nugent to purchase the Phillies. A lifelong fan of black baseball, Veeck secretly planned to secure the 1943 National League pennant by stocking the Phillies with the best Negro league players. Out of respect for the commissioner, however, Veeck informed Landis of his plans; Landis blocked the deal, ordered Nugent to return the team to the National League, and ensured that the Phillies' new owners adhered to the color line. Despite that setback, the movement to introduce black players into organized baseball refused to die and would gain momentum over the next three seasons.[44]

Stars and the War

For the Stars, the 1942 season again brought renewed promises of a second championship. Against the backdrop of raids from other professional teams and the growing momentum for integration, Bolden continued his efforts to sign the best players and to promote his team through the local black press. Prior to the start of the season, Bolden vowed to

After spending several seasons in Mexico and Puerto Rico, Barney Brown returned to the NNL in 1942 with the Philadelphia Stars. He remained with the Stars until the 1950 season and represented the team at several East-West Games (John W. Mosley Photograph Collection, Charles L. Blockson Afro-American Collection, Temple University Libraries, Philadelphia, Pennsylvania).

give his fans the youngest and best team in the region since the days of Hilldale's World Series championship.[45] To fulfill his pledge for a young team, Bolden announced that he intended to add "young blood, local variety preferred."[46] As Bolden explained, he hoped to avoid making another "grave mistake. That was permitting [Leon] Day and [Roy] Campanella, two good boys developed in our own local sandlots, to get away from us to become outstanding stars on the teams of our opponents."[47] He credited Duckett with changing his view on signing local sandlot stars. While the ongoing controversy concerning players from the folded St. Louis franchise blocked some of his plans, Bolden remained optimistic about his team's outlook. He hired Homer "Goose" Curry to serve as the team's field manager; Curry also patrolled the outfield with Parnell and Benson, who had returned from Mexico. Barney Brown and Henry McHenry anchored the Stars' pitching staff, and they received help from local product Larry Kimbrough and a big Texan named Joe Fillmore. The Stars infield consisted of Jim West, Pat Patterson, Duckett, James "Bus" Clarkson, and Henry Spearman. Bill Cooper and Clarence Palm shared catching duties.[48]

As in previous seasons, the 1942 Stars did not live up to Bolden's high expectations. Instead of traveling to the South for spring training, the Stars held all of their spring training session at the 44th and Parkside field, and many of the players reported late to those sessions. Consequently, the players remained ill-prepared to face league teams once the regular season started, and the team dropped in the standings. Early in the 1942 season, ace pitcher McHenry left for the Mexican league, and Bolden replaced him with Ches Buchanan, who had started the season with the Hilldale Daisies. Although the Stars finished the 1942 season in fourth place, the team had steadily improved during the season and seemed poised to contend seriously for the 1943 league championship. Benson, Patterson, and Brown continued to rank among the NNL's top players; Clarkson led the league in home runs.[49]

Bolden's hopes for a successful 1943 season disappeared when he lost six players, more than any other team, to the draft—Clarkson, Cooper, Duckett, Fillmore, Kimbrough, and Pat Patterson. In the *Philadelphia Tribune*, Saunders commented that Bolden needed "to assume the dimensions of a magician to field a team this season as potent and as popular as were the Stars of last season."[50] Due to those losses, Bolden resorted to raiding local independent teams for their best players. Additionally, the Stars altered their spring training schedule at the 44th and Parkside field to permit defense workers to practice at night, and Curry conducted a scouting tour through the South. Despite the efforts of Bolden and manager

Curry to find new talent, only one newcomer made the opening day roster; the previous year's reserve players inadequately replaced the drafted starting players. With their depleted roster of inexperienced players, the Stars struggled through the 1943 season and compiled another losing record.[51]

As Bolden and Curry strove to improve the team's depleted roster, a bizarre incident in July thwarted their plans and highlighted the weird workings of the NNL. Curry acquired three players from the Atlanta Black Crackers, a team that operated independently of the Negro leagues; therefore, the Black Crackers' players were the property of any owner who signed them to contracts. The *Philadelphia Tribune* insisted that Curry followed proper procedures and that the team paid a considerable amount of money to transport the three players from Atlanta. After a Stars and Grays game in Philadelphia, however, a "mysterious somebody"—probably NNL President Wilson—ordered the three players to return to Atlanta, and Grays owner Cum Posey hired one of the Stars' pitchers to drive the players back to their former club. An irate Bolden declared that he had suspended the pitcher, Willie Burns, and that he would protest any game featuring the three Atlanta players who had signed contracts with the Stars. Wilson, however, remained silent on the issue, allowing Posey to sign one of the Atlanta players without punishment and never compensating the Stars for the loss of the three players.[52]

In the midst of those disappointments, the Stars faced some of the limitations that other teams confronted during the wartime seasons. Like other owners, Bolden obtained a certificate from the Office of Defense Transportation (ODT) that gave the Stars the ability to purchase the gasoline needed to make their road trips. Additionally, Bolden and his fellow owners agreed to give the ODT ownership of their team buses from September 15, 1943, to April 15, 1944. He also responded to questions the ODT forwarded to the NNL. Acting in his authority as league secretary, Posey sent those letters back to the ODT and outlined the ways the NNL had modified its operations to meet the wartime demands. For example, Wilson's Elite Giants moved from Nashville to Baltimore due to travel restrictions, and the Cubans agreed to spend spring training in Philadelphia with the Stars. Posey also assured the ODT that Gottlieb had worked on the schedules and had reduced the travel mileage in the 1943 season by about fifty percent over the mileage traveled in the 1942 season. The Stars and other teams planned to spend multiple days in league cities and to travel by railroad on the weekends.[53]

During some of the wartime seasons, the Stars benefited from the heightened interest in the NNL. The NNL enjoyed an increase in atten-

Bill "Ready" Cash joined the Philadelphia Stars in the 1943 season, at time when World War II had depleted the Stars' roster. While the Stars struggled through a disappointing season, Cash finished the season with a .331 batting average (John W. Mosley Photograph Collection, Charles L. Blockson Afro-American Collection, Temple University Libraries, Philadelphia, Pennsylvania).

dance as millions of well-paid black workers from defense factories filled ballparks in every league city. Attendance at and receipts from the annual East-West Game attest to the league's popularity during the wartime seasons. In 1942, over forty-four thousand spectators helped the leagues accumulate a gross profit of over $33,000, for a net profit of $13,000 each after they took care of various expenses. The Stars and other NNL teams each received nearly $2,000. In 1943, the East-West Game resulted in a similar windfall for the Stars and other NNL teams.[54]

For the 1942 and 1943 seasons, the Stars continued to draw enthusiastic opening day crowds at the Parkside field. In 1942, Bolden also added wartime features to the traditional opening day festivities at the Parkside field. In that year, he invited Captain George J. Cole, company commander of the Anti-Tank 372nd Infantry, to toss the first pitch; for the 1943 season, Lieutenant Evelyn Green of the WAACs delivered the first pitch. Additionally, Bolden asked a committee of distinguished local citizens to reward players for certain opening day feats, such as the first base hit, the first home run, the first strikeout, and the most sensational play. Initially, the Stars also benefited from patriotism in the black community, attracting seven thousand fans to the Parkside Field for a Saturday double-header with the Louisiana Black Pelicans over the 1942 Memorial Day weekend. Later in the season, nine thousand fans watched an Independence Day double-header between the Stars and the Homestead Grays, and as many as thirty thousand fans watched the Stars in their numerous Yankee Stadium appearances. In August, eleven thousand spectators—the largest crowd to attend a black baseball game in Philadelphia since Hilldale's glory days—filled the Parkside field to watch the Kansas City Monarchs rout the Stars. By the 1944 season, however, interest in the Stars had waned due to persistent losing records and player departures, and the team no longer drew capacity opening day crowds to the Parkside Field.[55]

Shibe Park and the Parkside Field

In June 1943, the Stars added a new feature to their schedule by playing a Monday night game against the Kansas City Monarchs in Shibe Park, home of the A's and Phillies. During the 1940s, major league teams followed the lead of the New York Yankees in scheduling profitable Negro league appearances in their ballparks. Most teams, however, forbade black players from using their locker rooms and forced Negro league clubs to use nearby gyms or YMCA facilities. While A's owner Connie Mack disliked the idea of black players joining the major leagues, Ed Gottlieb convinced him that black baseball teams and their fans represented good tenants for Shibe Park. Ironically, Shibe Park sat in an increasingly black neighborhood in North Philadelphia. By the 1940s, Philadelphia boasted the country's third largest black population, and black workers had gradually infiltrated the previously white neighborhoods surrounding Shibe Park at 21st and Lehigh Avenue. In the fall of 1942, the Monarchs clinched their World Series title at Shibe Park, the first time that ballpark had hosted a black baseball contest since the 1920s. Surprisingly, Mack allowed the Stars to use the A's locker room and facilities; in addition to drawing their loyal fans, the Stars also attracted many white newcomers to their contests at Shibe Park.[56]

The *Philadelphia Tribune* extensively promoted every Monday night contest at Shibe Park for several weeks prior to the scheduled games, printing complete rosters of each team and mentioning the key performers who would appear in the games. The local white newspapers, however, only briefly mentioned the Stars' games in Shibe Park. Following the Stars' first successful outing at Shibe Park, the team's management expressed outrage over Satchel Paige's refusal to pitch more than three innings since most of the pregame advertisement had focused on his appearance. Despite that controversy, the Monarchs regularly appeared at Shibe Park during the wartime seasons; in one contest, Barney Brown outdueled Satchel Paige, and Bolden rewarded each of the players with a one-thousand-dollar bonus. For the first several seasons, the Stars hosted three-team double-headers that included at least one NAL team and played the winner of the first contest. In 1945, a bizarre situation arose when the Birmingham Black Barons failed to reach Shibe Park in time for their opening contest with the Monarchs. Consequently, Curry gathered a "motley crew" of Stars players to substitute for the Barons until they arrived in the fourth inning; a complete Stars team defeated the Barons in the second game. After their opening victory over the Monarchs that attracted twenty-five thousand fans, the Stars continued to amass an impressive record in their Shibe Park games and regularly drew ten thousand spectators to the local major league park.[57]

With the advent of Stars games at Shibe Park, the *Philadelphia Tribune*'s W. Rollo Wilson commented upon worsening conditions at the Parkside field. In the 1920s, the Pennsylvania Railroad had built a ballpark at 44th and Parkside Avenue, at the site of what had since 1903 been an athletic field. It was adjacent to a roundhouse, and the Stars had adopted the field as their home ballpark due to its accessibility. Wilson noted that rabid fans who had supported Hilldale refused to watch the Stars in action except when they played at the major league park because they objected to the Parkside field's dirty conditions. After enduring clouds of billowing smoke from the nearby roundhouse and absorbing grime and filth from the season, female fans needed to send their summer dresses to the dry cleaners. Additionally, fans suffered through soot showers every time a ball landed on the leaky roof, a roof that failed to shield fans during rainstorms; or when balls hit the rotting screens that offered fans little protection. Wilson commented that while the Stars had boasted good players, they never enjoyed the popularity of the old Hilldale team due to their rundown ballpark. Prior to the war, railroad officials had agreed to remove the roundhouse, but World War II had derailed those plans as well as any plans to repair the Parkside field or find another accessible ballpark. The Stars' management acknowledged and disliked the poor conditions at the Parkside field, but they lacked the financial resources to build a new field in a suitable location. Instead, the team's management asked their fans to endure the inconveniences until they could remedy the situation after the war ended.[58]

More Internal Dissension

Bolden prepared for the 1944 season without much hype; even though most of last season's disappointing team had returned, he expected them to enjoy a better season. Bolden expressed the most hope for Marvin Williams, a native of Texas who had played second base and had been an offensive force after Mahlon Duckett joined the Army. To revive his team, Bolden re-hired Oscar Charleston as a coach and signed highly touted shortstop Frank Austin, a native of the Panama Canal Zone who had produced impressive statistics in the Panamanian league. After another slow start, the Stars threatened the Homestead Grays for the second-half title, but President Tom Wilson gave the title to the Grays several weeks before the season officially ended. Rollo Wilson decried the decision, pointing out that the Stars and Grays played three scheduled games near the end of the season, games that the league suddenly classified as exhibition games. He also pointed out a continued problem with the league schedule—no two clubs played the same number of league games in the regular season.[59]

Bolden vainly filed a protest to president Tom Wilson, declaring that the "Stars have really won the second half fairly, by playing all the League games possible, and have not tried to win by canceling any League game or on any technicality."[60] He accused the Grays of refusing to play league games near the end of the season in order to remain in first place; on Labor Day, the Grays and New York Cubans played a double-header with only one game counting as a league contest. If both games had counted as league contests, then the Stars would have captured the second-half championship. As a result, Bolden asked Tom Wilson to order the Grays, who had won the first-half title, to play a series with the Stars that would determine the league championship. Bolden also asked for a prompt ruling since "fans and newspapermen are up in arms over the situation," adding that his "phone, Curry's, and Gottlieb's [have] been ringing without a stop" for the past several days. Not surprisingly, president Wilson refused to order a playoff and allowed the Grays to retain the second-half title because the league had already devoted too much publicity to a Grays and Birmingham Black Barons' World Series to make a change.[61]

As they had earlier in the war, the NNL owners proceeded to argue among themselves throughout the wartime era and consistently failed to resolve the league's lingering problems or to make the league a more solid organization. The owners continued to operate without a commissioner, allowed the highly partial Tom Wilson to serve as league president, and permitted the most powerful owners and booking agents to dominate league affairs. Despite their newfound wealth during the wartime seasons, the owners unwisely refrained from purchasing their own ballparks and grew increasingly reliant upon the major leagues' goodwill to stage important contests. More alarmingly, the NNL owners ignored the advice of black newspaper columnists to seek affiliation with the major leagues under the national agreement, thereby protecting themselves against player raids. Instead of ensuring that their teams completed their league schedules, the NNL owners only agreed to make a determined effort to follow schedules that required each team to play an equal number of league games. Furthermore, the owners weakly punished contract jumpers with light fines and merely pledged to make every effort to keep their best players from bolting to the Mexican league.[62]

In addition to avoiding lingering problems plaguing the league, the NNL owners refrained from discussing the possibility of black players entering white organized baseball, since none of the major league owners had approached them about signing their players. Instead, NNL owners vowed to maintain friendly relations with white baseball officials, since that friendship had allowed black teams to hold profitable contests in almost every major and minor league ballpark. In the *Philadelphia Trib-*

une, Don Deleighbur—a pen name for the *New York Amsterdam News's* Dan Burley—criticized the NNL owners for "upholding jim crow at this time when every body is pressing for progressive attitudes and real Americanisms."[63] He also lamented that the NNL's statement "points out the fallacious thinking that has dominated the eastern league in late years and has, in a measure, been the big block to advancement of the players and of the game."[64] Several months later, Deleighbur directed more criticism toward the NNL owners for their decision to hire the Monroe Elias Agency, a white statistical company, to keep the official league records. He decried the move as an affront to the black newspapers that gave the league thousands of dollars' worth of free advertising every year and lamented the amount of white influence in black baseball.[65]

The Integration Homestretch

Throughout 1943 and 1944, the campaign to reintegrate the Major Leagues persisted and became part of a larger movement against racial segregation in the United States. In December 1943, Commissioner Landis put the issue of integration on the agenda of the owners' winter meeting.[66] At that meeting Paul Robeson and others appealed to Landis to permit the entrance of black players into Major League Baseball. Black sportswriters joined Robeson and other activists in their appeal to the longtime commissioner. Landis responded by leaving the issue with individual teams: "Each club is entitled to employ Negro players to any and all extents it desires."[67] After making their appeal, the activists pushing for the signing of black players presented a four-point plan that they wanted Landis and the owners to accept. Nothing came of the meeting or Landis's announcement. The commissioner passed away one year later, and the issue of black players in the Major Leagues remained unresolved.[68]

In December 1944, Rollo Wilson commented upon the passing of Commissioner Landis, saying that the late commissioner should not receive all of the blame for keeping black players out of the major leagues. He joined Deleighbur in criticizing NNL owners for opposing the integration of organized baseball since it would prevent them from using major or minor league parks. According to Wilson, both Negro leagues needed to elect a commissioner who would appoint a special committee of owners, newspapermen, and major league officials to plan for baseball integration. Wilson, however, pessimistically noted, "Organized Baseball was able to get along without colored players during the past three seasons" when the wartime manpower shortage plagued the major leagues.[69] He also expressed pessimism about the NNL's winter meetings, seeing no indications that the owners would elect a commissioner or replace Tom Wilson with a more impartial president.[70]

Despite the Negro leagues owners' inactivity, the movement to integrate the major leagues continued, with the Brooklyn Dodgers giving a tryout to Terrie McDuffie and Dave Thomas. Recently, New York Governor Thomas Dewey had signed a bill outlawing racial discrimination in hiring practices in the state, and the Dodgers offered the tryout in response to the new legislation. Dodgers' President Branch Rickey and manager Leo Durocher decided against signing the players because of their "advanced" ages and their reputations for arguing with umpires. The *Philadelphia Tribune* criticized the workout as a cheap publicity stunt that gave the uninformed white public the incorrect perception that the two

Terris McDuffie spent one of his twelve Negro League seasons, 1942, with the Philadelphia Stars. His presence on the Stars' roster reflected Ed Bolden's efforts to sign notable players at a time when the Stars faced challenges from a wartime draft and the continued allure of leagues south of the American border (John W. Mosley Photograph Collection, Charles L. Blockson Afro-American Collection, Temple University Libraries, Philadelphia, Pennsylvania).

best Negro league players had failed to reach major league standards. Later in April, the Boston Red Sox held a tryout for the Stars' Marvin Williams, the Monarchs' Jackie Robinson, and the Buckeyes' Sam Jethroe; team officials praised both players, but refused to offer them contracts. With that flurry of tryouts, Rollo Wilson reported that Bolden differed from other NNL owners and would willingly negotiate with major league officials who wanted his players. Bolden believed that integration would improve the Negro leagues since the teams would attract talented players who wanted to join the major leagues and since players would perform better in order to impress major league scouts.[71]

Although Bolden acquired veteran pitcher Roy Partlow from the Homestead Grays before the 1945 season, the Stars never contended for first place in either half of the season since they lacked adequate personnel on their roster. The persistent problem of contract jumping devastated the Stars in 1945 when top second baseman Williams and veteran Barney Brown, the mainstay of the team's pitching staff, suddenly left for Mexico. Bolden expressed surprise since he had given both men new contracts with the salaries that they requested and noted that the players owed a combined total of nearly one thousand dollars to the Stars' franchise. In response to those latest departures, Bolden angrily proclaimed that he would introduce a motion at the upcoming NNL meeting to place lifetime bans on players who jumped their league contracts. He admitted that owners "have been too lenient with players who have gone to Mexico in other years and it is time we're tightening up on these fellows."[72] At the meeting, Bolden presided in the absence of president Tom Wilson, but he abdicated his position to Abe Manley in order to broker an agreement with other league owners. Due to Bolden's work, the owners reached a settlement that ordered Negro league players in Mexico to return to their clubs or face a five-year suspension; any future contract jumpers would automatically receive a five-year suspension.[73]

In the 1945 season, shortstop Frank Austin was the team's best player, and the *Philadelphia Tribune* even touted him as the key to major league integration. Quoting former Negro league stars, the newspaper declared that the twenty-one-year-old shortstop could compete at a major league level and urged other black press organizations to agitate for Austin to receive a tryout. In September, however, Austin extinguished his chances of breaking the color barrier when he threw his bat at an opposing pitcher in a game at Shibe Park after the pitcher threw a tight inside pitch. The umpire properly ejected Austin from the game, and the NNL fined him ten dollars for the incident and suspended him for three league contests.

Following that sorry incident, the Stars completed their season with little fanfare and finished in fourth place with a losing record.[74]

In October 1945, Jackie Robinson of the Kansas City Monarchs made history when he signed a contract with the Brooklyn Dodgers' organization. Although Robinson's signing represented a lifelong dream for many black baseball players, it also signaled the beginning of the end for Negro league baseball. Earlier in the season, Branch Rickey had vocally supported the United States League and used its Brooklyn Brown Dodgers franchise as a front to scout black talent. By contrast, Rickey refused to acknowledge the two other black professional circuits as legitimate leagues because they failed to complete balanced schedules, lacked territorial rights, and relied upon booking agents to schedule games. Most importantly, Rickey charged that the other "so-called" leagues failed to value their player contracts or institute a reserve clause into those contracts, thereby leaving themselves open to exploitation from outside forces. Rickey's statements angered many people in the NNL, particularly Ed Gottlieb, who unsuccessfully tried to arrange a conference between the Dodgers' president and NNL owners. At a joint meeting in November, NNL and NAL officials delivered a letter to Commissioner Happy Chandler protesting the raiding of Negro league clubs and demanding that major league owners consult with them and grant them compensation for their players.[75]

Throughout the wartime seasons, as the black press conducted its integration campaign, the Stars and other Negro league teams symbolized the United States' great hypocrisy in fighting a war against racism while enforcing racist principles at home. The Stars also reflected the league's difficulties in keeping team rosters intact during wartime—numerous players responded to the draft or to the lure of higher salaries in the Caribbean leagues. Although Bolden supported baseball integration, a majority of the NNL owners viewed integration with trepidation and publicly vowed to maintain the status quo since it benefited them financially. Jackie Robinson's signing with the Brooklyn Dodgers represented the culmination of the black press's efforts to expose the absurdity of segregated baseball leagues and to pressure major league organizations into acquiring black players. Ultimately, however, Rickey's signing of Jackie Robinson and his perception of the NNL and NAL had established a precedent that would lead to the downfall of the Negro leagues.

CHAPTER EIGHT

Twilight Time, 1946–1953

As the baseball world reacted to Jackie Robinson's joining the Brooklyn Dodgers' organization, both Ed Bolden and his Philadelphia Stars entered their twilights. Along with the rest of the NNL and NAL, the Stars enjoyed a deceptively successful 1946 season. Robinson's presence in the International League sparked interest in black professional baseball, yet his debut in April 1947 with the Brooklyn Dodgers had the opposite effect upon teams like the Stars. Due to declining attendance and revenue figures, the NNL folded after the 1948 season, and several teams also ceased operations. The Stars survived, yet they played their remaining years in near-obscurity. During their final seasons, the Stars effectively represented a traveling independent team. They had to share Shibe Park as well as the sports pages of the local black newspapers with both the Philadelphia Athletics and the Phillies. Like other all-black teams, the Stars seemed like an outdated relic from an earlier era, and the team could not compete with integrated Major League teams.[1]

Bolden remained at the Stars' helm as the franchise entered its twilight. His final years represented the toughest years of his baseball career since his messy divorce with Hilldale. While the Stars survived the NNL's dissolution, they lost their home ballpark at 44th and Parkside and had to use the already busy Shibe Park to stage their home contests. Though the Stars belonged to a reorganized NAL, Bolden could not rely upon a league structure to help support and promote his franchise. In addition to that hardship, Bolden lost players to Major League organizations and to teams outside of the United States. Bolden's death in September 1950 carried symbolic significance. The distinguished list of guests and pallbearers reflected Bolden's respected place within Philadelphia's society. As one of the last great black baseball leaders, Bolden's death unfortunately presaged the fate awaiting the Stars and the other remaining black professional baseball franchises.

Even though it came after a quiet offseason, Ed Gottlieb's announcement of the Stars' dissolution in March 1953 did not come as a surprise. During the two seasons following Bolden's death, the Stars played few games in Philadelphia and staged their home openers near midseason. As a result, the connections Bolden fostered between his franchise and the city unraveled. The Stars' final passing in April 1953, after Gottlieb's futile month-long attempt to sell the franchise, came with little fanfare in the *Philadelphia Tribune* and went nearly unnoticed in the *Philadelphia Independent*. The Stars' passing, however, marked the end of an era in Philadelphia sports since the team represented the final link to the region's great black baseball teams and powerful black baseball officials. With the Stars' dissolution, that link vanished, and the Philadelphia region lost an important cultural institution.

Fighting for Relevance

Prior to signing Robinson, Branch Rickey dropped a few hints about his interest in black baseball players. Before the start of the 1945 season, Rickey publicly supported the United States League (USL), a new league Gus Greenlee organized and that had six franchises, some in NNL and NAL cities. Greenlee served as the USL's vice-president and operated a revived Pittsburgh Crawfords. Across the state, Webster McDonald and Clarence "Fats" Jenkins operated the Philadelphia Daisies, a franchise named in honor of the great Hilldale franchise. Greenlee soon hired John G. Shackleford as the USL's president and added the Brooklyn Brown Dodgers, a franchise that brought Rickey directly into the new league.[2] In September 1945, Rickey admitted to the *Pittsburgh Courier* that he had met with Robinson in Brooklyn. When asked about the nature of the meeting, Rickey denied that they had discussed the possibility of Robinson's joining the Brooklyn Dodgers. He insisted that he remained focused on supporting a good Negro league and that signing Robinson to his Major League franchise "would bring in a lot of problems that I am unable to solve."[3] The article ominously noted that Robinson had a contract with the Kansas City Monarchs. Rickey, therefore, would face charges of "tampering" and of "violating the rules of organized baseball" if he did not consult with the Monarchs before signing Robinson.[4]

Greenlee's USL, along with Rickey's involvement in the new venture, brought a fresh round of attacks upon the NNL and NAL. When Greenlee announced the USL's founding, he directed bitterness at his former colleagues in the NNL. While insisting that the USL did not represent a rival of either the NNL or NAL, Greenlee noted that he had tried to return to the NNL, but the other owners blocked his return. Greenlee, furthermore, blamed the NNL owners for his failure to join the NAL, reasoning that the NAL owners did not want to anger their counterparts in the NNL.[5] A few months later, Greenlee directed more invective toward the NNL. He predicted, "There are going to be some very, very embarrassed persons … and they have a nice mighty banquet eating the words of poison that they have been circulating about the United States Baseball League."[6] He referred to the unnamed critics as his enemies who had hampered the progress of black professional baseball. Greenlee lauded the USL as "far and away superior to any Negro league set-up ever attempted" and said it would prove that a Negro league could achieve success "without the interference or dictatorship of booking agents."[7]

Rickey's involvement in the USL also provided him with the opportunity to vent his displeasure at the NNL and NAL. In a press conference that coincided with V-E Day, Rickey took questions from Effa Manley and others concerning his sudden interest in black baseball. Rickey insisted that he had long remained interested in the Negro leagues, but he lamented that "there does not exist in a true sense such a thing as organized Negro ball."[8] His comments prompted Manley to question him about his support for the NNL and NAL. In his response, Rickey refused to comment directly upon the two leagues, but he did issue a veiled threat against the other organizations. He professed his belief that "Negro baseball must be organized the same as any other clubs interested along this line."[9] Rickey, furthermore, described the USL "as the main structure around which to build" an organized black professional baseball league and as a potential addition to organized baseball.[10] He welcomed clubs to join the USL and expressed his openness to meeting "with owners of teams in what is called organized Negro baseball."[11]

Despite those threats and Rickey's obvious interest in Robinson, Bolden and other owners remained ill-prepared to confront the reality of black players in Major League organizations. In May 1945, shortly before Rickey's press conference in Brooklyn, Cum Posey outlined the NNL's ills. Posey, the NNL's secretary, identified the quality of umpires and control over the annual East-West game as two of the problems plaguing both the NNL and the NAL. He also lamented the lack of a commissioner in both leagues. As Posey noted, he had joined Bolden on a special committee tasked with the responsibility of securing a commissioner, but their committee had failed in its task. In December 1945, two months after Robinson's signing, both the NNL and the NAL owners held a meeting in Chicago, and neither set of owners made needed changes to their leagues. The owners announced plans to put reserve clauses into players' contracts and adopt the constitution of the National and American Leagues. At the same time, however, they did not elect a commissioner and reelected the same men, including Bolden, to their incumbent league offices. An article covering the meeting noted that the owners, along with Gottlieb and another booking agent, spent more time criticizing Rickey than they did on fixing problems within the leagues. Consequently, Bolden and other owners remained ill-prepared to make demands of any other Major League official who wanted to sign black players and to defend the relevancy of their own teams.[12]

The feebleness that the owners demonstrated in December 1945 reflected the feebleness of their immediate response to Rickey's actions. A few weeks after Robinson signed with the Dodgers organization, Bolden and other owners met in New York to plot a response. Both Bolden and Gottlieb joined in a resolution that came from the owners of both the NNL and the NAL. The resolution, directed at Commissioner Happy Chandler, expressed the deep concerns the owners had about the loss of their players to Major League organizations. The owners asked Major League officials to negotiate with them before signing any players and asked those same officials to refuse use of their ballparks to teams that signed black players without respecting those players' contracts with either the NNL or NAL. While the resolution contained some strong wording, it ultimately contained a note of defeatism and demonstrated the NNL's and NAL's weaknesses. The owners of those leagues lacked any leverage to force Chandler or other officials to respect their contracts and negotiate for black players. The owners, furthermore, conceded that they could not stop the movement of players from their leagues to the Major Leagues. Their joint resolution represented a desperate, empty, and futile gamble. Chandler rejected their resolution, saying that it did not represent a legitimate dispute that fell under the purview of his office. Major League owners subsequently refused to consider an appeal from the owners of the NNL and NAL for recognition as minor league organizations.[13]

Robinson's signing put owners like Bolden in a tricky situation. They could not voice their opposition to the signing, nor could they block entreaties from other Major League clubs for more black players. If Bolden and other owners took those stands, they would likely face opposition and charges that they supported segregation. Instead, Bolden and other owners had to support the signing while objecting to the methods Rickey employed to obtain Robinson. The fact that they had staged games in Major League stadiums, like Shibe Park, and had not consistently respected each other's player contracts further hampered their ability to demand respect from Major League owners. For Bolden, the reality of integration in the Major Leagues added another dimension to his job as he entered the 1946 season. Any good player on the Stars could also catch the attention of Major League scouts, and Bolden had little recourse to press for compensation for lost players.[14]

The Beginning of the End

Prior to the start of the 1946 season, Bolden retired from his full-time job at the Philadelphia Post Office, giving him more time to devote to his Stars. As he made plans for the 1946 season, ominous signs portended a bleak future for his franchise. Large headlines in the *Philadelphia Independent* announced the Stars' departure for spring training and Bolden's retirement from the post office. Underneath those headlines, however, the newspaper ran a story on Robinson's travails against segregation in Florida. A local segregation statute prohibited Robinson and his African American teammate, John Wright, from participating in a game with their white Montreal Royals teammates. Another story on that same page announced Kenny Washington's signing with the Los Angeles Rams of the National Football League. That story warranted a banner headline across the top of the sports page. The stories about Robinson and Washington came amidst stories about other players, notably Philadelphia native Roy Campanella, who had joined Major League organizations. While the Stars still warranted attention from the newspaper, the stories on players integrating their leagues signaled the beginning of a new era. The Stars' place in that new era remained uncertain.[15]

In the midst of that uncertainty, the Stars enjoyed an uneven 1946 season. Under the tutelage of Bolden and field manager Homer "Goose" Curry, the Stars boasted an impressive lineup of homegrown talent. Benson continued to patrol the Stars' outfield, while Duckett played at second base and other infield positions when needed. Joe Craig joined Benson in the outfield, while Henry Miller, Wilmer Harris and Larry Kimbrough occupied spots on the Stars' pitching staff. Bill Cash and Willie Wynn shared catching duties and brought the number of homegrown players on the Stars to eight. They joined other talented players like Roy Paltrow, Joe Fillmore, Henry McHenry, Barney Brown, Ed Stone, Frank Austin, Marvin

Williams, Henry Simpson, and William "Bus" Clarkson. With those players under contract, Curry confidently proclaimed that the team would finally capture that elusive second championship. At one point in the 1946 season, the Stars held first place in the NNL and appeared poised to fulfill Curry's prediction. As in previous seasons, however, the Stars slipped from contention for a league title and finished the season without capturing another championship.[16]

Several events during the Stars' uneven 1946 season captured the team's uncertain future and the difficult landscape confronting Bolden. In May, Bolden lost two of his players when Paltrow signed with the Dodgers organization and Stone jumped his contract for the Mexican League. Bolden did not issue any public statements about Partlow; Rickey purchased Partlow's contract, meaning Bolden received compensation, and then assigned him to the Montreal Royals. After staging a typical pomp-filled opening day game at their 44th and Parkside field, the Stars traveled across Philadelphia to play their first game of the season at Shibe Park. The game, which pitted the Stars against the Homestead Grays, attracted over ten thousand fans, yet it raised a troubling question about the Stars' dependency upon a Major League ballpark to stage important contests. The Stars, furthermore, had limited access to the ballpark since two Major League teams, the Athletics and the Phillies, used it as their home ballpark. Near the end of the 1946 season, Bolden faced more depletion of his roster when Clarkson and Fillmore jumped their contracts and joined the Mexican League. Clarkson, who had lost several seasons of his career to the armed forces, likely left the Stars because he had lost his starting shortstop job. On the heels of those departures, Bolden's Stars lost five straight games and limped through the rest of the 1946 season.[17]

The most troubling signs for the Stars appeared on the pages of the local black newspapers. Throughout the season, the black newspapers continued their coverage of Robinson and other black players who had signed with Major League clubs. In many instances, stories about those players carried banner headlines that dominated the sports pages and overshadowed stories on the Stars and other black teams. Such stories further emphasized the Stars' uncertain future in a world with black players in Major League organizations. The Stars seemed to represent the past, not the future, of professional baseball in the United States.[18]

As the Stars struggled through their uneven season and faced irrelevancy, Bolden, Gottlieb, and other officials sought to arrest the loss of players to the Major Leagues. Bolden's partner Gottlieb faced increased scrutiny over his role in black professional baseball. In one of the final acts of his life, Cum Posey spoke out against Gottlieb's attempts to increase the power of the NNL and NAL presidents. Posey sought to replace the current league presidents, Tom Wilson and J.B. Martin, with more effective leaders who did not hold interests in any league clubs.[19] Wendell Smith invited Posey to expound upon his views in his regular column for the *Pittsburgh Courier*. Posey accepted Smith's offer; in the column, Posey outlined his suggested reforms for the NNL and NAL. He lamented that the resolution the black leagues sent to Chandler did not contain any pledges from the leagues that would improve their operations. He also expressed respect for Gottlieb and for his work in booking well-attended games for black teams at Shibe Park. Posey, however, expressed alarm at the percentage of gate receipts Gottlieb kept for himself for games he booked at Yankee Stadium. As Posey reasoned, Gottlieb "is honest in his dealing, and a good baseball man, but he must come to realize that the Negro National League was not organized for his benefit."[20]

Following Posey's death, Smith carried on Posey's criticisms of Gottlieb and added a new dimension to the late mogul's concerns about Gottlieb's involvement in black professional baseball. In late 1946, Gottlieb secured a franchise, later named the Philadelphia Warriors, in the new professional basketball league, later named the National Basketball Association (NBA). When he first reported that news, Smith wondered if Gottlieb would sign black players to his new team. A few months later, Smith furthered his criticism of the man he referred to as "Brother Gottlieb" by noting the money he made promoting the recent World Series between the Newark Eagles and the Kansas City Monarchs as well as other NNL and NAL contests. According to Smith, the World Series contest netted $25,000 in receipts, and 158,000 watched NNL and NAL contests at Yankee Stadium during the 1946 season. He speculated that Gottlieb had earned approximately $50,000 through his dealings with black professional baseball over the previous five seasons. To Smith, those facts highlighted Gottlieb's hypocrisy since his new basketball franchise did not carry any black players.[21]

The troubles facing Gottlieb, Bolden, and the Stars continued into the 1947 season. In January 1947, the NNL owners elected a new president, the Reverend John H. Johnson, over the objections of Gottlieb. Since Gottlieb and Bolden worked together on the Stars, Bolden likely also opposed Johnson's election. Johnson served as the pastor of the St. Martin Episcopal Church in New York City and vowed to bring changes to the NNL's operations. His plans included adding the NNL to the realm of "organized" baseball that included the National and American Leagues. In the *Pitts-*

burgh Courier, Smith used Johnson's election as another opportunity to criticize Gottlieb's influence within the NNL and his refusal to include black players on his new basketball team. Smith also castigated a rumor that Gottlieb planned to organize a league composed of all-black professional basketball teams. He regarded Gottlieb's actions, both alleged and real, as insulting to black sports fans who had patronized Gottlieb-scheduled games at Yankee Stadium and other venues.[22]

The criticisms that Gottlieb faced served as a bad omen for the Stars' 1947 season. Bolden again named Curry as his field manager and worked to assemble a roster filled with returning and new talent. He succeeded in resigning Partlow after the lefty received his release from the Montreal Royals and decided to return to the NNL. The Stars celebrated another pomp-filled opening day at the 44th and Parkside field; Robert J. Nelson, the assistant director of public safety in Philadelphia, tossed the ceremonial first pitch. The Stars lost their opening day contest and amassed yet another losing record. Even worse, the Stars faced acute attendance shortages at both the 44th and Parkside field and Shibe Park. Robinson's debut with the Brooklyn Dodgers in April 1947, along with the continued influx of black players in Major League organizations, contributed to the declining attendance at Stars games. Stories about Robinson and other black players, including Larry Doby and Roy Campanella, again dominated the pages of the local black newspapers. At the end of the season, when the Dodgers secured a World Series berth, the Philadelphia Independent's editorial board devoted a lengthy editorial to Robinson's presence in the World Series. The editorial praised Robinson for establishing a good example for other black players and compared him to previous African American leaders like Frederick Douglass, Mary Bethune, and W.E.B. DuBois. The newspaper also invited readers to submit their opinions of Rickey using a form provided to them in the sports section.[23]

Around the NNL, other teams faced problems similar to the ones that the Stars endured during the 1947 season. After enjoying a prosperous 1946 season, both the NNL and NAL suffered a significantly worse 1947 season. Teams endured attendance declines and, like the Stars, lost newspaper coverage to Robinson and other black players in Major League organizations. The switch in coverage began with Robinson's debut in April 1947 as black sportswriters extensively covered Robinson's entrance into the Major Leagues and urged black fans to maintain good behavior at his games. While Wendell Smith urged his readers to continue to support the NNL and NAL, black fans chose to patronize Shibe Park and other venues in order to watch Robinson and the Dodgers. Due to high salaries and dwindling gate receipts, nearly every team lost money, including the NAL champion Cleveland Buckeyes and World Series champion New York Cubans. The dire situation facing teams in the NNL and NAL left owners like Bolden in an almost impossible situation. Bolden had to operate within a system that no longer seemed to value black professional baseball. The future did not look promising for him or for his Stars.[24]

On the Road

In response to a disappointing 1947 season, Bolden decided to make some changes in the Stars' management. He hired Oscar Charleston, who had previously managed the Stars, as his new field manager. In parting ways with Curry, Bolden praised his former field manager for helping lead the Stars through hard times. Bolden then worked with Charleston to restructure the Stars' roster and to focus on attracting young talent. Over the winter, the Stars' chances for a successful 1948 season appeared to vanish when Bolden and Gottlieb quietly announced that they had lost use of the field at 44th and Parkside due to financial problems. Although the Stars lacked a permanent home ballpark, Bolden decided to keep the franchise alive, and Gottlieb made tentative plans to schedule home games at Shibe Park and several out-of-city sites. Rollo Wilson lamented that the Stars had transformed into a "wandering Jew" of baseball and that the franchise stood at the mercy of major league baseball if it wanted to play any games in Philadelphia. With two major league teams already using Shibe Park, the Stars could no longer offer their fans daytime contests and could only present a limited number of nighttime contests. By playing a reduced number of games in Philadelphia, Wilson predicted, the Stars would represent a part-time club to local fans and that fans would not see enough of the team to evaluate its players.[25]

Prior to the start of spring training, the Stars opened their new headquarters at the Christian Street YMCA in Philadelphia; the players received full membership benefits from the YMCA and practiced daily at the Sons of Italy field. As part of his continued effort to improve the club, Bolden extended an invitation to all young players who wanted to try out with the Stars and promised them that they could replace the team's veterans. Despite the presence of hopeful young players at the training sessions, the Stars' opening day roster included many familiar names—Frank Austin, Gene Benson, Henry Miller, and Roy Partlow. A lack of financial resources prevented the team from training in the South, but manager

Gene Benson (left) played for the Philadelphia Stars until his retirement in 1948. His constant presence on the roster helped to provide Bolden and the rest of team with stability during a turbulent era (John W. Mosley Photograph Collection, Charles L. Blockson Afro-American Collection, Temple University Libraries, Philadelphia, Pennsylvania).

Oscar Charleston led his team on a barnstorming tour through the North to prepare them for league competition. For the beginning of the regular season, the Stars lost to the New York Cubans in Chester and then defeated the Black Yankees in the official NNL opener at Yankee Stadium before ten thousand spectators. The Stars celebrated their home opener in May at Shibe Park as part of a four-team double-header, and in the second game, they easily defeated the Newark Eagles behind solid pitching from Henry Miller.[26]

As the Stars faced their new future as a traveling team, Major League owners essentially dealt a death blow to the NNL by refusing to consider it as a minor league organization within the national agreement governing the American and National Leagues. While NNL President Johnson tried to minimize the impact of the decision, the denial essentially hastened the NNL's demise. The cumulative bad decisions NNL owners had made over the past fifteen years haunted them and left them with few options. The NNL's lack of territorial rights represented the biggest obstacle to obtaining some form of recognition from the Major Leagues. Since most NNL clubs used ballparks like Shibe Park and Yankee Stadium, their inclusion as minor league teams would create territorial conflicts in most major cities. Dwindling attendance and reduced attention in the black press compounded the problems facing the NNL. After a large crowd greeted the NNL teams at Yankee Stadium on the opening weekend, attendance at league games fell dramatically during the rest of the season.[27]

The problems facing the NNL deepened as the 1948 season progressed. In June, the Newark Eagles' Effa Manley unleashed a tirade against black baseball fans and the black press for neglecting the Negro leagues and for devoting an unwarranted amount of attention on the major leagues. The *Philadelphia Tribune* responded by arguing, "Negro Baseball is tottering under … its own colossal stupidity and lack of vision of which Effa's latest outburst is a typical and unshining example."[28] The newspaper also argued that neither black baseball fans nor the black press held any obligation to patronize the Negro leagues and that most fans no longer cared what happened in the Negro leagues. Despite the problems facing the NNL, the league managed to stage a World Series with the equally hurting NAL. Soon after winning the World Series, the Homestead Grays announced that they would no longer operate as a league team; owner Rufus Jackson revealed that the Grays had lost $45,000 in the past two seasons. The New York Black Yankees and Newark Eagles also disbanded after the season, leaving the Stars as one of the few teams left in the NNL. In December, however, the NNL also disbanded. The future again seemed uncertain for Bolden and his Stars.

Twilight Time

Instead of joining the NNL as a relic of baseball's segregated past, Bolden and Gottlieb kept the Stars viable and moved into a revamped NAL. Two other leftovers from the NNL, the Cubans and Elite Giants, also continued operations and joined the Stars. Those three teams, along with the Indianapolis Clowns and Louisville Buckeyes, joined a new eastern division within the NAL. The NAL western division included the Kansas City Monarchs, Chicago American Giants, Birmingham Black Barons, Houston Eagles, and Memphis Red Sox. All of the NAL teams drafted players from the defunct NNL franchises; the Houston Eagles took all of the players from the Newark teams except for Monte Irvin, who signed with the New York Giants. Despite the dire situation facing black professional baseball, NAL President Martin predicted a great year for the league in 1949. While he acknowledged the demise of the NNL and several of its teams, he noted the NAL's strong business practices and confidently predicted that black baseball fans would not abandon black teams. Martin also cited the strong performances of players like Robinson and Doby as proof of the NAL's continued value and as reasons for optimism for the league. In hindsight, Martin's confidence seems naïve. He likely sensed that organizations like the NAL remained in a precarious position, yet he needed to maintain a positive outlook in order to keep his outdated league viable.[29]

Sadly, the demise of the NNL and the declining interest in black professional baseball did not create harmony within the NAL. Prior to the 1950 season, rumors circulated that NAL owners from the western division, unhappy with the league's alignment, wanted to oust the former NNL teams that had joined the league on a one-year agreement. At an owners' meeting in February, the proposed elimination failed, and the Stars, Cubans, and Elite Giants rejoined the NAL eastern division. For the 1951 and 1952 seasons, the NAL operated with only eight teams due to the departures of the Cubans and the Cleveland Buckeyes, but the league remained aligned in two geographical divisions. Formal league play, however, largely disappeared, leaving owners like Bolden with few means of support. Though the Stars nominally belonged to the NAL, they essentially represented an independent team that lacked a true home ballpark. That reality put increased pressure on Bolden to field a team and to keep his franchise alive.[30]

Financial problems compounded the difficulties facing the Stars and other NAL franchises. From 1948 until 1952, the NAL suffered from dramatic declines in gate receipts, forcing the owners to make deep cuts in salaries and operational expenses. Consequently, most NAL teams fell into debt by the middle of each season, and the owners, including Bolden, sold players to major league organizations in futile attempts to make money. Over that period, the Stars typically started each season in debt due to salaries, operational expenses, and transportation costs; without a permanent home ballpark, the team grossed meager gate receipts of fifty to two hundred dollars per game. Only the Kansas City Monarchs and the Indianapolis Clowns, who mixed circus performances into their games, made money after the major league integrated. Despite those financial problems, Bolden and other owners kept their NAL teams alive in the vain hope that gate receipts would improve and that black baseball would co-exist with the integrated major leagues.[31]

Integration, the demise of the NNL, and the limited support coming from the NAL altered how Bolden conducted his business. While Bolden had used the local black press to generate interest for his Stars, he refrained from making public statements when he sold his players to Major League organizations. In June 1948, the American League–leading Cleveland Indians purchased pitcher Henry Miller for an undisclosed sum. When the *Tribune* contacted the Stars to confirm the story, Gottlieb refused to confirm or deny that the Indians had acquired Miller, and Bolden remained unavailable for comment at his Darby residence. The newspaper scolded Gottlieb and Bolden for their secrecy and pointed out that the Indians' public relations director had informed the Stars of his team's interest in Miller during a trip to Philadelphia last August. Before the 1949 season, the New York Yankees signed shortstop Frank Austin and assigned him to their Newark Bears farm club, another move that the Stars' management tried to hide from the public. Several weeks later, outfielder Harry Simpson

Oscar Charleston (left) had three separate stints as manager of the Philadelphia Stars. His final stint with the Stars lasted from 1947 through 1950. During that time, he had to help players like Henry Miller (center) and Harry Simpson (right) navigate a world with integrated major leagues (John W. Mosley Photograph Collection, Charles L. Blockson Afro-American Collection, Temple University Libraries, Philadelphia, Pennsylvania).

accepted an offer to play with the Eastern League's Wilkes-Barre club, an affiliate of the Cleveland Indians. Bolden offered minimal details about Simpson's signing and instead tried to shift the focus to the Stars and the purchase of a new bus and other equipment for his team.[32]

The 1950 season brought more bad news for Bolden and his Stars when five of his players jumped their contracts in May for teams in the Mexican League. While Bolden and Charleston had focused on using young players on the Stars, the Stars' roster still included some popular veterans. Those popular veterans—Henry Miller, Barney Brown, Bill Cash, and Joe Fillmore—turned their backs on the Stars and sought more lucrative contracts with teams in the Mexican League. The loss of those players added to the sense of gloom that accompanied the Stars and the rest of the NAL at the start of the 1950 season. Small crowds greeted NAL teams in their home openers in Chicago, New York, and other league cities. A lone bright spot for the Stars came in July 1950, when legendary pitcher Satchel Paige signed a one-month contract with the team. For the past several seasons, Paige had pitched for the Cleveland Indians, and his appear-

Harry Leon Simpson, a World War II veteran, symbolized the new reality facing the Philadelphia Stars in the late 1940s. Simpson played with the Stars for three seasons before signing with the Cleveland Indians organization in 1949; Ed Bolden never revealed what compensation, if any, he received for Simpson from the Indians. Simpson played in the major leagues for eight seasons (John W. Mosley Photograph Collection, Charles L. Blockson Afro-American Collection, Temple University Libraries, Philadelphia, Pennsylvania).

ance generated some positive coverage for the Stars. Paige, however, seemed to have little interest
in the Stars or in the NAL. After
his one-month contract ended,
Paige left the Stars and returned
to the Major Leagues.[33]

In a column for the *Pittsburgh Courier*, Wendell Smith
provided a bleak view of the situation facing Bolden and other
owners. Smith noted that none of
the NAL teams made money during the 1950 season, and eight of
the teams in the ten-team league
faced financial shortages. NAL
president J.B. Martin faced the
possibility of one or more teams
quitting. Smith soberly noted that
selling players to the Major
Leagues represented the only way
black teams could hope to make
money. He referred to "Negro
baseball" as the "orphan of baseball," an "illegitimate waif" that
existed because of segregation in
professional baseball.[34]

In the midst its many personnel losses, the Stars organization suffered its biggest lost when
founder and owner Bolden died
at the age of sixty-eight in September 1950. Prior to his death,
Bolden suffered a stroke at his
home in Darby; he died on September 28 at Darby's Mercy-
Fitzgerald Hospital. Bolden's wife

Bill "Ready" Cash remained with the
Philadelphia Stars until the 1950 season
and played in the Chicago White Sox'
farm system before his retirement in
1955. After his playing career ended,
Cash made his home in Philadelphia and
founded the Cobbs Creek Little League
Baseball Association (John W. Mosley
Photograph Collection, Charles L.
Blockson Afro-American Collection,
Temple University Libraries, Philadelphia, Pennsylvania).

Nellie had died in 1948; he was survived by their daughter Hilda, the director of a medical health center in Washington, D.C., and his two brothers.
Until he suffered his fatal stroke, Bolden remained involved in the Stars'

activities, and the Stars remained indelibly linked to him. The team's official stationery and business cards listed his home address, 300 Marks Avenue in Darby, and placed his name before the team's name.[35]

The response to Bolden's death and the turnout for his funeral at Darby's Mount Zion Church served as a testament to his place within Philadelphia society. Bolden's honorary pallbearers included Municipal Court Judge Herbert Millen, Philadelphia Postmaster Raymond Thomas, attorney Raymond Pace Alexander, and Lieutenant Colonel Elmber P. Gibson of the United States Army. The Reverend Marshall L. Shepherd, the Recorder of Deeds in Washington, D.C., Frederick Matheus, the assistant director of public safety, and Henry Deal, the superintendent of the Philadelphia Post Office's Middle City section, also served as honorary pallbearers. Other honorary pallbearers included people linked to Bolden through his baseball career—Charleston, Gottlieb, James "Artie" Lee, and Lloyd Thompson. The people who sent condolences to Bolden's daughter Hilda included the Liberian ambassador, the treasurer of the Citizens and Southern Bank Trust Company, the superintendent of Philadelphia's Mercy-Douglass Hospital, and Dr. J.B. Martins of the NAL. Wilson devoted one of his regular columns to delivering a heartfelt retrospective of his long relationship with Bolden and of Bolden's distinguished baseball career.[36]

Ed Bolden's Philadelphia Stars outlived Bolden. Though Hilda retained an ownership stake in the franchise, she did not follow in her father's footsteps and assume active control over the franchise's operations. Instead, Gottlieb kept the team playing, and Charleston took control over the team's personnel decisions. To replace the departed players, Charleston developed a youth movement and advertised for young local players in the *Tribune*, emphasizing that the Stars represented a proven training ground for major and minor league careers. Through Charleston's scouting efforts, the Stars attracted many local high school and sandlot players and, for the 1952 season, carried a youthful roster whose players averaged twenty-one years old. With their rosters of inexperienced players, the Stars consistently posted losing records; in 1952, the team endured a nightmarish beginning to the season with near-constant defeats and garnered the NAL's worst winning percentage. Charleston, however, always maintained a positive outlook and praised his young players for persevering through adverse conditions. Without a home ballpark, the young Stars faced a grueling schedule that required them to endure extended road trips through the southeast and Midwest, and they often played on consecutive days in different cities. For their long road trips, the Stars traveled on their old streamlined bus and, consequently, appeared fatigued on the playing field; in early 1952, the team purchased two new station wagons to make the traveling more comfortable.[37]

As the Stars continued to operate without a home field and to play ninety percent of their games on the road, the team's management came

During the franchise's final seasons, the Philadelphia Stars lost most of their popular players. The team carried young players on its roster and advertised itself as a stepping stone for careers in major league organizations (such as this unidentified group) (John W. Mosley Photograph Collection, Charles L. Blockson Afro-American Collection, Temple University Libraries, Philadelphia, Pennsylvania).

under fire for failing to lease another permanent home ballpark and schedule more games in Philadelphia. A letter to the *Tribune* from a West Philadelphia resident asked why the Stars refused to play in Hilldale Park and suggested that Gottlieb, as the team's business manager, disliked the idea of renting the park from its black owner. The writer also asserted that the Stars had harmed their popularity in Philadelphia by failing to give their loyal fans more home dates, particularly on the summer holidays. Speaking on behalf of black baseball fans in the Philadelphia area, the writer stressed that he wanted the Stars to remain in business and suggested that they "cut their prices ... and don't let 'foolish pride' stand in their way of renting Hilldale Park."[38]

In addition to spending long periods of time away from Philadelphia, the Stars also gradually delayed their debuts at Shibe Park. From 1948 until 1950, the team held their opener at Shibe Park in May, but rain washed out their scheduled opener in May 1950, and the Stars did not play in Philadelphia until early July. In their 1951 Shibe Park debut, the Stars lost a double-header to the Indianapolis Clowns and attracted a woeful crowd of three thousand fans; at the same time, the last-place Phillies and the Dodgers drew eighty-five thousand fans to a three-game series. For the 1952 season, the Stars' management refused to schedule their Shibe Park opener for May due to an increase in night games for the A's and the Phillies. They also indicated that the team would hold fewer games in Philadelphia after withstanding heavy financial losses at Shibe Park the previous season and grossing higher gate receipts on the road. When the Stars played their first game in Philadelphia in late July, they attracted four thousand fans to Shibe Park, more fans than they drew in any Shibe Park contest in 1951. Near the end of the season, Dr. Hilda Bolden announced that she would meet in Philadelphia with Gottlieb and attorney Carlyle Tucker to discuss the Stars' 1953 schedule and the future of black players in organized baseball. According to the *Tribune*, Dr. Bolden wanted to emulate her late father's role with Hilldale—she intended to direct the continued growth of the Stars into one of the largest gate attractions in professional black baseball.[39]

After a quiet off-season, Gottlieb suddenly announced in March 1953 that he had dissolved the franchise since he no longer wanted to risk losing money with a team that had lost money or barely broken even during the past six seasons. Several weeks later, however, Gottlieb contradicted his earlier announcement and promised that he would try to sell the team for ten thousand dollars, perhaps even less, given the franchise's poor financial situation. The *Tribune* blamed the Stars' financial losses on their decline in popularity—the team had failed to play in Philadelphia enough times to maintain its loyal fan base and had lost too many players to other leagues. The newspaper expressed hope that one of the city's financial leaders would purchase the team since the Stars' attendance at Shibe Park had improved last season, and since the team carried local players with promising baseball futures. In April, following unsuccessful attempts to sell the franchise, Gottlieb announced that he had officially disbanded the Stars and had given the players free agent status. Gottlieb insisted that he had considered every aspect of the situation and reached the conclusion that the Stars would endure more financial losses during the 1953 season. Although Gottlieb refused to rule out reorganizing the team in future seasons, Ed Bolden's Philadelphia Stars had played their final baseball game.[40]

While Bolden received a proper funeral following his death, his namesake franchise never received a proper memorial in the pages of the local black newspapers. The *Philadelphia Tribune* quickly moved on to cover other items of interest, while the *Philadelphia Independent* ignored the franchise's passing. By April 1953, the Stars had become an outdated reminder of an era when black baseball players had few outlets to pursue a professional career. The Stars no longer belonged in the American sports world of the 1950s. As the world moved on, both Bolden and his franchise faded into obscurity.

Conclusion

W. Rollo Wilson provided the best summation of Ed Bolden's career in black professional baseball. Writing after Bolden's death in 1950, Wilson argued that Bolden represented "the connecting link between the fabulous figures of diamond history, the in-between group, and the present-day magnates who have all but wrecked the game."[1] Bolden's career, in other words, spanned different eras in black baseball history in the first half of the twentieth century. With Hilldale and then the Stars, Bolden experienced all of the joys, frustrations, and challenges associated with black baseball teams that played both within and without a formal Negro League structure. Like many of his fellow Negro League owners, Bolden often acted in his own self-interest and undermined the fragile league structure present within black professional baseball. He effectively wrecked two leagues, the Eastern Colored League and the American Negro League, he established. None of that, however, should undermine Bolden's remarkable achievements in leading two baseball franchises to the heights of their respective leagues and in serving as a leader in three separate Negro Leagues.

Bolden fits comfortably into the history of leaders within the Philadelphia region's African American populace. While Bolden never overtly participated in civil rights–related protests or movements, his work offered parallels to the leaders and organizations that advanced civil rights in the seventeenth, eighteenth, and nineteenth centuries. He helped to establish and led an all-African American corporation, the Hilldale Baseball Corporation. Bolden also established two professional baseball leagues and, for several years in the 1920s, represented one of the dominating figures within Negro League baseball. He won championships with two different clubs and, despite his inglorious departure from Hilldale, enjoyed the respect of his peers. His respect and renown extended beyond Negro League baseball. Bolden actively cultivated relationships with the region's

African American leaders, and both of his franchises represented important cultural institutions within the black Philadelphia community. His funeral in 1950 attracted civil rights leaders, members of the city's legal system, colleagues from the Philadelphia Post Office, and partners from his long career in black baseball.

Ed Bolden's Philadelphia Stars outlived their namesake and founder by slightly more than two years. Perhaps it was for the best that Bolden did not live to see the disbanding of his second franchise. Both Bolden's death and the Stars' subsequent demise presaged the end of an era within American society. Teams like the Stars no longer served a definitive purpose because black baseball players no longer needed the services of the Stars and other all-black teams. Instead, those players could entirely bypass Negro League baseball and establish their professional careers within the confines of Major League Baseball. By the time the Stars ceased operations, any sort of formal league structure within black baseball had nearly evaporated. The Stars no longer occupied a favored spot in the *Tribune's* sports pages, and the team appeared to have little more than a tenuous connection to the region's baseball fans. As a relic of a segregated baseball world, the Stars no longer fit into an America that had black players in the Major Leagues and that stood on the cusp of other advancements in civil rights.

Similar to his Stars, Bolden represented a bygone era of American society. By the time of his death in September 1950, most of the great black baseball leaders of the twentieth century had passed away or moved on to other careers. Bolden survived his old nemesis, Andrew "Rube" Foster, by two decades. Sadly, it appeared as if Major League Baseball had no use for leaders like Bolden. While Major League franchises wanted black players, they refrained from hiring African Americans to work as managers or off-field executives and from welcoming African Americans as owners. Had Bolden lived longer than his Stars, he likely would not have found another sports outlet for his leadership abilities. When Bolden left Hilldale, he could and did find ways to revive his baseball career through the Darby Phantoms and then the Stars. A similar series of events would not have happened for Bolden in the early 1950s.

Though he operated within the confines of a segregated society, Bolden took full advantage of the opportunities available to him. He accepted the invitation to work for Hilldale in 1910, established the Hilldale Baseball Corporation, transformed his first franchise into one of the best teams in the United States, established two leagues, established his second franchise in the midst of the Great Depression, and served in a leadership role in yet another league. Bolden also maintained relationships with the *Philadelphia Tribune* and with local African American leaders, and he enjoyed a long and respected career with the Philadelphia Post Office. With his decades of work in Negro League baseball, Bolden left an indelible legacy in sports history and in the Philadelphia area's history.

Chapter Notes

Introduction

1. Gary B. Nash, "Slaves and Slave Owners in Colonial Philadelphia," in Joe William Trotter Jr. and Eric Ledell Smith, eds., *African Americans in Pennsylvania: Shifting Historical Perspectives* (University Park: The Pennsylvania Historical and Museum Commission and Pennsylvania State University Press, 1997), 43–72.

2. Julie Winch, *Philadelphia's Black Elite: Activism, Accommodation, and the Struggle for Autonomy 1787–1848* (Philadelphia: Temple University Press, 1988), 1–12; Richard S. Newman, *Freedom's Prophet: Bishop Richard Allen, the AME Church, and the Black Founding Fathers* (New York: New York University Press, 2008), 1–14, 60–76, 173–174.

3. Winch, 18–19, 35–39, 81–90.

4. Leslie A. Heaphy, *The Negro Leagues 1869–1960* (Jefferson, NC: McFarland, 2003), 10; Robert Peterson, *Only the Ball Was White: A History of the Legendary Black Players and All-Black Professional Teams* (New York: Gramercy Books, 1970), 16–18, 26–27; Christopher Threston, *The Integration of Baseball in Philadelphia* (Jefferson, NC: McFarland, 2003), 7–8; Anthony DiFiore, "Advancing African American Baseball: The Philadelphia Pythians and Interracial Competition in 1869, *Black Ball: A Journal of the Negro Leagues* 1, No. 1 (Spring 2008): 57–61; Harry C. Silcox, "Nineteenth-Century Philadelphia Black Militant: Octavius V. Catto (1839–1871)," in Trotter and Smith, eds., 208–209.

5. DiFiore, 59; Silcox, 199–208; Daniel R. Biddle and Murray Dubin, *Tasting Freedom: Octavius Catto and the Battle for Equality in Civil War America* (Philadelphia: Temple University Press, 2010), 355–365.

6. Silcox, 203–208.

7. Threston, 9; Silcox, 209; DiFiore, 60–61; Biddle and Dubin, 365–367.

8. DiFiore, 61–64; Biddle and Dubin, 370–376.

9. Silcox, 212–215; DiFiore, 64–65; Biddle and Dubin, 421–430.

10. Heaphy, 11–12; Threston, 9–11; and Peter Morris, *A Game of Inches,* vol. 2, *The Game Behind the Scenes* (Chicago: Ivan R. Dee, 2006), 248–249.

11. Threston, 10–23.

12. Heaphy, 11–32; Peterson, 105–107.

13. Program for Edward Bolden's funeral. Edward Bolden Papers Box 186–1 Folder 1; Manuscript Division, Moorland-Spingarn Research Center, Howard University.

Chapter One

1. For an overview of the gentlemen's agreement in Major League Baseball, see Neil Lanctot, "'A General Understanding': Organized Baseball and Black Professional Baseball, 1900–1930," in *Sport and the Color Line: Black Athletes and Race Relations in Twentieth-Century America,* ed. David K. Wiggins and Patrick B. Miller (New York: Routledge, 2004), 63–82; and James Overmyer and Lawrence D. Hogan, "Before Jim Crow" in *Shades of Glory: The Negro Leagues and the Story of African-American Baseball* (Washington, D.C.: National Geographic, 2006), 42–65.

2. For an overview of Foster's and Taylor's leadership in their respective cities, see Brian Carroll, "Rube Foster, C.I. Taylor, and the Great Newspaper War of 1915," *Black Ball* 4, No. 2 (Fall 2011): 36–54.

3. Christopher Threston, *The Integration of Baseball in Philadelphia* (Jefferson, NC: McFarland, 2003), 24–25; *Philadelphia: A 300-Year History* (New York: Barra Foundation, 1982), 415.

4. Neil Lanctot, *Fair Dealing and Clean Playing: The Hilldale Club and the Development of Black Professional Baseball, 1910–1932* (Syracuse: Syracuse University Press, 1994, 2007), 14–16; *Philadelphia Tribune*, 6 April 1912, 27 April 1912.

5. "Bon Ton Club Notes," *Philadelphia Tribune*, 6 April 1912.

6. *Ibid.*

7. "Hilldale Downed," *Philadelphia Inquirer* 4 June 1910.

8. Lanctot, 16–17.

9. "Notables to Attend Rites for Bolden," Folder 1, Edward Bolden Papers Box 186–1, Moorland-Spingarn Research Center, Howard University.

10. "Statement of Case Examination," November 15, 1921. Folder 3, Edward Bolden Papers Box 186–1, Moorland-Spingarn Research Center, Howard University.

11. "Games Not Published," *Philadelphia Tribune*, 22 August 1914.

12. "Hilldale A.C.," *Philadelphia Tribune*, 13 July 1912.

13. *Ibid.*

14. "Hilldale A.C.," *Philadelphia Tribune*, 22 June 1912.

15. Evergreen Hall Swamped Hilldale," *Philadelphia Tribune*, 3 August 1912.

16. "Hilldale Club," *Philadelphia Tribune*, 12 April 1913; "Hilldale Club," *ibid.*, 4 April 1914; "Hilldale Will Open Season April 17th," *ibid.*, 3 April 1915; "Hilldale Is Ready for April 17th," *ibid.*, 10 April 1915; "Hilldale Club," *ibid.*, 8 April 1916.

17. "Hilldale A.C.," *Philadelphia Tribune*, 5 June 1912.

18. "Bon Ton Loses Manager," *Philadelphia Tribune*, 29 June 1912.

19. "Hillside A.C.," *Philadelphia Tribune*, 6 July 1912.

20. *Ibid.*

21. "Philadelphia Defiance and Hilldale A.C.," *Philadelphia Tribune*, 14 September 1912.

22. "Hilldale A.C. and Philadelphia Defiance," *Philadelphia Tribune*, 21 September 1912.

23. *Ibid.*

24. Brian Carroll, "Rube Foster, C.I. Taylor, and the Great Newspaper War of 1915," *Black Ball* 4, No. 2 (Fall 2011): 36–54; "Rube Foster Speaks," *Chicago Defender*, 18 November 1916; "Rube Foster Speaks," *ibid.*, 25 November 1916.

25. Chad L. Williams, *Torchbearers of Democracy: African American Soldiers in the World War I Era* (Chapel Hill: University of North Carolina Press, 2010), 3.

26. "Draft Wrecks Foster's Team," *Chicago Defender*, 8 September 1917; "Draft Hits Foster Hard," *ibid.*, 27 July 1918; "Draft Hits Hilldale Club," *ibid.*, 27 July 1918; "Hilldale Team Hit Hard by Draft," *Philadelphia Tribune*, 20 July 1918.

27. V.P. Franklin, "The Philadelphia Race Riot of 1918," in *African Americans in Pennsylvania*, Joe William Trotter Jr. and Eric Ledell Smith, eds. (University Park: Pennsylvania State University Press, 1997), 316–329; Lloyd M. Abernathy, "Progressivism 1905–1919," in *Philadelphia: A 300-Hundred Year History* (New York: W.W. Norton, 1982), 530–532.

28. "Hilldale Club's Record Won 19; Lost 9; Tied 2," *Philadelphia Tribune*, 23 October 1916.

29. *Ibid.*

30. "Hilldale Makes Clean Up of Rioters," *Philadelphia Tribune*, 13 January 1917; "Hilldale Club," *ibid.*, 17 February 1917; Lanctot.

31. "Hilldale All Right," *Philadelphia Tribune*, 24 February 1917.

32. "Hilldale Lands Briggs and Presents Formidable Line Up," *Philadelphia Tribune*, 17 March 1917; "Hilldale Lands Pitcher Sykes," *ibid.*, 9 June 1917; "Hilldale Lands Sykes," *Chicago Defender*, 16 June 1917; Lanctot, 44.

33. "Hilldale Sparks," *Philadelphia Tribune* 31 March 1917; "Hilldale Drops Opener 8–1," *ibid.*, 28 April 1917.

34. "Major League Stars Take Second Game from Hilldale," *Philadelphia Tribune*, 20 October 1917; "Hilldale Closes Successful

Season," *ibid.*, 27 October 1917; "Hilldale Takes Another from Bacharachs, 5–1," *ibid.*, 25 May 1918; "Rube Foster's Giants Coming to Hilldale Park," *ibid.*, 6 July 1918; "Hilldale Takes Second Game of Big Series," *ibid.*, 10 August 1918; "Hilldale Trims Cuban Stars 4 to 3," *ibid.*, 31 August 1918; "Hilldale Holds Boston Red Sox," *ibid.*, 21 September 1918; "Hilldale Wins Final Game of Series from Bacharachs," 4 October 1919; "Hilldale Team Beats Chief Bender's Stars," *Chicago Defender*, 29 June 1918; "Fosterites Vs. Hilldales," 6 July 1918; "Hilldale Conquers Am. Giants in the 10th," *ibid.*, 10 August 1918; "Hilldale Team Is Coming to Chicago," *ibid.*, 9 August 1919; "American Giants, in Tenth, Drop Hilldale," *ibid.*, 30 August 1919.

35. Advertisement, *Philadelphia Tribune*, 28 July 1917; "Hilldale Club," *ibid.*, 2 March 1918; Advertisement, *Ibid.*, 11 May 1918; Lanctot, 51–52.

36. "Hilldale on Edge for Opening Clash with R.G. Dunn," *Philadelphia Tribune*, 13 April 1918; "Hilldale Vs. R.G. Dunn; Hilldale Lands Dilworth," *ibid.*, 20 April 1918; Lanctot, 51–52.

37. "Johnson Is Star," *Chicago Defender*, 29 June 1918; "Hilldale Beats M.L. Stars 11 to 3," *ibid.*, 14 September 1918; "Hilldale Cuts Loose," *ibid.*, 28 June 1919; "Defeats Bacharachs in 10-Inning Battle," *ibid.*, 30 August 1919; "Hilldale's Big Third Sends Yorkship Home," *ibid.*, 6 September 1919; Lanctot, 29.

38. "Hilldale Answers Wealthy Man Who Threatens Opposition, Then Offers to Amalgamate," *Philadelphia Tribune*, 13 April 1918.

39. "Hilldale Vs. R.G. Dunn; Hilldale Lands Dilworth," *Philadelphia Tribune*, 20 April 1918.

40. "Otto Briggs Also Writes Letter to the Hilldale Manager," *Philadelphia Tribune*, 1 June 1918.

41. "Poles Letter to the Hilldale Manager," *Philadelphia Tribune*, 30 March 1918; "Hero of Western Front Signs with Hilldale," *ibid.*, 15 March 1919.

42. "Benefit Game for Hilldale Players," *Philadelphia Tribune*, 28 September 1918.

43. *Ibid.*

44. *Ibid.*

45. "Bolden to Pilot Hilldale Another Year," *Philadelphia Tribune*, 8 November 1919.

Chapter Two

1. Michael E. Lomax and Lawrence D. Hogan, "The Great Independents," in *Shades of Glory*, 67–125. It should be noted that there is not unanimous agreement on the final year of NACBC operation. Baseball historian Gary Ashwill believes that the association's season never got under way in 1910. See "The Negro League You've Never Heard Of: The National Association 1907–1909," *Agate Type* (blog), February 5, 2014, http://www.agatetype.typepad.com.

2. Hogan, 109–123.

3. *Ibid.*, 107–131; F.A. Young, "Sporting," *Chicago Defender*, 18 October 1913.

4. "Call for National League Issued," *Chicago Defender*, 7 February 1920; "Baseball Magnates Hold Conference," *ibid.*, 14 February 1920.

5. For an overview of the events leading to the first World Series, see Larry Lester, *Baseball's First Colored World Series: The 1924 Meeting of the Hilldale Giants and Kansas City Monarchs* (Jefferson: McFarland, 2006).

6. Andrew "Rube" Foster, "Pitfalls of Baseball," *Chicago Defender*, 29 November 1919, 13 December 1919.

7. *Ibid.*, 13 December 1919.

8. *Ibid.*

9. *Ibid.*, 20 December 1919, 3 January 1920, 10 January 1920.

10. For an overview of Rube Foster's career, see Lester *Rube Foster in His Time: On the Field and in the Papers with Black Baseball's Greatest Visionary* (Jefferson: McFarland, 2012).

11. Lanctot, 22–23; Frederic Miller, "The Black Migration to Philadelphia: A 1924 Profile," in Joe William Trotter and Eric Ledell Smith, eds., *African Americans in Pennsylvania: Shifting Historical Perspectives* (University Park: Pennsylvania State University Press, 1997), 285–289.

12. Judith Stein, *The World of Marcus Garvey: Race and Class in Modern Society* (Baton Rouge: Louisiana State University Press, 1986), 61–107.

13. "Call for National League Issued,"

Chicago Defender, 7 February 1920; "Baseball Magnates Hold Meeting," *ibid.*, 14 February 1920; "Baseball Men Write League Constitution," *ibid.*, 21 February 1920.

14. "Baseball Magnates Hold Meeting," *ibid.*, 14 February 1920.

15. "Baseball Men Write League Constitution," *ibid.*, 21 February 1920.

16. "Philly Fans Look," *ibid.*, 24 April 1920; "Eastern Sports World; Rube Soothes the East," *ibid.*, 8 May 1920.

17. Lanctot, 59.

18. "Court Decision Favors Bachs," *Chicago Defender*, 12 June 1920; "Francis to Captain Team," *Philadelphia Tribune*, 31 January 1920; "Hilldale Club's Western Players Arrive on Time," *ibid.*, 10 April 1920; Sam West, "Baseball," *ibid.*, 13 March 1920; Lanctot, 82–84.

19. S.A. West, "'Darknight' Smith Meade and Briggs of Hilldale, Will Be Seen in Madison Stars Line-Up," *Philadelphia Tribune*, 10 April 1920.

20. Sam West, "Baseball! Baseball!" *Ibid.*, 6 March 1920.

21. *Ibid.*

22. Sam West, "Baseball," *ibid.*, 13 March 1920.

23. Quoted in *Ibid.*.

24. "Bolden's Hilldale Team: Was the Best Drawing and Most Largely Patronized Independent Team in the East Last Year," *ibid.*, 20 March 1920.

25. *Ibid.*

26. Edward Bolden, "Hilldale's Answer to Rube Foster," *ibid.*, 21 August 1920.

27. "Hilldale to Form Circuit: Schedule Covers 3 States," *ibid.*, 31 January 1920; "Hilldale Completes Her Line-Up for the 1920 Season," *ibid.*, 20 March 1920; "Opening Game at Hilldale," *ibid.*, 1 May 1920; "Week with Darby and Her Hilldale Clan," *ibid.*, 4 September 1920; "Stengels Stars Win 4 to 2 Verdict from Hilldale," *ibid.*, 16 October 1920; "Hilldale Goose-Eggs Babe Ruth and His Stars 5 to 0," *ibid.*; "Hilldale an Easy Winner of Independent Title," *ibid.*; Lanctot, 232.

28. "Rube Foster Re-Elected," *Philadelphia Tribune*, 18 December 1920; Lanctot, 86.

29. "Rube Foster Re-Elected," *ibid.*; "Baseball Magnates in Big Harmony Meeting," *Chicago Defender*, 11 December 1920.

30. "Bolden to Use Two Parks This Season," *Chicago Defender*, 26 February 1921; "Whitworth Wins from Red Ryan at Darby, 11–6," *ibid.*, 2 July 1921; "Whitworth Wins Pitching Duel Against Silk Sox, 6–4," *ibid.*, 16 July 1921; "Opening Game at Hilldale Park Today; Hon. Andrew F. Stevens to Throw Out New Ball," *Philadelphia Tribune*, 30 April 1921; "Darbyites Easily Win from Hebrew Association; Cuban Stars Divide Evening with Hilldale Bunch," *ibid.*, 9 July 1921; "Hilldale Ties Series with American Giants," *ibid.*, 22 October 1921; "Phil Cockrell, Star Pitcher Signs 1922 Contract," *ibid.*, 29 October 1921; "Hilldale Continues to Win as Biggest Season of Baseball Slowly Ends; Hilldale Adds a Few More to Her Splendid Record," *ibid.*, 5 November 1921; Lanctot.

31. "American Giants Cinch National League Championship," *Chicago Defender*, 17 September 1921; "East Vs. West Series to End Ball Season," *ibid.*, 1 October 1921; Rube Foster, "Rube Foster Tells What Baseball Needs to Succeed," *ibid.*, 10 December 1921; Foster, "Rube Foster Tells What Baseball Needs to Succeed," *ibid.*, 17 December 1921; Foster, "Players Prove Serious Drawback to Baseball," *ibid.*, 24 December 1921; Foster, "Future of Race Umpires Depends on Men of Today," *ibid.*, 31 December 1921.

32. Frank Young, "It's All in the Game," *Chicago Defender*, 14 January 1922; "Ed Bolden in City," *ibid.*, 18 February 1922; "National League News: American Giants Leave for South Monday—Hilldale Hops Back into Association—Ben Taylor to Lead A.B.C.S—Tates Announce Players—Season Opens in Chicago April 16," *ibid.*, 11 March 1922; J.H. Gray, "The Quaker City," *ibid.*, 25 March 1922; Lanctot.

33. "Rube Foster Pinched," *Chicago Defender*, 12 November 1921; "Rube Foster Confined to Bed with Throat Trouble," *ibid.*, 4 November 1922; "Charleston to Am. Giants; Dismukes to Manage A.B.C.S; Fourth Annual Meeting of the National League Peaceful," *ibid.*, 16 December 1922; Lanctot, 91–93.

34. "Baseball Men Gather Here for Annual Meeting on Dec. 7," *Chicago Defender*, 2 December 1922; "Rube Foster Confined to Bed with Throat Trouble," *ibid.*, 4 No-

vember 1922; "Charleston to Am. Giants; Dismukes to Manage A.B.C.S; Fourth Annual Meeting of the National League Peaceful," *ibid.*, 16 December 1922; Lanctot, 91–93.

35. Bill Dallas, "Six Colored Clubs in New Baseball League," *Evening Public Ledger*, 21 December 1922; Lanctot, 93.

36. Rube Foster, "Rube Foster Threatens Big Baseball War," *Baltimore Afro-American*, 12 January 1923.

37. "Fans Surprised at Actions of the Eastern League," *Chicago Defender*, 13 January 1923.

38. *Ibid.* The PBA folded in 1923. Lanctot, 69–70.

39. Edward Bolden, "Chairman of Eastern Club Answers Charges of Foster," *Pittsburgh Courier*, 20 January 1923.

40. *Ibid.*

41. *Ibid.*

42. "National League News," *Chicago Defender*, 20 January 1923; "Rube Foster Goes Eastward; Giants to Train in Texas," *ibid.*, 3 February 1923; "Bolden Worked at Night, Slept in Day, So He Didn't Have Time to Meet with 'Rube,'" *Ibid.*, 24 February 1923; "Eastern League Schedule Gives Fans Real Laugh," *ibid.*, 28 April 1923.

43. "Eastern League Moguls Meet in Philadelphia," *Pittsburgh Courier*, 7 July 1923; Lanctot, 99–101.

44. "Hilldale Wins Flag in Eastern League Race," *Pittsburgh Courier*, 29 September 1923; "Pennant Awarded to Darby Club in Eastern Circuit," *ibid.*, 6 October 1923; A.W. Shockly, "Hilldale Baseball Club an Achievement," *Philadelphia Tribune*, 1 December 1923; Lanctot, 102–106.

45. W. Rollo Wilson, "Eastern Snapshots," *Pittsburgh Courier*, 4 August 1923; "Mackey, Former A.B.C. Star, Is 'Babe Ruth' of Eastern League," *ibid.*, 8 September 1923; "Hilldale President Suspends Manager John Henry Lloyd," *ibid.*, 29 September 1923; Wilson, "Suspension of Lloyd Made Permanent by Darby Mogul," *ibid.*, 6 October 1923; "'Bizz' Mackey Leads Eastern Sluggers; Lloyd Is Second," *ibid.*, 13 October 1923; Wilson, "Eastern Snapshots," *ibid.*, 10 November 1923; "John Lloyd and Boss Bolden Have Run In," *Chicago Defender*, 29 September 1923; Lanctot, 102–103.

46. Shockly, "Hilldale Baseball Club."

47. *Ibid.*

48. "Eastern Colored League Magnates Hold Annual Session in City of Philadelphia," *Philadelphia Tribune*, 15 December 1923.

49. "Fans Getting Real Thrill as League Races Near Climax," *Pittsburgh Courier*, 11 August 1923; "Foster Begins to Wreck Once Great Machine," *Chicago Defender*, 11 August 1923; "Baseball Owners Will Meet Here Thursday, Dec. 6," *ibid.*, 17 November 1923; "Foster's Ire Aroused Over Ball Players' Charges," *ibid.*, 24 November 1923; "National League Owners in City Thursday, Dec. 6," *ibid.*, 1 December 1923; "Negro National Leaguers Are in Annual Session," *ibid.*, 8 December 1923; "National League Closes Peaceful Meeting," *ibid.*, 15 December 1923; Lanctot, 106.

50. "Record Crowd Expected at Hilldale Park Today," *Philadelphia Tribune*, 26 April 1924; "Hilldale Leads League as Lincoln Giants Lose Series," *ibid.*, 21 June 1924; "Hilldale Batting Averages," *ibid.*, 26 July 1924; "Eastern Champions," *Chicago Defender*, 4 October 1924; Lanctot, 109.

51. "Judge Landis Offers to Arbitrate Baseball Dispute," *Chicago Defender*, 6 September 1924; "Judge Landis Willing to Arbitrate Every Point in East-West Baseball War," *Philadelphia Tribune*, 6 September 1924; "Bolden for World's Series; Eastern Magnate Willing If Fans Desire Test Games," *ibid.*; "Contract Jumpers Greatest Menace to Negro Baseball Leagues Should Check Evil," *ibid.*; John Howe, "Hilldale and Kansas City to Meet in World's Series First Game Here, Oct. 3rd," *ibid.*, 13 September 1924; "East-West May Hold World Series," *Pittsburgh Courier*, 6 September 1924; Lloyd P. Thompson, "World Series to Be Held This Fall," *ibid.*, 13 September 1924; "Kansas City and Hilldale in 'Blue Ribbon' Classic," *ibid.*, 4 October 1924.

52. Frank A. Young, "Hilldale Leads in World Series," *Chicago Defender*, 11 October 1924; Young, "Kansas City Wins in 12th," *ibid.*, 18 October 1924; Young, "Kansas City Wins Championship," *ibid.*, 25 October 1924; Lloyd P. Thompson, "K.C. Monarchs Win Baseball Crown," *Philadelphia Tribune*, 25 October 1924; Thompson,

"Santop's Error in Ninth Paves Way for East's Defeat," *ibid.*; "World's Series Scores," *ibid.*; "How They Batted in the Big Series," *ibid.*; "Facts of the World Series as Told by the Figure," *Pittsburgh Courier*, 11 October 1924; W. Rollo Wilson, "Eastern Snapshots," *ibid.*, 1 November 1924; Lanctot, 112–121.

53. W. Rollo Wilson, "Beaten Eastern Champs Back 'Home,' Are Given Royal Reception by Philly Fans," *Pittsburgh Courier*, 1 November 1924; Lanctot, 118–121.

54. Andrew Rube Foster, "Rube Foster Reviews the World Series and Tells a Little Baseball History," *Chicago Defender*, 15 November 1924.

55. *Ibid.*

56. *Ibid.*; "World Series Report," *ibid.*, 1 November 1924; "Close to 50,000 Fans Witnessed World Series Games," *Pittsburgh Courier*, 1 November 1924.

57. "East and West in Joint Meet Come Together at Last," *Philadelphia Tribune*, 13 December 1924.

58. *Ibid.*

59. J.M. Howe, "Sport Sidelights," *Philadelphia Tribune*, 9 May 1925; Howe, "The Week in Sports," *ibid.*, 8 August 1925; "Beckwith and Judy Johnson Top the List of Heavy Hitters," *ibid.*, 29 August 1925; "Hilldale Clinches Pennant as Rally Beats the Senators," *ibid.*, 12 September 1925; "World Series Begins in West on October First," *ibid.*, 19 September 1925; "Carr Leads Hilldale at Bat for Entire Season with Average of .409," *ibid.*, 14 November 1925; Lanctot, 135.

60. J.M. Howe, "Sport Sidelights," *Philadelphia Tribune*, 10 October 1925; "Hilldale Ball Club Now National Champions; Kansas City Dethroned!" *Ibid.*, 17 October 1925; "Sport Sidelights," *ibid.*; "Hilldale Team Banqueted by Jubilant Fans," *ibid.*

61. "World Series Attendance-Receipts," *Chicago Defender*, 24 October 1925; "Baseball Commission Gives Statement on World Series," *Pittsburgh Courier*, 24 October 1925.

62. "Charges Against Hilldale False, Says Ed Bolden," *Chicago Defender*, 1 August 1925; "Hilldale Manager Takes Exception to Howe Cartoon," *Philadelphia Tribune*, 4 April 1925; J.M. Howe, "Sport Sidelights," *ibid.*, 19 September 1925; Cum Posey, "The Sportive Realm," *Pittsburgh Courier*, 5 December 1925.

Chapter Three

1. "White Newspaperman Is Picked by Eastern League as Supervisor of Umpires," *Pittsburgh Courier*, 28 March 1925; "Hilldale Manager Takes Exception to Howe Cartoon," *Philadelphia Tribune*, 4 April 1925.

2. Lanctot, 142–205.

3. Judith Stein, *The World of Marcus Garvey: Race and Class in Modern Society* (Baton Rouge: Louisiana State University Press), 248–273.

4. "Status of Umpires Discussed at Meet of Commissioners," *Philadelphia Tribune*, 19 April 1924.

5. *Ibid.*

6. "Final Arrangements and Complete Details Are Made for East-West Baseball Classic," *Pittsburgh Courier*, 20 September 1924; "The Sportive Realm," *ibid.*, 1 November 1924.

7. W. Rollo Wilson, "Eastern Snapshots," *ibid.*, 22 November 1924.

8. *Ibid.*

9. "White Newspaperman Is Picked by Eastern League as Supervisor of Umpires," *ibid.*, 28 March 1925.

10. "Hilldale Manager Takes Exception to Howe Cartoon," *Philadelphia Tribune*, 4 April 1925.

11. *Ibid.*

12. "Comes to Bat in Behalf of Umpires," *Pittsburgh Courier*, 18 July 1925.

13. "Foster Explains Action in Releasing Umpires," *Chicago Defender*, 22 August 1925.

14. *Ibid.*

15. J.M. Howe, "Sport Sidelights," *Philadelphia Tribune*, 1 August 1925; Wilson, "Eastern Snapshots," *Pittsburgh Courier*, 1 August 1925.

16. "Umpires Not Given Support Says Gholston," *Philadelphia Tribune*, 5 September 1925.

17. Wilson, "Eastern Snapshots," *Pittsburgh Courier*, 12 September 1925.

18. *Ibid.*

19. *Ibid.*

20. "Near Riot at Shore When Cops Beat Cockrell; Bacharachs Win Game 1–0," *Philadelphia Tribune*, 14 August 1926; "Diamond Dust," *ibid.*; William G. Nunn, "Diamond Dope," *Pittsburgh Courier*, 14 August 1926; Wilson, "Eastern Snapshots," *ibid.*, 21 August 1926.

21. Oscar Charleston, "Oscar Charleston Terms Eastern League a Farce," *Philadelphia Tribune*, 20 June 1925.

22. *Ibid.*

23. Edward Bolden, "Bolden Answers Charleston," *ibid.*, 27 June 1925.

24. J.M. Howe, "Sport Sidelights," *ibid.*

25. "Wilmington Potomacs Throw Up the Sponge," *Pittsburgh Courier*, 25 July 1925; William G. Nunn, "Diamond Dope," *ibid.*

26. "Right Back at You, Mr. Bolden," *ibid.*, 1 August 1925.

27. George W. Robinson, "George W. Robinson Throws Light on the Policies of the Eastern League," *ibid.*, 8 August 1925.

28. Wilson, "Eastern Snapshots," *ibid.*, 21 November 1925; "Newark Stars Quit Eastern League, Players Disbanded," *ibid.*, 10 July 1926; "Keenan Gives Big Lie to Rumors About Bolden," *Chicago Defender*, 6 March 1926; "Baseball Magnates of East and West Hold Harmonious Session at Local Y.M.C.A.," *Philadelphia Tribune*, 16 January 1926; "League Heads Thresh Out Differences, Eastern League Moguls to Alleviate Ills of Base Ball Circuit That Was Ailing," *ibid.*, 7 August 1926.

29. Edward Bolden in Howe, "Sport Sidelights," *ibid.*, 14 August 1926.

30. Lloyd Thompson, "Keenan Goes West with Rest of League Moguls; May Have Changed His Mind," *ibid.*, 15 January 1927; Wilson, "Eastern League Elects Nutter Pres. to Succeed Bolden," *Pittsburgh Courier*, 22 January 1927.

31. "Detroit Will Have Baseball in 1925; Rube Foster Still Head of the Westerners," *Chicago Defender*, 3 January 1925; "Foster Releases Several Ball Players," *ibid.*, 7 March 1925; "Cuban Stars Remain but Elites Quit," *ibid.*, 31 July 1926; "Gas Nearly Kills Andrew Rube Foster," *ibid.*, 6 June 1925; "Foster Releases Practically Entire Team," *Pittsburgh Courier*, 7 March 1925; "Foster Has Narrow Escape from Death in Indianapolis," *ibid.*, 6 June 1925.

32. "N.N. League Moguls in Meeting," *Pittsburgh Courier*, 26 June 1926 ; "Affairs in N.N. League Muddled," *ibid.*, 24 July 1926; "Rube' Foster Insane; in Chicago Hospital," *ibid.*, 4 September 1926; "St. Louis Man Elected President N.N. League," *ibid.*, 11 September 1926; Wilson, "Eastern Snapshots," *ibid.*, 20 November 1926; Posey, "The Sportive Realm," *ibid.*, 27 November 1926; Frank A. Young, "Directors of National League Hold Future of Our Baseball in Their Hands," *Chicago Defender*, 11 September 1926.

33. "Rain Wrecks Opening Day for Hilldale," *Philadelphia Tribune*, 7 May 1927; Howe, "Sport Sidelights," *ibid.*, 19 May 1927; "'Nip' Winters George Carr and Washington Suspended Indefinitely by Bolden," *ibid.*, 9 June 1927; "Daisies Lose Thursday, Win Saturday to Senators," *ibid.*, 19 June 1927; Howe, "Sport Sidelights," *ibid.*; Howe, "Sport Sidelights," *ibid.*, 14 July 1927; Lanctot, 143–157.

34. "Ed Bolden, Hilldale Mentor, Suffers Nervous Breakdown," *Philadelphia Tribune*, 29 September 1927; "Bill Francis Signs as Manager of Hilldale for 1928," *ibid.*, 15 December 1927; "Charlie Freeman Succeeds Bolden as Hilldale Head," *Chicago Defender*, 26 November 1927; "Bill Francis Will Manage Daisies," *ibid.*, 17 December 1927; "Ed Bolden Suffers Nervous Breakdown," *Pittsburgh Courier*, 1 October 1927; Wilson, "Sport Shots," *ibid.*, 29 October 1927; "Bolden 'Let Out' as Head of Hilldale Baseball Club," *ibid.*, 10 December 1927; Wilson, "Sport Shots," *ibid.*

35. Edward Bolden, "Bolden Back in Perfect Health, Proffers Views," *Philadelphia Tribune*, 2 February 1928; Randy Dixon, "Hilldale and Giants Quit Eastern Loop," *ibid.*, 15 March 1928; "Freeman Out as Hilldale Quits Eastern League," *Chicago Defender*, 17 March 1928.

36. Quoted in "Nutter Backed by Magnates Defies Bolden," *Philadelphia Tribune*, 15 March 1928.

37. Quoted in Wilson, "Hilldale Withdraws from League," *Pittsburgh Courier*, 17 March 1928.

38. "Ed Bolden Explains Hilldale's Position," *ibid.*, 31 March 1928.

39. Edward Bolden, "Bolden Tells Why

Hilldale Quit Circuit," *Philadelphia Tribune*, 29 March 1928.

40. *Ibid.*

41. "Eastern League, Punctured Already, Gets Flat Tire," *Chicago Defender*, 21 April 1928; Wilson, "Eastern League Will Continue," *ibid.*, 28 April 1928; "Eastern League Bubble Bursts as Moguls Disagree," *ibid.*, 5 May 1928; "Eastern League Disbands," *Pittsburgh Courier*, 21 April 1928; "Jap Champs to Play Hilldale," *ibid.*, 12 May 1928; "Eastern League Disbands; Fate Long Predicted," *Philadelphia Tribune*, 18 April 1928; Randy Dixon, "Sport Sidelights," *ibid.*; "Veteran Outfielder and Star Pitcher Will Play for Daisies; Report Soon," *ibid.*, 29 March 1928; "Hilldale Club Battles House of David Sat.," *ibid.*, 28 June 1928; "Bolden's Pets Wreck House of David; Divide with the Bacharachs at the Seashore," *ibid.*, 5 July 1928; "12,000 Watch Hilldale and Rivals Split," *ibid.*, 19 July 1928; "Fandom Eagerly Awaits Initial Fray of Series to Determine Supremacy," *ibid.*, 13 September 1928; Dixon, "Sport Sidelights," *ibid.*, 20 September 1928; Lanctot.

42. Dixon, "Need of Baseball in East Apparent; Bolden the Logical Reorganizer," *Philadelphia Tribune*, 9 August 1928; Wilson, "Baseball League in East Vital to Future Welfare of All Clubs," *Pittsburgh Courier* 18 August 1928.

43. *Ibid.*

44. *Ibid.*; Wilson, "Sport Shots," *Pittsburgh Courier*, 24 November 1928; Otto Briggs, "New League Is Unlikely Says Baseball Star," *Philadelphia Tribune*, 13 December 1928; Bolden, "Hilldale Directors Recommend League," *ibid.*; Briggs, "Fan Proposes a Mixed League," *ibid.*, 20 December 1928; Lanctot, 190–191.

45. "Eastern League Formed, Grays Join," *Pittsburgh Courier*, 19 January 1929; Wilson, "American Negro League Flays Barnstorming; Reserves Named," *ibid.*, 2 March 1929; "A.N. League Makes Laws," *ibid.*, 8 June 1929; "Possibility of New Baseball League to Replace Defunct Eastern Circuit Looms in Conclave Here Next Month," *Philadelphia Tribune*, 3 January 1929; "System of Rotating Umps Agreed by Baseball Magnates at Parley Here," *ibid.*, 28 February 1929; Lanctot, 192–193.

46. "A.N. League Makes Laws," *Pitts-*

burgh Courier, 8 June 1929; "Baseball War Looms as East Raids Western Clubs," *Chicago Tribune*, 13 July 1929; Dixon, "Sport Sidelights," *Philadelphia Tribune*, 25 April 1929; "Baseball War Between American and National Negro Leagues Looming," *ibid.*, 15 July 1929; Dubbia Ardee, "Antics of Cum Posey Are Likely to Harm Future of Organized Baseball," *ibid.*, 1 August 1929.

47. Isaac H. Nutter, "Ike Nutter Threatens New League," *Pittsburgh Courier*, 26 January 1929.

48. Syd Pollock, "Syd Pollock Calls New League 'Joke,' Makes Grave Charges," *Pittsburgh Courier*, 3 August 1929.

49. Syd Pollock, "Fur Flies in Posey-Pollock Verbal Battle as Syd Answers," *ibid.*, 24 August 1929.

50. Wilson, "Sport Shots," *ibid.*, 31 August 1929.

51. *Ibid.*

52. *Ibid.*

53. Dixon, "Sport Sidelights," *Philadelphia Tribune*, 7 March 1929; Orrin C. Evans, "Hilldale Park Murderer Is Penitent; Lays Killing of Mate to Insane Passion," *ibid.*, 23 May 1929; "Fists Fly as Daisy Outfit Ties H'stead," *ibid.*; "Clan Rallies in Eleventh to Top Foes," *ibid.*

54. The "Scout," "Strong, Hilldale Hurler, Sustains Fractured Skull When Struck by Brick," *ibid.*, 5 September 1929.

55. *Ibid.*; Joseph H. Rainey, "'No Malice' Says Strong, Daisy Hurler," *ibid.*, 12 September 1929.

56. Ardee, "Antics of Cum Posey," *ibid.*, 1 August 1929.

57. *Ibid.*

58. "Negro Umps at Hilldale," *ibid.*

59. "Hilldale Again," *ibid.*, 8 August 1929.

60. Dixon, "Sport Sidelights," *ibid.*, 5 September 1929.

61. Wilson, "Sport Shots," *Pittsburgh Courier*, 12 October 1929; Wilson, "Sport Shots," *ibid.*, 30 November 1929; "American Negro League Votes to Disband," *ibid.*, 22 February 1930; "American Negro League Disbands; Teams Enter Independent Field," *Philadelphia Tribune*, 20 February 1930.

62. Wilson, "Sport Shots," *Pittsburgh Courier*, 1 March 1930.

63. "Clan Darby Status in Doubt," *ibid.*,

5 April 1930; Wilson, "Sport Shots," *ibid.*, 19 April 1930; Wilson, "Sport Shots," *ibid.*, 26 April 1930; "Bolden Loses in Effort to Bust Daisies," *Philadelphia Tribune*, 3 April 1930; Lanctot, 202–204.

64. "Ed Bolden to Head Up New 'Hillsdale' Club," *Pittsburgh Courier*, 19 April 1930; Wilson, "Sport Shots," *ibid.*, 26 April 1930; "Ed Bolden to Organize New Ball Outfit," *Philadelphia Tribune*, 10 April 1930; Dixon, "Sport Sidelights," *ibid.*; "Lincoln Giants, Hilldale and Bolden's Latest Club to Furnish Pastime," *ibid.*, 17 April 1930; Dick Sun, "Original Hilldale Club to Open Home Season on May 3 with Camden Nine," *ibid.*, 24 April 1930.

65. Dixon, "Sport Sidelights," *ibid.*, 24 April 1930.

Chapter Four

1. *Ibid.*

2. Randy Dixon, "Sports Sidelights," *Philadelphia Tribune*, 29 January 1931.

3. *Ibid.*

4. Dixon, *Philadelphia Tribune*, 26 February 1931.

5. *Ibid.*

6. Dixon, "Sports Sidelights," *ibid.*, 5 March 1931.

7. Frank "Fay" Young, "Fay Says," *Pittsburgh Courier*, 19 September 1931; W. Rollo Wilson, "Sport Shorts," *ibid.*, 31 October 1931; *Ibid.*, 31 October 1931.

8. Cumberland Posey, "'Cum' Posey's Pointed Paragraphs," *ibid.*, 26 December 1931.

9. *Ibid.*

10. *Pittsburgh Courier*, 2 July 1932; Leslie Heaphy, *The Negro Leagues 1869–1960* (Jefferson, NC: McFarland, 2003), 56–68.

11. *Philadelphia Tribune*, 18 February 1932, 25 February 1932.

12. *Ibid.*, 21 April 1932, 26 May 1932.

13. *Ibid.*, 23 June 1932.

14. *Ibid.*, 28 July 1932.

15. *Ibid.*, 28 July 1932.

16. *Ibid.*

17. *Ibid.*, 8 September 1932.

18. Neil Lanctot, *Negro League Baseball: The Rise and Ruin of a Black Institution* (Philadelphia: University of Pennsylvania Press, 2004), 25.

19. *Philadelphia Tribune*, 8 September 1932.

20. *Ibid.*

21. *Ibid.*

22. *Pittsburgh Courier*, 14 January 1933, 11 February 1933.

23. *Ibid.*, 11 March 1933.

24. *Ibid.*, 18 March 1933.

25. Leslie Heaphy, *The Negro Leagues 1869–1960* (Jefferson, NC: McFarland, 2003), 93.

26. Find info later.

27. *Pittsburgh Courier*, 1 July 1933, 29 July 1933, 5 August 1933, 30 September 1933.

28. Quoted in W. Rollo Wilson, "Sport Shots," *ibid.*, 4 February 1933.

29. *Ibid.*

30. *Philadelphia Tribune*, 9 February 1933.

31. *Ibid.*

32. Wilson, "Sport Shots," *Pittsburgh Courier*, 25 February 1933.

33. Quoted in *Ibid.*.

34. *Philadelphia Tribune*, 16 March 1933.

35. *Ibid.*

36. *Philadelphia Tribune*, 16 March 1933.

37. *Philadelphia Tribune*, 23 March 1933.

38. *Ibid.*

39. *Ibid.*, 13 April 1933.

40. *Ibid.*

41. "Philadelphia Stars, Greatest Defensive Club in the East," *Colored Baseball and Sports Monthly* 1, No. 4 (October 1934): 18, in Edward Bolden Papers, Box 186–1, Folder 21; Manuscript Division, Moorland-Spingarn Research Center, Howard University.

42. *Ibid.*

43. *Philadelphia Tribune*, 27 April 1933, 4 May 1933, 11 May 1933.

44. *Ibid.*, 11 May 1933.

45. *Ibid.*

46. *Ibid.*, 18 May 1933.

47. James E. Overmyer, *Black Ball and the Boardwalk: The Bacharach Giants of Atlantic City, 1916–1929* (Jefferson, NC: McFarland, 2015), 188.

48. *Philadelphia Tribune*, 6 April 1933, 4 May 1933.

49. *Ibid.*, 22 June 1933.

50. *Ibid.*, 22 June 1933, 24 August 1933.

51. *Philadelphia Tribune*, 17 August 1933.

52. *Ibid.*

53. *Ibid.*, 22 June 1933; Lanctot, 225.

54. *Philadelphia Tribune*, 29 June, 6 July, 10 August 1933.

55. Holway, 80–88.

56. "Philadelphia Stars, Greatest Defensive Club in the East," *Colored Baseball and Sports Monthly* 1, No. 4 (October 1934): 18, in Edward Bolden Papers, Collection 186–1, Folder 21; Manuscript Division, Moorland-Spingarn Research Center, Howard University.

Chapter Five

1. *Pittsburgh Courier*, 30 December 1933.

2. *Ibid.*

3. *Ibid.*

4. Chester Washington, "Sez 'Ches,'" *Ibid.*, 13 January 1934, 20 January 1934; *Ibid.*, 10 February 1934.

5. *Ibid.*, 17 February 1934; W. Rollo Wilson, "Sport Shots," *ibid.*, 24 February 1934; *Philadelphia Tribune*, 15 February 1934.

6. *Philadelphia Tribune*, 15 March 1934.

7. *Ibid.*

8. *Ibid.*, 1 February 1934.

9. *Philadelphia Tribune*, 22 March 1934.

10. *Philadelphia Tribune*, 1 February 1934, 22 March 1934.

11. *Philadelphia Tribune*, 17 May 1934.

12. *Philadelphia Tribune*, 31 May 1934.

13. *Philadelphia Tribune*, 14 June 1934, 28 June 1934, 5 July 1934, 12 July 1934.

14. *Philadelphia Tribune*, 7 June 1934.

15. *Philadelphia Tribune*, 5 July 1934.

16. *Philadelphia Tribune*, 12 July 1934.

17. *Philadelphia Tribune*, 19 July 1934.

18. *Philadelphia Tribune*, 9 August 1934.

19. Lanctot, 30–33; Rich Westcott, *The Mogul*, 84–85.

20. *Philadelphia Tribune*.

21. *Philadelphia Tribune*, 12 July 1934, 6 September 1934, 13 September 1934; Lanctot, 35–39.

22. *Philadelphia Tribune*, 3 August 1934, 9 August 1934, 16 August 1934, 23 August 1934; Jack Pace, "Slim Jones," *Colored Baseball and Sports Monthly* 1, No. 4 (October 1934) in Edward Bolden Papers Box 186–1 Folder 21; Manuscript Division Moorland-Spingarn Research Center, Howard University.

23. *Philadelphia Tribune*, 30 August 1934.

24. *Philadelphia Tribune*, 6 September 1934.

25. *Philadelphia Tribune*, 13 September 1934.

26. *Philadelphia Tribune*, 4 October 1934.

27. *Philadelphia Tribune*, 26 July 1934.

28. *Philadelphia Tribune*, 3 August 1934, 16 August 1934.

29. *Philadelphia Tribune*, 20 September 1934, 27 September 1934, 4 October 1934.

30. *Ibid.*

31. Quoted in Ed Harris, "And Bright Stars," *Philadelphia Tribune*, 11 October 1934.

32. *Philadelphia Tribune*, 27 September, 4 October, 11 October 1934.

33. Ed Harris, "To Be or Not to Be," 4 October 1934.

34. *Ibid.*

35. *Ibid.*

36. *Ibid.*

37. Harris, "And Bright Stars," 11 October 1934.

38. *Ibid.*

39. Harris, "Cole Refuses to Pay League Salaries Due," 8 November 1934.

40. Harris, "Second the Motion," 15 November 1934, 20 December 1934.

41. Lanctot, 30–33.

Chapter Six

1. *Philadelphia Independent*, 3 February 1935; Randy Dixon, "The Sports Bugle," *ibid.*, 10 February 1935.

2. *Ibid.*, 10 March 1935; *Philadelphia Tribune*, 14 March 1935.

3. *Ibid.*

4. Ed R. Harris, "Now the Fun Begins," *Philadelphia Tribune*, 14 March 1935.

5. John L. Clark, "1934 Season Considered Successful; Baseball Highlights Recalled," *Pittsburgh Courier*, 5 January 1935.

6. *Ibid.*

7. *Ibid.*

8. Randy Dixon, "Ed Bolden Completes 25 Years in Baseball with Clean, Unmatched Record," *Philadelphia Independent*, 22 September 1935.

9. *Ibid.*

10. *Ibid.*

11. Randy Dixon, "Bolden, Ill in Hospital, Sees Pennant for Stars," *Philadelphia Independent*, 31 March 1935.

12. *Ibid.*

13. "Bolden Charges League with 'Dirty Politics,'" *Ibid.*, 7 April 1935.

14. Quoted in *Ibid.*

15. "Bolden Eyes Loop Start with Porter Charleston Topping Ace Mound Staff," *ibid.*, 28 April 1935; "Fate of League Baseball Here Rests on 3 Members of Bolden's Stars," *ibid.*, 5 May 1935; "Baseball League Launches Saturday with Boldenmen Meeting Grays," *ibid.*, 5 May 1935; "Stars Vs. Eagles in Opener Saturday," *ibid.*, 12 May 1935; Dixon, "Record Opening Day Crowd See Boldenmen Rule," *ibid.*, 19 May 1935; "Philly Stars Start Season with Victory," *Philadelphia Tribune*, 18 April 1935; "Stars Collect 3 Victories O'er Weekend," *ibid.* 2 May 1935; "Eagles Furnish Opposition for Home Opener," *ibid.*, 9 May 1935; "Stars Tag Brooklyn for 3," *ibid.*, 16 May 1935.

16. Dixon "Spearman Expected to Be First Man Obtained by Boldenmen in Shakeup," *Philadelphia Independent*, 23 June 1935: Dixon, "Shakeup Sure in Stars' Camp as Bolden Gets Mad," *ibid.*, 30 June 1935; "Owners Try to Block Bolden," *ibid.*, 7 July 1935; Dick Sun, "Stars Back in Form, Start 2nd Half Flag Fight Taking 3 of 4," *ibid.*, 14 July 1935; Dixon, "Stars Keep First Place as Casey Breaks Leg; New Hurler Signed," *ibid.*, 21 July 1935: "Boldenmen on Run Rampage, Annihilate Grays and Sweep Series with Newark Nine," *ibid.*, 28 July 1935'; "Slim Jones Suspended, Two Others Are Fined," *ibid.*, 11 August 1935; Dixon, "Charleston Hero as Craws Snare World Series," *ibid.*, 29 September 1935.

17. "Slim Jones Suspended, Two Others Are Fined," *ibid.*, 11 August 1935.

18. *Ibid.*

19. *Ibid.*

20. Quoted in "Bolden to Wreck Present Phila. Stars Outfit; Will Assemble Great Machine," *ibid.*

21. *Philadelphia Tribune*, 29 August 1935.

22. *Ibid.*

23. Jules Tygiel, *Past Time: Baseball as History* (Oxford: Oxford University Press, 2000), 136–137.

24. Roberta Newman and Joel Nathan Rosen, *Black Baseball, Black Business: Race Enterprise and the Fate of the Segregated Dollar* (Oxford: University of Mississippi Press, 2014), 1266–1411; Rob Ruck, *Sandlot Seasons: Sport in Black Pittsburgh* (Urbana: University of Illinois Press, 1993), 137–165.

25. *Ibid.*

26. Dixon, "The Sports Bugle," *Philadelphia Independent*, 18 August 1935.

27. *Ibid.*

28. Dixon, "Baseball Moguls Establish Record for Doing Nothing," and "Sports Bugle," *Philadelphia Independent*, 2 February 1936; "Bolden League Prexy," *ibid.*, 15 March 1936.

29. *Ibid.*, 2 February 1936; Dixon, "Fans Put Baseball on Spot," *ibid.*, 16 February 1936; John L. Clark, "Official Warns Magnates of Impending Pitfalls," *ibid.*, 8 March 1936.

30. Dixon, "Stearns, Suttles, Brown Head Here, Stevens Jumps," *ibid.*, 5 April 1936; "Stars Fail to Land Chicago Aces; Slim Jones Ailing," *ibid.*, 12 April 1936; Dixon, "The Sports Bugle," and "Bolden Faces Problem with Gaps in Infield," *ibid.*, 19 April 1936; Dixon, "Bolden Cracks Whip as Campaign Nears," *ibid.*, 3 May 1936. "Ed Bolden Will Actively Manage Stars in Title Dash; Cockrells Ready," *Philadelphia Tribune*, 26 March 1936; Ed Harris, "Ed Bolden Expects to Be Strong Contender in 1936 Nat'l. Assn. Race," *ibid.*, 16 April 1936.

31. "Local Fans Acclaim Phila. Stars' Feat," *Philadelphia Independent*, 17 May 1936; Dixon, "The Sports Bugle," *ibid.*, 14 June 1936; Dick Sun, "Stars Lose League Lead; Drop Three in Row to Elites," *ibid.*, 28 Jun3 1936; "Stars-Elites Tied, League Title Decided This Week," *ibid.*, 5 July 1936; "First Half Ends with Title Undecided," and Dixon, "Sports Bugle," *ibid.*, 12 July 1936.

32. Ed Bolden, "Bolden Says League Secretary Guilty of Misusing Office," *ibid.*, 23 August 1936. Bolden, "Bolden Gives Views on 1st Half Title," *Pittsburgh Courier*, 22 August 1936; Cumberland Posey, "Posey's Points," *ibid.*, 25 July 1936, 1 August 1936, and 29 August 1936.

33. Harris, "Empty Barrels," *Philadelphia*

Tribune, 8 October 1936; "Elites Okay Title Frays," *Philadelphia Independent*, 6 September 1936; Dixon, "Loyal Roots Go Broke When Greenlee's Serfs Form Link with Gamblers," *ibid.*, 13 September 1936; Dixon, "Craws-Elites Give Fans Bum's Rush," *ibid.*, 4 October 1936.

34. Harris, "Players and Fans Handed Gold Brick as Owners Run League Any Way They Care," *Philadelphia Tribune*, 8 October 1936.

35. *Ibid.*; Harris, "Empty Barrels," *ibid.*

36. Dixon, "Craws-Elites Give Fans Bum's Rush," *Philadelphia Independent*, 4 October 1936.

37. Bolden, "Ed Bolden Answers Scribe's Blast on Organized Baseball," *ibid.*, 18 October 1936; Bolden, "League Chairman Answers Critics of Negro Baseball," *Pittsburgh Courier*, 31 October 1936.

38. *Ibid.*

39. John L. Clark, "Clark Says Sepia Loop Will Operate in 1937," *Philadelphia Independent*, 25 October 1936.

40. Posey, "Naming of President, Sec'y Set for Jan. 19," *Pittsburgh Courier*, 16 January 1937; "Greenlee Named President of National Association as Josh Gibson Goes to Grays," *Philadelphia Tribune*, 25 March 1937; "Declines to Head National League," *Philadelphia Independent*, 14 February 1937.

41. "Baseball Leagues Far Apart as Opener Nears," *Chicago Defender*, 3 April 1937; "Two Leagues May Combine If the Status of Six Ball Players Can Be Determined," *Philadelphia Independent*, 28 March 1937.

42. Robert Peterson, *Only the Ball Was White: A History of Legendary Black Players and All-Black Professional Teams* (Oxford: Oxford University Press, 1970), 93–94, 135–136.

43. Chester Washington, "Sez Ches," *Pittsburgh Courier*, 31 July 1937; "Negro Leaguers Top Outlaws; Taylor Is Star," *Philadelphia Tribune*, 25 September 1937; Earl Barnes, "Baseball Briefs," *Philadelphia Independent*, 11 July 1937; Barnes, "Prodigal Sons Return but Get Nixed by League," *ibid.*, 25 July 1937; Barnes, "Baseball Briefs," 15 August 1937.

44. Dixon, "Report 'Ump' Forbes Beaten by Yanks in Club House Brawl," *Philadel-*

phia Independent, 13 June 1937; Barnes, "Baseball Briefs," *ibid.*, 11 July 1937; "National League Heads to Back Umpires in Enforcing Discipline," *ibid.*, 1 August 1937.

45. Posey, "Posey's Points," *Pittsburgh Courier*, 14 August 1937.

46. *Ibid.*

47. Greenlee, "Greenlee Claims Proposed 'World Series' Is Unsanctioned by League," *ibid.*, 18 September 1937.

48. Greenlee Letter to Unknown Recipient, 8 September 1937, Effa Manley Papers, Newark Public Library.

49. "Scrappy Infielder to Be Boss of Boldenmen," *Philadelphia Independent*, 28 February 1937; Barnes, "Stars Take Three from Yanks as Umpires' Decisions Irk Both Fans and Players," *ibid.*, 13 June 1937.

50. *Philadelphia Tribune*, 1 July 1937, 24 July 1937.

51. *Ibid.*

52. "Ed Bolden Predicts Pennant," *Philadelphia Tribune*, 28 April 1938; Dixon, "The Sports Bugle," *ibid.*, 5 May 1938; Dick Sun, "Stars Near League Lead," *ibid.*, 9 June 1938; Dixon, "The Sports Bugle," 23 June 1938; Barnes, "Perkins, Patterson, Carter to 'Stars' for Benson, Cash; Signs Giles and Spearman; Reds Parnell to Return," *Philadelphia Independent*, 13 March 1938; Barnes, "Stars Arrive in Texas; Wilson in Shape; Casey, Page, Roberts Release," *ibid.*, 10 April 1938; "Ed Bolden Visions 1938 Flag; Slim Jones Flashing 1934 Form," *ibid.*, 1 May 1938; Barens, "Baseball Briefs," 29 May 1938; Barnes, "Beat Eagles; Win Three in a Row from Senators; Sign Miller; Patterson Plays," *ibid.*, 12 June 1938; Barnes, "Baseball Briefs," *ibid.*, 19 June 1938; Barnes, "Perkins, Wilson Hurt; Stars Beat Eagles, Elites; Lose to Grays, Yanks," *ibid.*, 21 August 1938; "Stars Toss Away Two to Baltimore Elites in Labor Day Games," *ibid.*, 11 September 1938.

53. Dixon, "The Sports Bugle," *Philadelphia Tribune*, 26 May 1938 and 21 July 1938; Dixon, "S. American Loop Lures Players," *ibid.*; Barnes, "Baseball Briefs," *Philadelphia Tribune.*, 12 June 1938, 17 July 1938, 14 August 1938, and 25 September 1938; "Better Organization and Umpiring Needed for Negro Circuits," *ibid.*, 31 July 1938.

54. Dixon, "The Sports Bugle," *Philadelphia Tribune*, 23 June 1938.

55. *Ibid.*

56. Ed R. Harris, "The Stars Are Stars," *ibid.*, 4 August 1938.

57. Harris, "Our Jud," *ibid.*, 18 August 1938.

58. "'Stars' Southpaw Dies in Baltimore," *Philadelphia Tribune*, 27 November 1938.

59. Ed Gottlieb Letter to Effa Manley, 4 April 1939; Ed Gottlieb Letter to the Owners of the Negro National League, 4 April 1939; Effa Manley Letter to Ed Gottlieb, 5 April 1939; Ed Gottlieb Letter to Effa Manley, 5 April 1939; Ed Gottlieb Letter to Effa Manley, 7 April 1939; Ed Gottlieb Letter to Effa Manley, 20 April 1939; Ed Gottlieb Letter to Effa Manley, 28 April 1939; Effa Manley Letter to Ed Gottlieb, 28 April 1939; Ed Gottlieb Letter to Effa Manley, 5 May 1939; Ed Gottlieb Letter to Effa Manley, 27 May 1939, Effa Manley Papers, Newark Public Library. Barnes, "Tom Wilson Elected President of N.N.L.; Greenlee Resigns," *Philadelphia Independent*, 26 February 1939.

60. Barnes, "Seek Hughes, Snow; Hunter's Status Puzzles Bolden," *Philadelphia Independent*, 12 February 1939; Barnes, "Williams Rounds Out Infield; Team Stronger as Spring Grind Starts," *ibid.*, 16 April 1939; Barnes, "New Men Impress; Williams' Status Still Doubtful," *ibid.*, 7 May 1939; Barnes, "Bolden Nine on Edge for Opening Fray with Strong Elite Giants," and "Baseball Briefs," *ibid.*, 14 May 1939; Barnes, "Dunn Replaces Wilson as Pilot; New Hurler Signed; Lose to Grays and Eagles," *ibid.*, 25 June 1939; Barnes, "Lefty Missouri, McHenry Pitch Masterful Games," *ibid.*, 9 July 1939; Barnes, "Baseball Briefs," 16 July 1939; Barnes, "Baseball Briefs," 30 July 1939; Barnes, "Stars Win 13 Straight; Beat Newark 4 in a Row; 'Pat's' 2 Bagger Wins 15 Inning Fray; in 2nd," *ibid.*, 20 August 1939; Barnes, "Baseball Briefs," *ibid.*, 24 September 1939.

61. Barnes, "Baseball Briefs," *Ibid.*, 28 May 1939.

Chapter Seven

1. *Philadelphia Tribune*, 15 February 1940, 14 December 1939.

2. *Ibid.*, 15 February 1940, 29 February 1940.

3. Effa Manley, Letter to William H. Hastie, 12 February 1940. Effa Manley Papers, Newark Public Library.

4. *Ibid.*

5. *Ibid.*

6. *Ibid.*, 29 February 1940, 14 March 1940, 11 and April 1940; "Vote by Pompez Breaks Tie; Manley's Moves Defeated," *Philadelphia Independent*, 3 March 1940; Cum Posey, "Posey's Points," *Pittsburgh Courier*, 24 February 1940; "Baseball Moguls Meet in Chicago," *ibid.*

7. Ed Gottlieb, Letter to Effa Manley, 20 September 1940, 27 September 1940, and 16 October 1940, Effa Manley Papers, Newark Public Library.

8. Gottlieb, Letter to Effa Manley, 4 December 1939, Effa Manley Papers, Newark Public Library.

9. *Ibid.*

10. *Ibid.*

11. Gottlieb, Letter to Effa Manley, 5 August 1940, Effa Manley Papers, Newark Public Library.

12. *Ibid.*

13. Barnes, "McHenry Threatens to 'Jump' Stars; Parnell, Williams, Harris, Patterson, Thompson May Join New 'Outlaw' Team," *Philadelphia Independent*, 24 March 1940; Barnes, "Bolden Reports Nine Philly Stars Signed Up; to Start Training April 15," *ibid.*, 31 March 1940; Barnes, "Ace Right Hander Still Seeking Pay Increase; Benson Ready to Sail," *ibid.*, 7 April 1940.

14. Rogosin, 168–170.

15. *Ibid.*, 170–175.

16. *Philadelphia Tribune*, 7 August 1941.

17. Effa Manley, Letter to Dr. J.B. Martin and Tom Wilson, 15 April 1940; Effa Manley Papers, Newark Public Library.

18. Effa Manley, Letter to Dr. J.B. Martin, 25 November 1940, Effa Manley Papers, Newark Public Library.

19. *Ibid.*

20. Barnes, "Baseball Briefs," *Philadelphia Independent*, 16 June 1940; Barnes, "Duckett's 'Pinch' Single Knocks Yanks into Cellar; Stars Take Double-Header," *ibid.*, 7 July 1940; Barnes, "Baseball Briefs," *ibid.*, 14 July 1940; "Benson, McHenry in East Vs. West Classic; Benson to Start in Center," *ibid.*, 18 August 1940; "1940 Philadelphia Stars," Baseball-Reference.com.

21. Barnes, "Dunn Re-Appointed as Manager of Stars," *Philadelphia Independent*, 9 June 1940; "Bea, Hayes, Thompson Made Free Agents in Bolden Team Shake-Up," *ibid.*, 4 August 1940.

22. Barnes, "Poor Food, Climate Cause Tossers to Leave Mexico," *ibid.*, 28 July 1940; Barnes, "Baseball Briefs," 11 August 1940; "Dandridge, Roberts Barred as Stars Beat Royals 3–1," *ibid.*, 25 August 1940.

23. "Nat'l-Amerk Leagues to Try Joint Schedule; Map Plans for 1941 at Big Meeting in Baltimore," *Pittsburgh Courier*, 11 January 1941; "Leagues Agree to Drop Ban on Contract 'Jumpers'; Fine of $100 Only Penalty Imposed," *ibid.*, 1 March 1941; "Ed Bolden Plans to Expose Conditions Reported Harmful," *Philadelphia Independent*, 19 January 1941.

24. Maurice Teal, "Bolden Planning Deals; Duckett Signs Contract; Patterson Returning to Stars; Bankhead, Young Brewer May Join Locals," *ibid.*, 30 March 1941; Teal, "Patterson, Duckett, Dunn, McHenry, Benson, Jordan Sure of Posts on Stars," *ibid.*, 13 April 1941; "Stars Only N.N.L. Club to Train at Home Park," *ibid.*, 20 April 1941; Teal, "Jake Dunn, Philly Stars' Pilot, Faces Army Draft; Dunn Awaits Decision of California Board; West in Great Shape," *ibid.*, 4 May 1941; Barnes, "Baseball Briefs," *ibid.*, 18 May 1941; Barnes, "Stars Strong Despite 61-Loss to Cubans," *ibid.*, 18 May 1941; Barnes, "Jake Dunn in Army; May Draft Zollie Wright; N.Y. Black Yanks Play 2 Saturday; Parnell Manager," *ibid.*, 25 May 1941; Barnes, "Oscar Charleston May Pilot Ed Bolden's Stars; Bolden Awaits Reply from Ex-Hilldale Slugger; Stars Sign Johnson; Split Two," *ibid.*, 8 June 1941; Barnes, "Baseball Briefs," *ibid.*, 15 June 1941; Barnes, "Campbell, Miller Go; Sign Three Players; Other Trades Loom," *ibid.*, 22 June 1941; Barnes, "Patterson, Benson Jump Stars; Leave for Mexico; Elites and Grays Lose to Stars; Pass Yankees; Charleston Plays," *ibid.*, 29 June 1941; Barnes, "Baseball Briefs," *ibid.*, 28 September 1941.

25. "Statement of Employee's Record, William Penn Annex of the Philadelphia Post Office," 1 July 1944, Edward Bolden Papers, Box 186–1, Folder 21; Manuscript Division, Moorland-Spingarn Research Center, Howard University.

26. Ed Bolden, Press Release; Henry McHenry Letter to Ed Bolden, 9 October 1941; Ed Bolden Letter to Henry McHenry, 12 October 1941; Bolden Letter to Mr. James Bell, 12 October 1941; Bolden Letter to Edward A. Davis, 12 October 1941; Bolden Letter to L.C. Davis, 12 October 1941, Edward Bolden Papers, Box 186–1, Folder 21; Manuscript Division, Moorland-Spingarn Research Center, Howard University.

27. McKinley "Bunny" Downs Letter to Edward Bolden, 22 August 1941; Downs Letter to Bolden, 8 September 1941; Bolden Letter to Downs, 12 September 1941, Edward Bolden Papers, Box 186–1, Folder 21; Manuscript Division, Moorland-Spingarn Research Center, Howard University.

28. Raymond Pace Alexander Letter to Ed Bolden, April 14, 1942, Edward Bolden Papers, Box 186–1, Folder 8; Manuscript Division, Moorland-Spingarn Research Center, Howard University.

29. Edward Bolden Letter to Walter Purnell, 12 April 1942; Bolden Letter to Robert H. Johnson, 3 May 1942; W. Howard Still Sr. Letter to Bolden, 25 June 1942; Bolden Letter to Still, 26 August 1942. Edward Bolden Papers, Box 186–1, Folder 21; Manuscript Division, Moorland-Spingarn Research Center, Howard University.

30. Kent Jackson Letter to Edward Bolden, 17 April 1942; Bolden Letter to Jackson, 19 April 1942; Bolden Letter to Jackson, 17 May 1942; Leon M. Snead Letter to Bolden, 15 August 1942; Bolden Letter to Snead, 23 August 1942, Edward Bolden Papers, Box 186–1, Folder 21; Manuscript Division, Moorland-Spingarn Research Center, Howard University.

31. Negro National League Treasurer's Report for the Season of 1941; Ed Gottlieb Letter to Effa Manley, 11 May 1942; Gottlieb Letter to Effa Manley, 7 August 1942, Effa Manley Papers, Newark Public Library.

32. John L. Clark Letter to Effa Manley, 11 December 1942, Effa Manley Papers, Newark Public Library; "Tom Wilson Retained as NNL Prexy," *Pittsburgh Courier*, 21 February 1942; Wendell Smith, "Smitty's Sports Spurts," *ibid.*, 28 February 1942; Cum Posey, "Posey's Points," *ibid.*, 7 March 1942.

33. "Failure to Agree on Player Transfers

May Soon Cramp Negro Organized Baseball," *Philadelphia Independent*, 14 March 1942; "Baseball Outlook Dark; N.A.L. Decree, War May Cripple Philly Stars Hope," *ibid.*, 22 March 1942.

34. Roscoe Coleman, "New League Formed to Operate East-West," *ibid.*, 29 March 1942; "New Baseball Circuit Doomed to Early Death," *ibid.*, 19 April 1942.

35. *Philadelphia Tribune*, 4 April 1942.

36. Quoted in "Dykes Would Use Negro Ball Players," *Philadelphia Independent*, 22 March 1942.

37. *Ibid.*

38. *Ibid.*

39. "Six Big League Clubs Scout Stars-Eagles, Grays-Monarchs, Games," *ibid.*, 26 March 1942.

40. *Ibid.*

41. David K. Wiggins, "Wendell Smith, the *Pittsburgh Courier-Journals*, and the Campaign to Include Blacks in Organized Baseball, 1933–1945," *Journal of Sport History* 2, No. 1 (Summer 1983): 5–29.

42. *Philadelphia Tribune*, 18 April, 25 April, 25 July, 1 August 1942.

43. Wiggins, "Wendell Smith," 5–29.

44. *Philadelphia Tribune*, 1 August 1942, 22 August 1942, 12 December 1942; Bruce Kuklick, *To Every Thing a Season: Shibe Park and Urban Philadelphia 1909–1976* (Princeton: Princeton University Press, 1971), 145–148.

45. Coleman, "Phila. Stars to Field Best Team in History," *Philadelphia Independent*, 8 March 1942.

46. Quoted in Coleman, "Bolden Seeks Players; Will Give Local Sandlotters a Fair Chance, Bolden Says," *ibid.*, 5 April 1942.

47. *Ibid.*

48. Coleman, "Phila. Stars Strong; Should Take League Pennant, Bolden Says," *ibid.*, 26 April 1942.

49. *Philadelphia Tribune*, 23 May 1942, 30 May 1942, 8 August 1942, 15 August 1942.

50. *Philadelphia Tribune*, 6 February 1943.

51. *Philadelphia Tribune*, 10 April 1943, 15 May 1943.

52. *Philadelphia Tribune*, 10 July 1943; "Baseball War On; Posey Berates Martin on Player 'Steal' Deal," *Philadelphia Independent*, 9 May 1943; "Must Return 10 Players; Vote Baseball Moguls; Owners Kiss, Makeup at Quaker City Powwow," *ibid.*, 6 June 1943; Coleman, "Ed Bolden Peeved; Accuses Posey of Taking Players Gotten from Atlanta," *ibid.*, 11 July 1943.

53. Marty Weintraub Letter to Effa Manley, 23 February 1943; Cum Posey Letter to Mr. Eastman of the Office of Defense Transportation, 13 March 1943; Effa Manley Papers, Newark Public Library; "Baseball's Future Dark Bus Travel Curtailed," *Philadelphia Independent*, 4 April 1943; Coleman, "12 Race Baseball Clubs Doomed by ODT Edict," *ibid.*, 11 April 1943; "NNL Owners Decide to Operate Baseball with 7 Teams; NAL in Quandary," *ibid.*, 18 April 1943.

54. Leslie Heaphy, *The Negro Leagues 1869–1960* (Jefferson, NC: McFarland, 2003), 120.

55. *Philadelphia Tribune*, 16 May 1942, 30 May 1942, 8 August 1942, 15 August 1942, 15 May 1943.

56. *Philadelphia Tribune*, 12 June 1943; Kuklick, 145–148; Rich Westcott, *Philadelphia's Old Ballparks* (Philadelphia: Temple University Press, 1996), 186.

57. *Philadelphia Tribune*, 26 June, 3 July 1943; 30 June 1945.

58. *Philadelphia Tribune*, 9 October 1943, 5 February 1944, 20 May 1944; Coleman, "Baseball Moguls Hedge; Owe Debt of Gratitude to White Park Owners," *Philadelphia Tribune*, 16 January 1944; Westcott, 6.

59. *Philadelphia Tribune*, 1 March 1944, 6 April 1944, 16 September 1944.

60. *Philadelphia Tribune*, 16 September 1944.

61. *Ibid.*, "Phila. Stars Jockeyed Out of NNL Flag Race; Protest Filed Against Grays' Claim; Wilson Silent," *Philadelphia Independent*, 17 September 1944.

62. *Philadelphia Tribune*, 8 January 1944.

63. *Ibid.*

64. *Ibid.*

65. *Philadelphia Tribune*, 18 March 1944.

66. "Landis Makes Race Ball Players Part of Powwow; Move Drives Owners into Open on Issue," *Philadelphia Tribune*, 5 December 1943.

67. "'Up to Clubs'—Landis; Robeson Pleads Cause of Negroes in Majors," *ibid.*, 12 December 1943.

68. *Ibid.*

69. *Philadelphia Tribune*, 16 December 1944, 13 September 1944, 7 October 1944.

70. *Philadelphia Tribune*, 9 December 1944, 16 December 1944.

71. *Philadelphia Tribune*, 14 April 1945, 21 April 1945, 5 May 1945; "Players Too Old? Branch Rickey Nixes Thomas, McDuffie's Brooklyn Dodger Bid," *Philadelphia Independent*, 14 April 1945; "Boston Red Sox Give 3 Tryouts; Robinson, Williams, Jethro Get Tryouts with Boston Red Sox," *ibid.*, 21 April 1945; "2 N.Y. Groups Fight for Negroes in Majors; N.Y. Solons Speed Up Fight to Place Negroes in Majors," *ibid.*, 18 August 1945.

72. *Philadelphia Tribune*, 30 June 1945, 8 January 1944.

73. *Philadelphia Tribune*, 30 June 1945.

74. *Philadelphia Tribune*, 11 July 1945, 21 July 1945, 8 September 1945, 22 September 1945.

75. *Philadelphia Tribune*, 12 May 1945, 25 August 1945, 27 October 1945, 17 November 1945; *Philadelphia* Independent, 27 October 1945.

Chapter Eight

1. Lanctot, *Negro League Baseball*, 320–362.

2. "'Gus' Greenlee Organizes New Six Club League," *Pittsburgh Courier*, 6 January 1945; "Brooklyn Franchise Added to League," *ibid.*, 28 April 1945.

3. Quoted in "Rickey Admits Calling in Jackie Robinson," *ibid.*, 1 September 1945.

4. *Ibid.*

5. "'Gus' Greenlee Organizes New Six Club League."

6. Quoted in "Greenlee Lashes Critics," *ibid.*, 21 April 1945.

7. *Ibid.*

8. Quoted in Wendell Smith, "Join U.S. League or Else," *ibid.*, 12 May 1945.

9. *Ibid.*

10. *Ibid.*

11. *Ibid.*

12. Cum Posey, "Many Problems League Must Solve," *ibid.*, 5 May 1945; "Meeting Winds Up with Same Officers, Same Old Problems," *ibid.*, 22 December 1945.

13. Resolution, Effa Manley Papers, Newark Public Library; "Chandler Turns Down Negro Baseball Protest," *Philadelphia Independent*, 17 November 1945; "Peace or War? Prexy Seeks Baseball Tieup," *ibid.*, 24 November 1945; "Organized Baseball 'Igs' Bid of Colored Leagues," *ibid.*, 22 December 1945.

14. Effa Manley Letter to Dr. J.B. Martin, 26 October 1945; Dr. J.B. Martin Letter to Effa Manley, 29 October 1945, Effa Manley Papers, Newark Public Library. "'Will Not Protest' Says Owner of Kansas City," *Pittsburgh Courier*, 27 October 1945; "Martin Congratulates Rickey on Signing," *ibid.*, 3 November 1945; "Chandler Fails to Recognize Protest of Sepia Moguls," *ibid.*, 17 November 1945.

15. "Race Players May Be in Majors by Spring," *Philadelphia Independent*, 8 December 1945; "Grays Hurler May Play with Dodgers," *ibid.*, 29 December 1945; "Philadelphia Stars Leave for Spring Training Camp; Bolden Retires from P.O., Devote Full Time to Baseball," *ibid.*, 30 March 1946; "Fla. City Bars Robinson, Wright in Mixed Game," *ibid.*; "Kenny Washington Signs to Play with Cleveland Rams," *ibid.*

16. *Philadelphia Tribune*, 26 January 1946, 12 April 1946; "Brown, McHenry, Fillmore, Harris Hurl Stars into Nnl Loop Lead," *Philadelphia Independent*, 15 June 1946; "8 Home Grown Players in Phila. Stars Berths," *ibid.*, 27 July 1946.

17. "Rickey Signs Partlow; Phila. Stars Open Sat.; Stone Jumps to Mexico," *Philadelphia Independent*, 4 May 1946; "Phila. Stars Split Two with N.Y. Cubans, Grays," *ibid.*, 18 March 1946; "Roy Partlow Called Home to Ink Non-Shanghai Note," *ibid.*, 20 July 1946; "Clarkson, Fillmore Leave for Mexico," and "Phila. Stars Drop Last Five Starts," *ibid.*, 3 August 1946.

18. "Montreal Royals Win International Loop Flag; Jackie Robinson Stars," *ibid.*, 31 August 1946; "Montreal Royals Win Little World Series; Jackie Sheds Big Tears of Joy as Season Ends," *ibid.*, 12 October 1946.

19. Wendell Smith, "Posey Balks at 'More Power' Plan for League Presidents," *Pittsburgh Courier*, 5 January 1946.

20. Posey, "The Sports Beat," *ibid.*, 2 February 1946.

21. Smith, "The Sports Beat," *ibid.*, 21 December 1946.

22. Smith, "N.Y. Minister New President of Nat'l League," and "The Sports Beat," *ibid.*, 11 January 1947; Smith, "The Sports Beat," 22 February 1947.

23. "R. Partlow Rejoins Phila. Stars in Ala.," *Philadelphia Independent*, 26 April 1947; "Phila. Stars Tripped by Elites in Opener," *ibid.*, 10 May 1947; "Dodgers' Manager Bert Shotten Says ... Jackie Robinson Will Make Grade in Majors," *ibid.*, 31 May 1947; "Cleveland Indians Buy Larry Doby from Eagles," *ibid.*, 12 July 1947; "Jackie Robinson in the World Series," *ibid.*, 4 October 1947.

24. Brian Carroll, *When to Stop the Cheering?: The Black Press, the Black Community, and the Integration of Professional Baseball* (New York: Routledge, 2007), 159–174.

25. *Pittsburgh Courier*, 14 February 1948, 13 March 1948.

26. *Philadelphia Tribune*, 27 March 1948, 6 April 1948, 1 May 1948, 8 May 1948, 18 May 1948.

27. *Philadelphia Tribune*, 3 February 1948, 28 February 1948; Peterson, 202.

28. *Philadelphia Tribune*, 15 June 1948, 3 February 1948, 28 February 1948; Peterson, 202.

29. "Negro National League Folds," *Philadelphia Tribune*, 4 December 1948; "Dr. Martin Predicts Great Year for Negro Baseball," *ibid.*, 23 April 1949.

30. *Philadelphia Tribune*, 15 February 1949, 18 February 1950; Peterson, 202, 286.

31. *Philadelphia Tribune*, 3 October 1950, 9 January 1951, 10 March 1951, 11 April 1953.

32. *Philadelphia Tribune*, 26 June 1948, 19 March 1949; "Harry Simpson Sold to Cleveland Indians," *Philadelphia Independent*, 29 January 1949.

33. "5 Phila. Star Players 'Jump' to Mexican Loop," *Philadelphia Independent*, 20 May 1950; "4 Negro American League Openers Draw Small Crowds," *ibid.*, 20 May 1950.

34. Wendell Smith, "The Sports Beat," *Pittsburgh Courier*, 17 June 1950.

35. *Philadelphia Tribune*, 3 October 1950, 10 October 1950; W. Rollo Wilson, "Through the Eyes of W. Rollo Wilson"; "Notables to Attend Rites for Bolden," Edward Bolden Papers Box 186–1 Folder 1; Manuscript Division, Moorland-Spingarn Research Center, Howard University

36. Funeral program for Ed Bolden; Wilson, "Through the Eyes of W. Rollo Wilson"; Western Union Telegram, George B. Stevenson to Doctor Hilda Bolden, September 30, 1950; Condolences from Harriet Wright Lemon to Hilda Bolden; Condolence from Russell F. Minton, M.D. to Hilda Bolden; Western Union Telegram, Dr. J.B. Martins, President of the NAL, to Hilda Bolden, October 2, 1950; Western Union Telegram, Ambassador & Mrs. King, Liberian Embassy, to Hilda Bolden; Western Union Telegram, Memphis Red Sox to Family of Edward Bolden, October 2, 1950; Western Union Telegram Wayne L. Hopking to Hilda Bolden, October 2, 1950, Edward Bolden Papers Box 186–1 Folder 1; Manuscript Division, Moorland-Spingarn Research Center, Howard University.

37. *Philadelphia Tribune*, 3 March 1951, 20 January, 22 March, 12 April, 25 June 1952; Letter from McKenzie Wilkins II to Ed Bolden, 28 May 1951, Edward Bolden Papers Box 186–1, Folder 15; Manuscript Division, Moorland-Spingarn Research Center, Howard University.

38. *Philadelphia Tribune*, 19 March 1949.

39. *Philadelphia Tribune*, 10 July 1951; 20 January, 26 July, 26 August 1952.

40. *Philadelphia Tribune*, 14 March 1953, 28 March 1953, 11 April 1953.

Conclusion

1. W. Rollo Wilson, "Through the Eyes of W. Rollo Wilson," Ed Bolden Papers 186–1, Folder 1; Moorland-Spingarn Research Center, Howard University.

Bibliography

Primary Sources

NEWSPAPERS

Chicago Tribune
Philadelphia Independent
Philadelphia Tribune
Pittsburgh Courier

ARCHIVAL COLLECTIONS

Edward Bolden Papers, Manuscript Division, Moorland-Spingarn Research Center, Howard University.

Effa Manley Papers, Newark Public Library.

Lloyd Thompson's Personal Papers, Cash-Thompson Collection, African American Museum in Philadelphia.

Secondary Sources

Bankes, Jim. *The Pittsburgh Crawfords.* Jefferson, NC: McFarland, 2001.

Biddle, Daniel R. *Tasting Freedom: Octavius Catto and the Battle for Equality in Civil War America.* Philadelphia: Temple University Press, 2010.

Browne, Paul. *The Coal Barons Played Cuban Giants: A History of Early Professional Baseball in Pennsylvania, 1886–1896.* Jefferson, NC: McFarland, 2013.

Clark, Dick, and Larry Lester, eds. *The Negro Leagues Book.* Cleveland: The Society for American Baseball Research, 1994.

Carroll, Brian. *When to Stop the Cheering? The Black Press, the Black Community, and the Integration of Professional Baseball.* New York: Routledge, 2007.

DiClerico, James M., and Barry J. Pavelec. *The Jersey Game: The History of Modern Baseball from Its Birth to the Big Leagues in the Garden State.* New Brunswick: Rutgers University Press, 1991.

Debano, Paul. *Indianapolis ABC's: History of a Premier Team in the Negro Leagues.* Jefferson, NC: McFarland, 2007.

Heaphy, Leslie. *The Negro Leagues, 1869–1960.* Jefferson, NC: McFarland, 2013.

Hogan, Lawrence D., ed. *Shades of Glory: The Negro Leagues and the Story of African-American Baseball.* New York: National Geographic, 2006.

Holway, John. *Voices from the Great Black Baseball Leagues.* New York: Dodd, Mead, 1975.

Kuklick, Bruce. *To Every Thing a Season: Shibe Park and Urban Philadelphia 1909–1976.* Princeton, NJ: Princeton University Press, 1991.

Lanctot, Neil. *Fair Dealing and Clean Playing: The Hilldale Club and the Development of Black Professional Baseball 1910–1932.* Jefferson, NC: McFarland, 1994.

_____. *Negro League Baseball: The Rise and Ruin of a Black Institution.* Philadelphia: University of Pennsylvania Press, 2008.

Lester, Larry. *Baseball's First Colored World Series: The 1924 Meeting of the Hilldale Giants and Kansas City Monarchs.* Jefferson, NC: McFarland, 2006.

_____. *Rube Foster in His Time: On the Field and in the Papers with Black Base-*

ball's Greatest Visionary. Jefferson, NC: McFarland, 2012.

Lomax, Michael. Black Baseball Entrepreneurs, 1860–1901: Operating by Any Means Necessary. Syracuse, NY: Syracuse University Press, 2002.

_____. Black Baseball Entrepreneurs, 1902–1931: The Negro National and Eastern Colored Leagues. Syracuse, NY: Syracuse University Press, 2014.

Luke, Bob. The Most Famous Woman in Baseball: Effa Manley and the Negro Leagues. Washington, D.C.: Potomac, 2011.

Miller, Randall, and William Pencak, eds. Pennsylvania: A History of the Commonwealth. State College: Pennsylvania State University Press, 2002.

Nash, Gary B., and Jean R. Soderlund. Freedom by Degrees: Emancipation in Pennsylvania and Its Aftermath. New York: Oxford University Press, 1991.

_____. Forging Freedom: The Formation of Philadelphia's Black Community, 1720–1840. Cambridge, MA: Harvard University Press, 1991.

Newman, Richard S. Freedom's Prophet: Bishop Richard Allen, the AME Church, and the Black Founding Fathers. New York: New York University Press, 2008.

Newman, Roberta J., and Joel Nathan Rosen. Black Baseball, Black Business: Race Enterprise and the Fate of the Segregated Dollar. Oxford: University of Mississippi Press, 2014.

Overmeyer, James. Black Ball and the Boardwalk: The Bacharach Giants of Atlantic City, 1916–1929. Jefferson, NC: McFarland, 2014.

Peterson, Robert. Only the Ball was White: A History of Legendary Black Players and All-Black Professional Teams. Englewood Cliffs, NJ: Prentice-Hall, 1970.

Plott, William J. The Negro Southern League: A Baseball History 1920–1951. Jefferson, NC: McFarland, 2015.

Riley, James A. The Biographical Encyclopedia of the Negro Baseball Leagues. New York: Carroll & Graf, 1994.

Rogosin, Donn. Invisible Men: Life in Baseball's Negro Leagues. New York: Athenaeum, 1983.

Trotter, Joe W., and Eric Ledell Smith, eds. African Americans in Pennsylvania: Shifting Historical Perspectives. State College: Pennsylvania State University Press, 1997.

Tygiel, Jules. Baseball's Great Experiment: Jackie Robinson and his Legacy. New York: Oxford University Press, 1983.

_____, ed. The Jackie Robinson Reader: Perspectives on an American Hero. New York: Plume, 1997.

_____. Past Time: Baseball as History. Oxford: Oxford University Press, 2000.

Saunders, John A. 100 Years After Emancipation: History of the Philadelphia Negro. n.p.: n.p., n.d.

Weigly, Russell F., ed. Philadelphia: A 300-Year History. New York: W.W. Norton, 1982.

Westcott, Rich. The Mogul: Eddie Gottlieb, Philadelphia Sports Legend and Pro Basketball Pioneer. Philadelphia: Temple University Press, 2008.

_____. Philadelphia's Old Ballparks. Philadelphia: Temple University Press, 1996.

Winch, Julie. The Elite of Our People: Joseph Wilson's Sketches of Black Upper-Class Life in Antebellum Philadelphia. State College: Pennsylvania State University Press, 2000.

_____. Philadelphia's Black Elite: Activism, Accommodation, and the Struggle for Autonomy, 1787–1848. Philadelphia: Temple University Press, 1993.

Index